A Challenge to Social Security

**THE CHANGING ROLES OF
WOMEN AND MEN IN AMERICAN SOCIETY**

A Challenge to Social Security
THE CHANGING ROLES OF WOMEN AND MEN IN AMERICAN SOCIETY

A 1980 conference sponsored by
The Institute for Research on Poverty
and
The Women's Studies Research Center
of
The University of Wisconsin

This is a volume in the

Institute for Research on Poverty Monograph Series

A complete list of titles in this series appears at the end of this volume.

A Challenge to Social Security

THE CHANGING ROLES OF
WOMEN AND MEN IN AMERICAN SOCIETY

Edited by

RICHARD V. BURKHAUSER

Department of Economics
Vanderbilt University
Nashville, Tennessee

KAREN C. HOLDEN

Department of Economics
Institute for Research on Poverty
University of Wisconsin–Madison
Madison, Wisconsin

ACADEMIC PRESS
A Subsidiary of Harcourt Brace Jovanovich, Publishers
New York London
Paris San Diego San Francisco São Paulo Sydney Tokyo Toronto

This book is one of a series sponsored by the Institute for Research on Poverty
of the University of Wisconsin pursuant to the provisions of the
Economic Opportunity Act of 1964.

The views expressed in this book are those of the authors; they do not necessarily
represent the official views of the institutions with which the authors are affiliated.

368.43
C437

ACADEMIC PRESS, INC.
111 Fifth Avenue, New York, New York 10003

United Kingdom Edition published by
ACADEMIC PRESS, INC. (LONDON) LTD.
24/28 Oval Road, London NW1   7DX

Library of Congress Cataloging in Publication Data
Main entry under title:

A Challenge to social security.

   (Institute for Research on Poverty monograph series)
   Bibliography: p.
   Includes index.
   1. Social security--United States. 2. Survivors'
benefits--United States. 3. Family policy--United
States. I. Burkhauser, Richard V. II. Holden, Karen C.
III. Series.
HD7125.C476   368.4'3'00973   82-1596
ISBN 0-12-144680-8   AACR2

m.R.

PRINTED IN THE UNITED STATES OF AMERICA

82 83 84 85   9 8 7 6 5 4 3 2 1

The Institute for Research on Poverty is a national center for research established at the University of Wisconsin in 1966 by a grant from the Office of Economic Opportunity. Its primary objective is to foster basic, multidisciplinary research into the nature and causes of poverty and means to combat it.

In addition to increasing the basic knowledge from which policies aimed at the elimination of poverty can be shaped, the Institute strives to carry analysis beyond the formulation and testing of fundamental generalizations to the development and assessment of relevant policy alternatives.

The Institute endeavors to bring together scholars of the highest caliber whose primary research efforts are focused on the problem of poverty, the distribution of income, and the analysis and evaluation of social policy, offering staff members wide opportunities for interchange of ideas, maximum freedom for research into basic questions about poverty and social policy, and dissemination of their findings.

Contents

1
Introduction   1

RICHARD V. BURKHAUSER and KAREN C. HOLDEN

2
Concepts Underlying the Current Controversy about Women's Social Security Benefits   21
ROBERT J. LAMPMAN and MAURICE MACDONALD

3
Supplemental OASI Benefits to Homemakers Through Current Spouse Benefits, a Homemaker Credit, and Child-Care Drop-Out Years   41
KAREN C. HOLDEN

Discussion   66
EDITH U. FIERST

4
Earnings Sharing: Incremental and Fundamental Reform   73
RICHARD V. BURKHAUSER

Discussion   92
VIRGINIA P. RENO

Discussion   190

PAUL N. VAN DE WATER

8
Occupational Pension Plans and Spouse Benefits   201

FRANCIS P. KING

Discussion   224

JAMES C. HICKMAN

9
The Housewife and Social Security Reform:
A Feminist Perspective   229

BARBARA R. BERGMANN

10
Incremental Change in Social Security Needed to
Result in Equal and Fair Treatment of
Men and Women   235

ROBERT J. MYERS

11
The Changing Nature of Social Security   247

STANFORD G. ROSS

List of Figures and Tables

Contributors

Numbers in parentheses indicate the pages on which the authors' contributions begin.

HENRY AARON (124), The Brookings Institution, 1775 Massachusetts Avenue, N.W., Washington, D.C. 20036

BARBARA R. BERGMANN (229), Department of Economics, University of Maryland—College Park, College Park, Maryland 20740

DAVID E. BERRY (131), Institute for Research on Poverty, University of Wisconsin—Madison, Madison, Wisconsin 53706

WILLIAM B. BURFIELD (169), Health Studies Program, Syracuse University, Syracuse, New York 13210

RICHARD V. BURKHAUSER (1, 73), Department of Economics, Vanderbilt University, Nashville, Tennessee 37240

COLIN D. CAMPBELL (161), Department of Economics, Dartmouth College, Hanover, New Hampshire 03755

EDITH U. FIERST (66), 1140 Connecticut Avenue, N.W., Washington, D.C. 20036

IRWIN GARFINKEL (131), School of Social Work, and Institute for Research on Poverty, University of Wisconsin—Madison, Madison, Wisconsin 53706

JAMES C. HICKMAN (224), School of Business, University of Wisconsin—Madison, Madison, Wisconsin 53706

KAREN C. HOLDEN (1, 41), Department of Economics, and Institute for Research on Poverty, University of Wisconsin—Madison, Madison, Wisconsin 53706

WILLIAM G. JOHNSON (169), Health Studies Program, Syracuse University, Syracuse, New York 13210

FRANCIS P. KING (201), Teachers Insurance and Annuity Association–College Retirement Equities Fund (TIAA–CREF), 730 Third Avenue, New York, New York, 10017

ROBERT J. LAMPMAN (21), Department of Economics, and Institute for Research on Poverty, University of Wisconsin—Madison, Madison, Wisconsin 53706

MAURICE MACDONALD (21), Institute for Research on Poverty, University of Wisconsin—Madison, Madison, Wisconsin 53706

ALICIA MUNNELL (101), Federal Reserve Bank of Boston, 600 Atlantic Avenue, Boston, Massachusetts 02210

ROBERT J. MYERS (235), National Commission on Social Security Reform, 736 Jackson Place, N.W., Washington, D.C. 20503

VIRGINIA P. RENO (92), Office of Policy Analysis, Social Security Administration, 330 C Street, S.W., Washington, D.C. 20201

STANFORD G. ROSS (247), Califano, Ross and Heineman, 1575 I Street, N.W., Washington, D.C. 20005

LAURA E. STIGLIN (101), North Andover, Massachusetts 01810

PAUL N. VAN DE WATER (190), Congressional Budget Office, 2nd and D Streets, S.W., Washington, D.C. 20515

JENNIFER L. WARLICK (131), Department of Economics, and Institute for Research on Poverty, University of Wisconsin—Madison, Madison, Wisconsin 53706

Acknowledgments

No book can go to press without the hard work and advice of many people other than the editors and writers. This is especially true for volumes that originated in a conference which itself took a great deal of effort to organize and execute successfully. In many ways the final editing of the conference papers was the easiest part of the entire effort. Although we cannot mention all those who were involved in one way or another in the preparation of the conference and of this book, a few should receive special acknowledgment. We are grateful for the encouragement and financial support of the Institute for Research on Poverty and of its directors, Irv Garfinkel, who was director at the time we proposed the conference, and Eugene Smolensky, who had assumed the directorship by the time the conference took place. Suzette LaVigne was indispensible in planning the conference. Bob Lampman, Irv Garfinkel, and Paul Van de Water made many invaluable comments on the initial draft of the Introduction.

The Women's Studies Research Center of the University of Wisconsin enthusiastically cosponsored the conference and the Administration on Aging of the U.S. Department of Health and Human Services provided financial assistance for the editing of the manuscript.

Although the final manuscript reflects the input of many people other than those named, the authors are of course responsible for the views expressed.

NA

Director's Foreword

A veritable concatenation of trends makes this a timely volume indeed. Women have voluntarily entered the work force in large numbers and therefore pay social security taxes and become entitled to social security benefits—on the face of it, a happy enough development. The probability that marriages will end in divorce has risen dramatically—on the face of it, not so happy a development. The social security system has reached maturity, as new beneficiaries have contributed to the retirement system over the whole of their working lives—on the face of it, an inevitable event bringing neither great joy nor sorrow, even to actuaries. Coming together now, in the early 1980s, these three events coalesce into one large and widely recognized problem, but there is no agreed-upon solution. An informal public discourse must start us toward consensus. This book moves us down that road.

The purpose of this conference, say its organizers, is "to sharpen the debate over social security reform." I would say that the intent of the participants is not so much to sharpen the debate as to flatten the debaters. Karen Holden tells us that the spouse benefit makes rich women richer while widows are consigned to poverty, all in honor of the proposition that the traditional role of woman as homemaker should be encouraged. If that is the goal, says Holden, she can do it better and cheaper, but the implication is that she would just as soon forget it. Burkhauser, Warlick, Berry, Garfinkel, Munnell, and Stiglin base their reforms on the utopian view that family income is (or should be) equally shared by husband and wife but that a divorcée should renounce the idea that an ex-husband is an asset in her portfolio, meager as that portfolio may be. Is it any wonder that Robert Myers, that wiliest of old veterans of the social security wars, finds that reforms and reformers are sadly misguided? No timid scholars honing precious and esoteric points here. Indeed, the prose is polite, academic, sometimes pedantic, sometimes very technical, but the content adds up to a no-holds-barred slugfest.

The choices concern deeply held social values—insurance or redistribution, neutrality or subsidy to traditional homemaker roles for women, joint or individual work decisions within the family. The choices to be made also concern highly technical issues: double-decker or two-tier, high marginal tax rates or high average tax rates. And the choices involve the passions of people who have played a role in forging the current system— do proposals for change reform or rape the current system?

The questions argued in this volume involve sensibilities, intellect, and prejudice. That is an unusually rich mix even among income security policy debates, and it makes for rewarding reading. As Institute director, I am proud to have it on our list.

Eugene Smolensky
Director, Institute for Research on Poverty

A Challenge to Social Security

**THE CHANGING ROLES OF
WOMEN AND MEN IN AMERICAN SOCIETY**

9/50
U.S.

1

Book Title:

Introduction

RICHARD V. BURKHAUSER

KAREN C. HOLDEN

The Old Age, Survivors, and Disability Insurance System (OASDI)—or social security—is the largest of all federal income maintenance programs.[1] In 1981 it paid benefits to over 35 million retired or disabled workers and their spouses, widows, and dependents. Monthly OASI benefits in that year exceeded $12 billion, second only to defense expenditures in the federal budget. Funds for the system are raised by a payroll tax which in 1981 was equal to 10.7%, shared equally by employer and employee, on the first $29,700 of wage income for the 98% of workers in OASI-covered employment.[2]

Over its 45-year history, social security has been widely accepted as the appropriate means for providing income support for the elderly. Yet now critics at various points of the political spectrum are assailing the system

[1] Since 1965 social security has included a hospital insurance program for the aged; thus the full initials of the system are OASDHI. Because the papers in this volume do not discuss Medicare, we shall use the initials OASI as a general term and in those papers that discuss the old age and survivors components of the system. We shall use the initials OASDI when dealing as well with the disability component.

[2] Including the payroll tax used to finance the Medicare program, the total tax rate in 1981 was 13.3%. This rate increased to 13.4% in January 1982. The payroll tax ceiling increases automatically with inflation and is $32,400 in 1982.

1

with charges that range from insufficiently protecting covered workers and their dependents to totally abandoning its traditional insurance principles in an attempt to redistribute income. Even some of those who consistently supported the system over the years now question whether its mounting costs can be sustained and whether it is flexible enough to meet the needs of today's society.

Not since the original debates over the establishment of social security in the 1930s has the system been so severely criticized, with academics, public policy makers and, more important, the current and future beneficiary population attacking the relevance of OASI policy to the stated goals of the system and to the methods used to attain them. In this new debate no issue has been more vigorously argued than the treatment of the family, especially its alleged bias toward the traditional roles of women and men.

OASI's treatment of women and men follows from a particular vision of the family and the responsibility of government to provide protection to family members. Thus, before considering any proposed reforms, we must look at the development of the OASI system and its logic. We intend, therefore, to explore the underlying principles of OASI as well as its current treatment of women and men within the family and proposals for change in that treatment. This perspective should make it apparent that the choices made by OASI about the treatment of individuals and family units parallel those faced by other government income maintenance programs as well as by many tax laws.

First, we define some crucial concepts used in the public policy debate on OASI and sketch a brief history of "how we got to where we are." The reader is then invited to view the potpourri of proposals for "where we should be going" contained in the body of the book.

The Current System: How It Works

The basic insured unit of OASI is the worker. Upon reaching age 62 covered workers are eligible for retired-worker benefits if they have worked sufficient *quarters* in covered work to attain *insured status* (see Glossary for definitions of quarters and other program variables—in italics here). Benefits are based on *average indexed monthly earnings* (AIME), the average covered earnings between age 21 (or 1950, if later) and age 62, with the five lowest years of earnings dropped. A worker's earnings are indexed so that amounts earned early in his or her career are stated in terms of overall earnings levels prevailing at the time he or she becomes eligible for benefits. This means that the actual number of years of earnings used in calculating AIME depends on a retiree's year of birth. All retirees born in 1929 or later will have AIME calculated over a constant 35 years, whether or not income was earned during all years of the averaging period.

The retired-worker benefit for which a person is eligible at 65 is the *primary insurance amount* (PIA) and is equal to some proportion of the AIME. This proportion is different for different AIME amounts such that higher-income earners have a lower proportion of their AIME replaced and thus a lower return on their past contributions than do low-income earners. The actual benefit received by a worker will be less than the PIA if benefits are *actuarially reduced* for each month benefits are received prior to age 65 or if earnings after acceptance are higher than the earnings allowed by the *earnings test* relevant to that year.[3]

The tilt in the PIA and the earnings test affect the distributional properties of OASI. By reducing the marginal increase in benefits to higher-income contributors in the system, the PIA tilt redistributes income from high-wage earners to low-wage earners at retirement. The earnings test is a kind of means test which reduces benefits to those who continue to work past age 65. For those workers who delay applying for OASI benefits, the benefit is increased by 3% for each year acceptance is postponed past age 65 up to a maximum of 15%. This increase, the *delayed-retirement credit*, however, is less than the actuarial adjustment for the shorter life expectancy of older retirees. Thus continued work past age 65 by a person eligible for a retired-worker benefit means a real loss in benefits over his or her remaining lifetime, although this actuarial loss may be offset in part by the higher PIA resulting from additional years of earnings.

OASI also grants benefits to dependents of a retired, disabled, or deceased worker. In most cases these are spouse, widow(er) and children under 18. When one member of a couple receives retired-worker benefits, the other partner may be eligible for a *spouse benefit* equal to 50% of the former's PIA.

Survivors of an insured worker are eligible for a *survivor benefit* based on the past earnings of the deceased worker.[4] For aged widows and widowers this is generally equal to the worker's PIA. Thus an aged spouse upon widowhood will receive two-thirds of the total benefit for which the

[3]In 1983 the earnings test is scheduled to apply only to beneficiaries less than 70 years old. The earnings test continues to be a controversial part of social security and several proposals to change the age or eliminate the earnings test entirely are pending before Congress.

[4]Eligible survivors include children under 18, their mother or father, aged widows and widowers, and dependent parents of the deceased worker. Eligibility for all OASI benefits is tied to the age of the potential beneficiary. Some of the more critical ages are given as part of the definitions in the Glossary.

couple was eligible prior to the worker's death, or an amount exactly equivalent to what the deceased covered worker could have received as a single retired worker. A divorced spouse may receive an amount equal to 50% of the former mate's retired-worker benefit, and the divorced widow an amount equal to 100%. However these benefits are conditional upon the marriage having remained intact for at least 10 years. It must be emphasized that receipt of either spouse or *divorced-spouse benefits* depends on the actions of the insured worker; dependents may receive benefits only after the insured worker has started to draw benefits. In addition, all such benefits may be reduced by further market work of the primary beneficiary.

Although every spouse or survivor is theoretically entitled to a benefit based on the insured worker's earnings, the so-called *dual entitlement* provision determines the person's actual social security benefit. Under this provision a person may not receive multiple benefits. In effect a person may receive only the higher of the retired-worker benefit and the spouse or survivor benefit for which he/she is eligible. Thus a person with a sufficiently long history of earnings covered by social security will be eligible for a benefit based on this past work record. The spouse or survivor of a worker with insured status will receive the higher of his/her own benefit and that for which he/she may be eligible as a spouse.

Many people regard the dual entitlement provision as a serious inequity, since families which contribute equal amounts into the system and have equal earnings over their lifetimes can receive substantially different OASI benefits depending on how the earnings were divided between the husband and wife. Because benefits received by a single-earner couple are often higher than those received by a two-earner couple with identical combined lifetime earnings, the provision of spouse benefits is often considered an unjustified income transfer to wives of higher earners, or to result in redundant OASI taxes paid by working wives.

Disability benefits to disabled workers and their families are based on AIME, as are retired-worker benefits—except that the quarters of coverage required for insured status for these benefits and the averaging period are adjusted to account for the disabled person's shorter work life. Eligibility for benefits also requires that a person meet a *work recency test*. Because families of disabled workers are younger and more likely to include minor children than those of retired workers, these families are more likely to have benefits limited by the *maximum family benefit.*

Historical Conflicts in OASI

Government income maintenance programs are often evaluated with reference to two models—the first is based on a strict insurance principle, and the second on pure income transfer principles. In general, the latter is designed to achieve some level of social adequacy through the redistribution of income among groups classified by income. Insurance programs, on the other hand, are meant to provide protection to individuals against an event whose occurrence cannot be predicted with certainty. In the case of retirement pensions, this uncertainty occurs in the timing of retirement and the length of the individual's remaining lifetime (and that of dependents), during which retirement benefits must be paid. Although neither public or private pension programs conform entirely to these types, it is useful to develop the principles underlying strict insurance and pure income transfer programs and apply these principles in evaluating the goals and achievements of the current OASI program. Rather than consider all the many differences between these two types of programs, we focus on the crucial difference between them in the relationship between contributions made and subsequent benefits derived.

In private pension programs of the defined-benefit type (in which benefits are based on wages and length of service, as are those of social security), contributions are calculated on the basis of accrued or projected liabilities. That is, contributions are made either by individuals or by their employers at the level necessary to finance the benefits the worker is expected to receive on retirement. While benefits are not likely to equal actual payments plus interest for a given individual,[5] the funding plan of a private pension program calls for contributions on behalf of a cohort of workers to cover the expected retirement benefits of the group as a whole.

A pure income transfer program, in contrast, is one in which benefits are divorced from contributions. Benefits are defined by law or regulation and awarded on the basis of individual or family characteristics such as income or family size. The actual method of paying benefits is not critical in either type of program. Income transfers could be means-tested, as in the Supplemental Security Income program (SSI), or they could be a flat benefit related only to age. Pension payments through an insurance program could be provided through a lump-sum benefit upon retirement or regular payments to the retiree for his or her remaining lifetime. The critical difference is that in a program based on insurance principles, benefits are related to a worker's prior contributions, whereas this is not true of benefits from a pure income transfer program. In addition, the financing of an insurance program is based on a principle that imposes a balance between the *expected present value* of retirement income and

---

[5]This inequality results because it is impossible to accurately predict a given worker's mortality, withdrawal from the program, or disability, and wage changes and because investment income will almost certainly deviate from the assumptions made in estimating required contributions.

contributions for an individual or group. Pure income transfer programs depend on more general sources of financing.

An insurance-type pension system will significantly affect the pattern of income receipts over an individual's lifetime by insuring against substantial losses at some future time at the cost of a yearly premium. Such a system, which bases final benefits on prior contributions and investment earnings, will have no effect on the distribution of lifetime income across groups of individuals. However, by its very nature, a benefit paid solely on the basis of presumed or measured need alters both the distribution of an individual's lifetime income and the distribution of income across individuals.

The social security system—the cornerstone of United States income support policy toward the aged and disabled—is generally considered insurance, yet it clearly has many aspects typical of a pure income transfer program. The continuing tension between the insurance and adequacy goals inherent in this program are at the heart of much of the debate now going on concerning social security policy.

In 1935 there was no OASI. Income support for the aged was provided through their own earnings or those of their families, savings for retirement, limited private and public employee pensions, state-administered old-age assistance programs, and private charities. In that year of deep depression and high unemployment the call for political action to provide an adequate income maintenance program for the aged was overwhelming. The political conflict over the various approaches to increasing the incomes of the retired aged and the final compromises made, which we can only highlight here, have been discussed both by those closely involved in the development and early administration of the social security program (Cohen, 1957; Witte, 1963; Altmeyer, 1966; Ball, 1978) and by current students of its history (Pratt, 1977; Derthick, 1979; Ferrara, 1980; Stein, 1980). The final outcome was a compulsory, contributory insurance program containing both insurance and redistributive features. Over time the mix of insurance and redistributive elements was to change with successive program amendments.

The intent of the original program was to provide a safe annuity to workers upon retirement. Benefits were to be related to total covered wages of workers over their work life and were to be financed with wage-related contributions paid by employees and their employers. This was in stark contrast to the major political alternative at the time, the Townsend Old Age Revolving Pension Plan, a pure income transfer scheme, which would have given every citizen of the United States age 60 and over, a $200 per month demogrant. However, it is worth noting that the original program (OAI) through its progressive benefit structure redistributed income from higher- to lower-income workers.

Long before 1942 (when the first benefits were scheduled to be paid) it became apparent that for many years even a partially funded, earnings-related retirement program would provide only minimal benefits not much above those paid by old-age assistance.[6] In the near term this was especially true, since workers already close to retirement in 1935 would have few remaining years of work life upon which to accrue retirement benefits. But even in the long term, after the system had fully matured, benefits would still be low for lifelong low earners and those with interruptions in earnings.

In recognition of this deficiency and motivated in part by the fear that the fledging OAI plan would be replaced by a Townsend type plan, the architects of the program amended the program in favor of greater redistribution so that the first generation of workers might have an adequate standard of living upon retirement and their dependents would have sufficient income if the primary wage earner died. The 1939 amendments shifted the balance away from insurance principles in favor of adequacy goals. Note, however, that unlike the Townsend Plan, social security continued to maintain a link between taxes paid while working and benefits, in that benefits were paid only to workers who had contributed to the program for a minimum number of years.

It is in this context that the introduction of special benefits to wives and widows, part of the 1939 amendments to the Social Security Act, must be considered. Spouse and survivor benefits were one of many compromises of insurance principles to achieve income adequacy for a group of workers in presumed need of higher income.[7] The method used to achieve that goal was a noncontributory benefit to spouses and survivors based on the earnings record of the worker. (It was not until 1977, however, that husbands and widowers were eligible on the same basis as wives and widows.) In addition, the 1939 amendments largely abandoned the original funding principles, which were akin to private plans, switching to pay-as-you-go funding in which accrued liabilities remained unfunded.

[6]In 1935 cost estimates projected an ultimate trust fund of $47 billion by 1980 (in 1935 dollars). Although even this fund would not be sufficient to fund all projected liabilities, the projected fund was almost twice the national debt in 1935 of $27 billion. Even partial funding at this level represented a major commitment to the insurance principle during the Depression.

[7]It should also be noted that the 1935 Social Security Act established, as well as the social security system, a system of federal grants to the states for the cost of old-age assistance programs. Thus the act recognized through these two programs the need for a basic guarantee of income to all persons. Since a welfare program partially financed by federal funds had been created by the same act that established the social security system, the later shift toward the accomplishment of welfare goals through social security is somewhat curious.

Current retirement benefits were to be financed through the contributions of current workers.[8]

In reviewing these compromises, which arose out of concerns of earlier generations for the economic hardships of the aged, it is important to recognize that they were based on the political conflicts and priorities of that time. Rather than debate the merits of these original choices, we will consider whether they continue to meet the economic and political priorities of the current generations of OASI beneficiaries and contributing workers.

Two crucial changes in general socioeconomic conditions have occurred. First, many of the assumptions about a typical family which were taken for granted in 1939 may not be relevant today. The OASI system of 1939 was tailored to provide old-age income to the typical family of that day: a family headed by a male who worked full time in the labor force and a wife who worked full time caring for children and maintaining the home. This family was stable and divorce was rare. Whether in fact, even in 1939, this could be described as the typical family, clearly in the 1980s it is not.

Second, and perhaps even more important, OASI approaches maturity (i.e., retirees are increasingly likely to have been covered by the system throughout their working lives) at the same time that demographic changes have caused the number of taxpaying covered workers to grow at a slower rate than the number of retirees drawing benefits. These changes make the conflict between insurance and adequacy goals of the system greater than at any time in the past.

Throughout the history of social security, benefits received by all retirees have been greater than those that could have been financed by their prior contributions alone (Burkhauser and Warlick, 1981). The contributions of the cohorts of workers earning high wages were sufficient to compensate for additional benefits granted to retirees on the basis of adequacy considerations (e.g., to compensate for lower lifetime income, dependent children, a noncontributing spouse, and price rises since retirement). Yet even workers with high covered earnings throughout their life received a higher rate of return on their contributions into the system than would have been the case in a fully funded wage-related pension system.

Because everyone gained from the system it was easy to overlook its redistributive aspects, and thus the myth was perpetuated that social security was a system based on insurance principles. The reality is that

---

[8]Although the 1939 amendments in effect abandoned the principle of a fully funded system, the debate over whether the system should in the long run be fully funded continued into the early 1950s. This has once more become a seriously discussed proposal.

without continuing increases in OASI tax rates, the intergenerational transfers inherent in this pay-as-you-go program will no longer be sufficient to provide *all* contributors within a cohort with a pension at least equivalent to that they would have received under a fully funded wage-related system. This problem becomes more acute as either real productivity or labor force growth slows, two features of today's economy that put an even greater burden on the current working population in fulfilling the promises made to the current retired population. Under these conditions any additional benefits to one particular group in an age cohort above the level which would be generated from their past contributions can be achieved only if other members of that cohort receive less.

The political reality of this situation is that OASI will never again enjoy the degree of support it had in the past. Now a decision to increase benefits to some will mean real losses and higher taxes to others. As a result, OASI will be perceived increasingly—and correctly—as an income redistribution system as well as an insurance system.

The current controversy over the treatment of women and men by OASI must therefore be considered in the light of the limited choices now available. The realization that OASI is an important income redistribution mechanism in which some families will be taxed in excess of benefits they will receive makes it imperative that we openly bring the tools of income distribution analysis to bear to ensure that such redistribution is done in the most equitable and efficient manner. Too often because spouse and survivor benefits are received primarily by women, the rationale and adequacy of these benefits are defined as a "women's issue." Such a view is too narrowly focused. The discussion of spouse and survivor benefits in this volume takes a broader view, one that considers the ramifications of various program features which attempt to satisfy either the insurance or social adequacy goals of social security.

The Controversy over Spouse Benefits

Spouse and survivor benefits were part of the 1939 amendments to the Social Security Act. For the first time benefits were to be paid to persons who had not worked in covered employment and therefore had not directly paid into the system. Yet the extension of benefits to spouses and survivors of covered workers only was consistent with the program's original and continuing emphasis on the worker population. Because benefits to the spouse were proportionate to the benefits of the husband, a strong link between earnings and benefits was maintained. In fact, the introduction of supplemental, noncontributory benefits for wives and widows of insured workers may be considered a further step in providing income adequacy for the retired population—a goal which had been partially achieved in the 1935 act through the progressive benefit structure and the failure to account, in calculating benefits, for actuarial differences in the expected lifespans of men and women.

Spouse and survivor benefits arose from the social conditions prevalent in the late 1930s. Between 1935 and 1937 both supporters and detractors debated the ability of social security to meet its adequacy goals in the near future, arguing that paying benefits based almost entirely on earnings of insured workers during the early years of the program would not shield beneficiaries, especially married couples, from economic hardship in old age. According to their published recommendations the 1937–1939 Advisory Council on Social Security sought primarily to increase "average old-age benefits in the early years." In this spirit, the Advisory Council recommended that the benefit schedule, which was already slightly tilted in favor of low earners, be changed so that benefits would be higher than originally planned during the early years of the program, and lower as the system approached maturity in 1980. This change would affect all retired beneficiaries. But, in the council's words, "the inadequacy of the benefit payable during the *early* years of the program is more marked where the benefit must support not only the annuitant himself but also his wife." The council therefore recommended that "the enhancement of the *early* old-age benefits under the system should be partly attained by the method of paying in the case of a married annuitant a supplementary allowance on behalf of an aged wife [Brown, 1977, Appendix, p. 9; emphasis added]." The council report also contained a proposal for paying survivor benefits to aged widows and to widows caring for the children of deceased, insured workers. Supplementary benefits to wives and widows were proposed because, at a time when all benefits were low, they were a means of meeting "the greatest social need with the minimum increase in cost [U.S. Department of Health, Education, and Welfare, 1979a, p. 15]."

The council made this recommendation at a time when family structure, and the division of work within a family were far different from those of today. In 1939 only one woman in four participated in the labor market and in only three out of twenty households were both the husband and wife in the labor force at the same time. The assumption that males were the primary wage earners in families while wives were most likely to be dependents was instrumental in the decision by the council to raise benefits to retirees through the payment of supplemental benefits to wives and widows. Because benefits to wives and widows were designed specifically to help a particularly needy group, the method of determining eligibility was designed such that those presumed better off would not be eligible. At a time when little research had been done on the determinants of work by married women, the presumption was that couples with a working wife were better off than couples with only one earner. Marriage itself was adopted as an indicator (though not proof) that one retired-worker benefit might have to support two aged individuals. To be eligible for a spouse or survivor benefit, a woman had to (a) be a wife or widow of a retired or deceased worker; and (b) not be eligible for a retired-worker benefit higher than the spouse or survivor benefit. The dual entitlement provision, by which a women could receive only the higher of her retired-worker or spouse benefit, was similar to income-offset provisions of other income assistance programs in which benefits were reduced as other income rose. For dually entitled wives and widows the implicit tax on retired-worker benefits was 100%.

Although the one-earner model of the household may have been accurate for the 1930s, it is not for the 1980s. By 1981 over one-half of all women (52%) age 16 and over were in the work force, and both wife and husband worked in 51% of all married couples. In addition, the rise in divorce has increased the dependence of women on old-age benefits based on their own earnings. Although elderly one-earner couples may have been the group in 1939 most likely to have low per capita income relative to needs, changing work and marriage patterns among women and men suggest that two-earner couples and divorced women are now more likely to be among the low-income aged.

The social security program has not ignored the importance of the changing roles of women and men. Amendments since 1939 have extended *dependent benefits* to husbands and widowers, implying the legitimacy of males in "nontraditional" roles. Recognition that divorce was a frequent occurrence led to extension of spouse and widow benefits to divorced women in 1965 and to divorced males in 1977. The 1977 amendments also reduced the duration-of-marriage requirement for a divorced person to receive a benefit based on their former spouse's earnings from 20 to 10 years. However, the dual entitlement provision remains: a provision that may have addressed the economic and political realities of the 1930s but is bitterly contested today.

A good indicator of the importance of this issue is the rising concern about it expressed in the reports of successive advisory councils. It is notable, however, that not until 1975 did a council recommend that provisions of the social security law which treated women and men differently should be made the same for both. This recommendation was implemented by 1979, when the most recent Advisory Council report found that no differential treatment because of sex remained in the system.

But of more importance to the issues of concern in this book, the 1975 council was the first to give explicit recognition in its report to the major socioeconomic changes which have occurred since the 1939 amendments. The council's Subcommittee on the Treatment of Men and Women recommended changes that would have increased benefits to dually entitled women, but this issue was still treated as minor in the full report and evoked no changes in the system. Between 1975 and 1979, however, a great change in the intellectual and political climate took place. The 1979 Advisory Council report acknowledged that the council spent more time on reviewing the current treatment of working and nonworking women under social security than on any other issue. Yet in recognition of the lack of a consensus on alternatives to that treatment, the council was unable to agree on any single fundamental change. It did recognize the need to establish equity in benefits between working and nonworking wives and concluded that a system of shared earnings in which benefits for husbands and wives would be based on one-half the couple's combined earnings represented the most promising approach to correcting the current bias in favor of single-earner families at a time when the majority of women no longer fit that pattern. This was a complete reversal of the position of the previous advisory council, which refused to endorse the principle of benefits based on a married couple's combined earnings. Nevertheless, the 1979 council did not endorse a full-scale "*earnings sharing*" plan. A narrow majority did, however, recommend earnings sharing in two circumstances: at divorce for couples married at least ten years and in calculating survivor benefits for widows and widowers.

The recognition by the 1979 Advisory Council of the inequities in the treatment of working and nonworking wives clears the way for a major political debate on this issue. But equally significant is the tacit recognition by the council that we have entered a new age with respect to OASI. Derthick (1979) in her discussion of the history of OASI argues that in the past, "policy choices can be summed up in two maxims: A little bit more is always a good thing; anything less is inconceivable [p. 412]." Thus it is notable that one of the two specific changes in the current system recommended by the council—that divorced homemakers should be credited with earnings equal to one-half the combined earnings of the household—would clearly benefit one group of beneficiaries, divorced homemakers, at the expense of another group of beneficiaries, divorced workers. That is, promised benefits would actually be reduced for workers to allow divorced-spouse benefits to rise. This is in sharp contrast to the past method of increasing the benefits of some group by enlarging the liabilities of the system and thus increasing taxes paid by the current generation. More in keeping with Derthick's assessment is the other recommendation of the council—to increase survivor benefits by increasing taxes raised from the current generation of workers.

The inconclusive or conflicting recommendations of previous advisory councils indicate that these deliberations are only the first round in what promises to be major debate on the shape of the social security program in a world radically altered by changing work and earnings behavior, as well as by a new recognition of the limits on program growth.

A Look at Alternative Reforms

This volume brings together researchers and policymakers from both the public and private sectors to examine the major alternatives for altering the treatment of women and men by social security.[9] The contributors reflect the diversity of views presented in the debate. Some papers discuss particular reform proposals, others examine particular problem areas that must be addressed by all proposed changes. Neither the authors of the papers nor the editors reach a consensus on the desirability of any specific reform. We believe this inability to settle on a single plan of action accurately reflects the mood of the public debate. Although persons advocating change may agree that the old model of work and earnings upon which the current structure of benefits is based is obsolete, they nevertheless find it difficult to agree on an appropriate model for the present. The proposed reforms contain different assumptions about family structure and society's obligations to provide support for the aged and survivors and the disabled. This volume clarifies the debate by examining the major alternatives to the current treatment of women and men by OASI. We leave to the reader the choice of which of several "reasonable" remedies are preferable.

Even a cursory examination of the definitions of an economic unit shows that no consistent model of the family or of societal obligations to families has been applied by the federal government either in its tax policies or in its income maintenance programs. Hence, in evaluating such programs it is not always clear which unit is the relevant one to hold constant in determining issues of horizontal equity. Although most people would agree that equals should be treated equally, no clear resolution emerges as to the manner in which the economic unit should be defined or as to

[9]The reforms examined in detail are those discussed by the 1979 Advisory Council on Social Security and which would result in major changes in the way benefits are calculated for retired workers and their dependents and survivors. Some changes, such as the reduction or elimination of spouse benefits or a cap on the size of these benefits, though not specifically dealt with, can be inferred from the results reported in this volume.

whether the same definition should be applied in all circumstances. This problem is behind the criticism made of current OASI policy, whereby two families who pay equal contributions into OASI over their lifetime and earn equal amounts of income can expect to receive vastly different benefits net of payroll taxes depending on how the earnings were split between the marriage partners. Yet it is equally true that such a matched pair of couples would also pay different federal income taxes depending on whether they were legally married or not. Robert Lampman and Maurice MacDonald, in examining U.S. tax policies, property law, and the old-age income support programs of other nations, conclude that it is not obvious which model of the family (or economic unit) is the most appropriate. Other Western countries which have experienced changes in work, earnings, and family relationships similar to those that have taken place in the United States have adopted widely different methods of ensuring adequate income to their elderly populations.

Inequities in OASI (the different treatment of beneficiaries who are identical in some ways) reflect past perceptions which no longer hold true about marriage patterns, the roles of women within marriage, and the relative income needs of married couples in old age. One assumption underlying our current provision of spouse and widow benefits was that supplemental benefits paid to homemakers was an effective means of redistributing income to the poor. Karen Holden argues that in fact today spouse benefits are paid primarily to wives of high-earning males (in part because wives of wealthy men are less likely than other wives to work outside the home) while widows' benefits still leave a high proportion of widows with incomes below the poverty line. This result reinforces suspicions that social security benefits for spouses and survivors do not accomplish their goal of income redistribution. Rather this goal and the system's insurance goal are compromised for a third and perhaps less understood and more debatable goal, which is to reward the family in which the traditional roles of working man and dependent wife are sustained at the expense of those families with less traditional roles.

Holden looks at the ramifications of *homemaker credits* as an alternative means of providing security to women. She argues that in fact the spouse benefit is already a form of homemaker credit but that it fails on income distribution grounds by rewarding higher-income groups more than lower-income groups. It also fails on insurance grounds by further dissociating earnings from benefits. It serves today as a subsidy to encourage traditional family roles. If this is the real purpose of such a benefit (a question not yet resolved), some form of alternative homemaker credits are preferable to our present system. A homemaker credit in place of spouse and survivor benefits would address the dependency issue either by providing a benefit to homemakers based on an estimated wage for work in the home or by increasing the average market earnings record of homemakers by allowing them to drop years of low earnings in their AIME calculations. This type of reform is particularly appealing, since it would not significantly increase the cost of the system if it replaced the present spouse benefit.

Richard Burkhauser notes that the current OASI system is based on the proposition that earnings of a husband and wife are the sole property of the individual who actually received them. If a community-property notion of family earnings were used instead (i.e., earnings sharing), this would fundamentally change property rights within the household, end the bias toward traditional family roles, and maintain a link between contributions and benefits. It would furthermore have only a minor effect on the total cost of the system and on income distribution if it replaced the current provision of spouse benefits.

Both of these proposals—homemaker credits and earnings sharing—accept the basic mix of insurance and redistributive goals present in the current OASI system, but they differ on the issue of whether traditional family roles should continue to be subsidized. Earnings sharing is neutral with respect to the roles of husband and wife, in that one- or two-earner couples who had the same total earnings records would receive identical benefits. Homemaker credits would continue to subsidize work in the home, with the result that, unless homemakers were required to pay taxes, benefits would continue to be tilted to favor one-earner couples. Both would end the dependency role of homemakers by providing them an earnings record in their own right. Earnings sharing, however, would explicitly develop that record based on an equal-sharing concept. Homemaker credits would divorce both the receipt and size of the homemaker's benefits from the earnings or retirement of her spouse.

The *double-decker system* discussed by Jennifer Warlick, David Berry, and Irwin Garfinkel, and the *two-tier system* discussed by Alicia Munnell and Laura Stiglin challenge the concept that both redistributive and insurance features should be mixed in one benefit. The plans discussed in both papers adopt earnings sharing in the top tier or deck as the proper means of abolishing spouse benefits but make drastic changes in the insurance–welfare mix of the present OASI system.

A double-decker system would provide benefits at two levels. The lower deck would provide a fixed *demogrant* to all people reaching age 65 regardless of prior contributions or current income. General revenues would be used to finance this benefit. This plan is similar to the Townsend movement in the 1930s. Additional benefits would be paid on the top deck based on insurance and earnings-sharing principles. On this level benefits to both husband and wife would be proportional to the combined covered earnings of the couple. There would be no spouse or survivor benefits, since eligibility for benefits would be based solely on prior contributions to the system.

A two-tier system would also completely separate the redistributive features of the social security system from the insurance features. It would base top-tier benefits solely on covered earnings but would rely solely on Supplemental Security Income, a *negative income tax* program for aged and disabled persons established in 1974, rather than a demogrant to provide benefits for the low-income aged. The spouse benefit, survivor benefits, and redistributive tilt of OASI would be dropped from the top, earnings-related tier. The double-decker and two-tier systems have much in common. Both are based on the belief that the present social security system requires explicit attention to the proper mix of redistributive and insurance goals. The proponents of these systems argue that their plans are superior to the current system in that these goals are directly addressed and more effectively attained even when total expenditures are held constant.

Both sets of authors explicitly recognize that our current social security program is attempting to fulfill both insurance and redistributive goals. They believe the inequities of the present system would best be alleviated by separating the insurance and redistribution objectives. They see the issue of the changing roles of women and men within this broader context. According to Garfinkel (forthcoming), the major differences are that total revenue collected and distributed by a double-decker system will be much greater than by a two-tier system, since a double decker provides a demogrant to rich and poor alike. Thus the marginal tax rate on all but the low-income population will be greater under a double-decker system than under a two-tier system, but, on the other hand, the marginal tax rate for the low-income population will be greatly reduced.

In reviewing the four major proposals for change, it is important to recognize the underlying assumptions made by each about family decisions and who should bear responsibility for them. Earnings sharing assumes that labor force withdrawal is a joint decision by husband and wife and that both worker and homemaker should share the cost of this decision. Earnings sharing, by splitting total earnings between spouses, forces the working spouse to share this cost through lower benefits and explicitly recognizes the contribution of the nonworking or lower-earning spouse in the higher-paid accomplishments of the other spouse. Proposals for providing earnings credits to homemakers or child-care providers are based on the assumption that the service performed is of value to society and thus that the cost of partial compensation for the OASI benefit loss of the spouse should be shared by *all* workers. If a homemaker credit were enacted, the OASI system would for the first time determine the economic value of work, rather than accepting the value placed on it by the market. Homemakers would be protected against a decline in covered earnings in the labor market up to the amount of this credit. The remaining cost of labor force withdrawal would be borne by the home-maker alone. Under both a two-tier and double-decker system with earnings sharing, the cost of withdrawal would be borne entirely by the family, although minimal old-age benefits would be guaranteed by a demogrant or improved SSI.

Unlike the present system, all four proposals share a basic assumption that a person divorced from a covered worker should not benefit from the latter's postdivorce earnings and should be free to accept benefits independent of the former spouse's retirement decision. In a system of earnings sharing, benefits would be derived from those of the working spouse only for the duration of the marriage. The adoption of any of these proposals would thus be an important rejection of a major controversial implication of the current system, that divorced spouses should be treated no differently from currently married women and men at the time of the worker's retirement. Each proposal rests on a unique judgment about the appropriate sharing of earnings during marriage. Are they the joint property of a couple, or do they belong entirely to the earner?

Different expectations about the future work behavior of women are implied by the various proposals. The underlying assumption of spouse benefits, as explained above, was that the pattern of work and earnings of married women was radically different from that of men. If there had been no difference, the rationale for spouse benefits would not have existed, since most married couples would receive two benefits. Current contro-versy over the dual entitlement provision arises in part because of the growing percentage of female beneficiaries who are eligible for both their own benefits as retired workers and for spouse or widow benefits. However, because women continue to have shorter work histories and lower earnings than men, retired-worker benefits for many women are lower than the benefits for which they are eligible as spouses or widows. The persistence of earnings differentials between men and women com-plicates the debate over social security reforms, since for many couples and divorced and widowed women, spouse and survivor benefits are still a necessary source of income in old age. In a world of complete equality in earnings and identical work behavior, the simple elimination of spouse benefits would reduce the inequality of benefits net of payroll taxes paid between one-earner and two-earner couples without causing widespread hardship for future generations of retirees. Should the social security system continue to compensate for differences in the work behavior of men and women? A demogrant or means-tested SSI program would assure that most aged units would have incomes above a given minimum. But beyond that, retirement income would depend in part on a homemaker's ability to obtain additional income in market work. Only the homemaker-credit proposal explicitly recognizes that homemaking should be given special consideration as a socially beneficial function and that some subsidy out of payroll tax revenue should be given for it.

In reviewing the proposals and the discussions in the body of this book, the reader is urged to continually question the underlying assumptions about the purpose of a multi-part social security system, the appropriate unit to be insured or assisted, the future work behavior of women and men, and the obligations of couples or society to share the financial responsibility of labor force withdrawal to care for home and family. Only then can the reader evaluate the pattern of gainers and losers under each of the reforms.

Although we, as the editors, hesitate to draw conclusions about the relative merits of specific proposals, other contributors express strong opinions. Barbara Bergmann judges the relative importance of gainers and losers under each proposal. Her discussion points out sharply that predictions about the work behavior of women in the future will be an important ingredient in the final decision on social security reform. Robert Myers, Chief Actuary between 1947 and 1970, who became Deputy Commissioner of Social Security (for Programs) in the Reagan administration, after having participated in this conference, argues that the underlying models of the current social security program are not obsolete, that it continues to fulfill the goals both of the original designers and of current society far better than would any of the major reform proposals. In his paper he discusses various incremental reforms that he argues would equally well reduce current inequities without the large administrative costs involved in more comprehensive reform proposals. Stanford Ross, a social security commissioner during the Carter administration, presents a quite different view. He believes the current controversy over social security is in part owing to public misunderstanding of the basic purposes of the program and its inability to meet these purposes under changed social conditions.

Social security was designed during a time when other private and social income maintenance programs paid retirement income to only a small fraction of the elderly population. The expansion of federal and state income transfer programs and the increased coverage of workers by private and public employee pension plans require that social security reform be considered within the context of other income support programs. The integration of social security with these other programs is at the heart of the Munnell–Stiglin and Warlick–Berry–Garfinkel papers and the discussions of them by Henry Aaron and Colin Campbell.

One alternative to improving the protection of dependent spouses by OASI is to require that they be eligible for survivor benefits under private pensions. Indeed, a step was taken in this direction with the passage in 1974 of the *Employee Retirement Income Security Act* (ERISA), mandating that all pensions must offer a *joint and survivor's benefit* to retired workers. The use of increased regulation in the private sector, however, is only as effective as the scope of private pension coverage. Coverage by private pension plans is now at about 50% and has remained at this level for the past decade. Thus, without further extensions of coverage, half of all workers and their dependents will not benefit from federal regulation of private pension plan provisions.[10] In addition, the present law, by allowing retirees to choose not to receive a joint and survivor's benefit, assumes that the worker covered by such a plan will make the most appropriate decision considering the current and future needs of his or her family. Francis King's discussion of spouse benefits under private pensions addresses both of these considerations. A further complication with respect to the protection of women is the wide variation among states as to whether pension benefits are property rights that can be transferred. This is most critical in the case of divorce, and it is clear that public policy makers cannot assume divorced spouses will uniformly share in the private pension rights accumulated by their spouses during marriage.

In the discussion of all reforms, the issue of disability protection for dependent spouses remains unresolved. Because the current OASDI system provides protection directly to workers, it assumes no responsibility (with the single exception of disabled widows) for providing disability benefits to full-time homemakers or those who become disabled after having been out of the labor force for several years. This is true whether or not the family experiences a large increase in expenses due to the loss of the homemaker's services. William Johnson and William Burfield point out that the various reform proposals would alter and in most cases increase disability protection for persons out of the paid work force. Their paper estimates the potentially large cost of such protection. Financing is the most significant problem with all the proposed reforms of disability coverage. Unless increased disability protection to homemakers is countered by reduced coverage of workers (as would be the case in the

[10]The President's Commission on Pension Policy recommended a system of required minimum private pension coverage for all workers. Such a policy, of course, would make private pension coverage universal and reduce the burden on public programs to alone meet minimum insurance and welfare goals (President's Commission on Pension Policy, 1981).

earnings-sharing system), tremendous costs would accrue to the system. Even in the earnings-sharing case, they predict large cost increases, which are lower than in the case of the double-decker system or homemaker credit only because of the reduced protection afforded the primary worker and the exclusion from coverage of never-married women.

Conclusions

The purpose of this monograph is to sharpen the debate over social security reform. The papers advance our knowledge of the insurance and pure income transfer aspects of each proposal as well as point out different assumptions about family and work behavior underlying each. Whether or not gaps or inequities in the program are justified and whether the minimum income provided is sufficient depend upon the weight put on achieving the goals of adequacy and equity. It is increasingly clear that spouse benefits are a relatively wasteful means of redistributing income to the poor. Examining how nonearners—primarily wives and widows—are treated under OASI forces one to articulate the purpose of this program in the context of current work and earnings behavior and in concert with other income maintenance programs. Each of the major proposed reforms discussed in this volume seeks to eliminate deficiencies in the current OASI program, often at the cost of reducing the subsidy to women who remain at home or, in the case of a homemaker credit, by altering the nature of the subsidy. Other nations have resolved this issue in different ways. Thus the answer is not clear, and the path to reform will be neither easy nor without controversy.

We can only approximate the changes in income distribution that will result from each proposed change. Actual gainers and losers (compared to what they would have had under the current program) cannot be predicted with certainty, since the ability of families to adjust future work and earnings decisions in reaction to these changes is difficult to estimate. It is apparent, however, that any change in the current treatment of women and men by OASI should not be accepted until its rationale is fully developed. Only then will the final distribution of benefits among the population be accepted. This is the message of Ross's chapter—that only understanding, not myths, will save the social security program. Whereas Ross concludes that structural change is required, Myers, who pushes for only incremental reforms, argues that better understanding will increase acceptance of the present system. We agree that greater understanding of social security and how it fits current social conditions is central to the debate.

2

Concepts Underlying the Current Controversy about Women's Social Security Benefits

ROBERT J. LAMPMAN
MAURICE MACDONALD

Reconsideration of how women are treated by social security (i.e., the taxes they pay and the benefits they receive and the terms on which they receive them), drives us back to fundamental questions of equity, adequacy, and efficiency. In turn, those questions take us to issues of whether the appropriate unit for a tax–transfer program is the individual or the family; whether benefits should be related to contributions, to presumed or demonstrated need, to age, or to family status; and whether—and in what degree—social insurance should be supplemented by other income transfer programs.

These questions have been addressed at every stage in the historical development of the social security system. After initially assigning retirement protection to covered workers as individuals, the Congress, with the 1939 amendments, instituted spouse benefits and survivor benefits to meet the greater needs of retired couples and to insure against the loss of a primary earner.[1] Both disability and health-care benefits have been

---

[1] A review of historical writings does not suggest any great controversy about these family benefits. Arthur Altmeyer (1966, pp. 92, 106) notes that they were paid for in part by reducing benefits for single workers and also reducing lump-sum death benefits. Edwin E. Witte (1962, pp. 165, 199) objected to the denial of benefits to wives who were less than 65 years old. Martha Derthick (1979) states that reducing the long-run benefits promised to

added to make up Old Age, Survivors, Disability, and Health Insurance (OASDHI). Recently, Supplemental Security Income (SSI) replaced Old Age Assistance, Aid to the Blind, and Aid to the Disabled. Aid to Families with Dependent Children (AFDC) and Medicaid, along with SSI, are the leading public-assistance parts of what is often loosely referred to as a "social security system."[2] In this paper, our attention is centered on OASI and SSI.

This paper has two main parts. The first identifies concepts that have been important in the development of social insurance and related government programs. Some fundamental differences between an individualistic and familistic approach to benefits and taxes are defined, and applications of these approaches are illustrated with reference to marital-property law and federal income taxation. Related ideas from the "new home economics" and feminist thought are mentioned. Then the implications and incentive effects of the familist and individualist orientations for defining the beneficiary unit are considered. A discussion of the main alternatives for scaling social insurance benefits completes the first part of the paper. This discussion highlights equity issues that stem from different views about the purposes of social insurance.

The second part of the paper uses concepts developed in the first part to evaluate several proposals for the reform of social security. These include earnings sharing, homemaker credits, a two-tier system, and a double-decker proposal. Precedents for these proposals are examined, including those embodied in the social security systems of other nations. A summary reviews the main points.

Basic Concepts in Social Insurance and Related Programs

INDIVIDUALISM VERSUS FAMILISM

Continued expansion of women's role in the labor force has led to increased awareness of the implications of OASI's practice of taxing workers as individuals and at the same time paying benefits that take into

---

single workers was "a rare instance of benefit reduction." She comments as follows, "Single persons, however, were a small and politically inactive portion of the population—a statistical category, not an organized interest group—and so the program's bias against them was not transferred into a political issue [p. 261]." See also Flowers (1979).

[2]Unemployment insurance, workers' compensation, temporary disability insurance, and other public programs are sometimes included in a more broadly defined system.

account their family relationships. Tax-transfer policy is always in tension between the concepts of individualism and familism. On the one hand, we have the concept of freestanding individuals defining by contract their rights and obligations toward one another. But, on the other hand, members of a family live under a set of rights and obligations imposed on them by law and custom and ethics. Hazel Kyrk (1953, p. 17) identified the family as a status system surviving in what is otherwise largely a regime of contract.

A pure individualist might assert complete indifference about how people choose to relate themselves to other adults or to children. Presumably such a choice is freely made as a way to maximize one's own utility given one's income. Hence, a transfer of income from a single person to a married person at the same income level will not increase total utility any more than a transfer from a non-car-owner to a car-owner. The earner is seen as the appropriate taxpaying and beneficiary unit, and the dependents who presumably share his or her earnings are irrelevant to tax and benefit policy. It follows, then, that taxes and benefits should not vary with marital status nor with size of family. With respect to women's roles, an individualistic tax–benefit policy would not recognize homemaking and/or child-rearing responsibilities as bases for varying taxes or benefits.

A familist is one who recognizes the family rather than the individual as the basic self-reliant unit and who sees the family not simply as the outcome of consumer choice but also as an ongoing transfer or insurance institution whereby income is shared. Such a person sees it as appropriate for tax and benefit policy to take into account the needs and ability to pay of any family constellations which appear. A familist is comfortable with a social policy that legitimizes family membership as a status that qualifies one for benefits without proof that one has done anything to deserve them. This unconditional willingness to assist family members may be motivated by the fact that the family rears and socializes children; it reproduces the labor force and transmits social and spiritual values across generations. Familists might disagree about what these special contributions imply for women's roles and for assigning benefits to women in family filing units. Some may believe that homemaking ought to be rewarded because it is uniquely responsible for the important social contributions of the family. Other familists might hold that women have special nurturant skills that facilitate parenting.

Both the individualist and the familist face a cross-cutting difficulty with the concept of family responsibility. How far does it extend? The individualist may find it offensive to legislate a detailed code of responsibilities to relatives but at the same time tends to believe that it is wrong for government to aid persons until relatives have done all they are able to do. This is consistent with the belief that the individual should be responsible for his own free choices about marriage and family size. The familist, on the other hand, is more likely to see the case for outside aid to meet the needs of family members to facilitate the desirable functions families perform. This is consistent with recognition of a social interest in the well-being of dependents. However, familists, just like individualists, are likely to divide on the question of which responsibilities should be enforced against potentially responsible family members and which should be assumed by the state. Both groups also divide on the question of whether relatives' responsibility extends beyond the nuclear family.

It is important to note that many of the functions of the present-day "welfare state" could be handled by mandating that responsibility for current benefits be assumed not by the taxpayer but by all relatives, broadly defined, of current beneficiaries. Of course, the trend has been in the opposite direction. In the past, AFDC held the parents of the mother as well as the absent father of the child to be responsible (i.e., their income and assets were countable in determining the eligibility of the mother). At one time most states required adult children to contribute to the support of parents on Old Age Assistance. However, SSI has no general require- ment that holds relatives responsible for the support of recipients. It also abolished the lien law that restricted the rights of OAA recipients to pass property on to their heirs. SSI does state that the countable income and assets of a spouse ineligible for SSI are deemed available to the SSI applicant and counted against benefits. Similarly, the parents' resources are countable for disabled children. In addition, SSI payments are reduced by one-third if the beneficiary person or couple lives in another person's household.

Property Law

The history of property law reflects the conflict between the individual- ist and familist approaches. The thought that individuals should have undisputed sway over the use and disposition of their earnings and property was a radical challenge to feudalistic doctrines, which taught that spouses, children, and aged parents have claims to the income and property of another. Contemporary English and American common law reflect the feudal and modern views. Primary property right run to the individual owner, but at the same time some claims reside with other family members. Such claims come into play in cases of nonsupport, divorce, and inheritance. But in general the law is reluctant to look inside the family unit to direct how income and property are to be shared.

The Napoleonic code, with its concept of community property, identified earnings and property acquired during a marriage as belonging half to
each spouse.[3] This familistic principle governs the division of property in
case of divorce.[4] At time of death, only the decedent's share of property
passes, and the surviving spouse has no automatic claim to that share.
Community property prevails in eight states that have a background of
French or Spanish colonization. And, in 1948, one principle of community-property tax law was incorporated in federal income taxation, allowing spouses in non-community-property or common-law states to split
their combined incomes. This allowed many couples to pay lower taxes
because one spouse usually had either no earnings or lower earnings than
the other.[5] With a progressive tax rate schedule, the tax payable on two
$50,000 incomes is substantially less than the tax on one $100,000
income. The percentage reduction in tax due to splitting rises with
income. In that sense, income splitting was said to have lessened the
progressivity of the tax. This "pro-family" change also reduced the tax
liability of married as compared to single persons, and of one-earner as
compared to two-earner couples. In response to demands from single
taxpayers for relief from this "discrimination," the Tax Reform Act of
1969 reduced the rates for single individuals. This, in turn, gave rise to the
so-called marriage penalty. The magnitude of this penalty varies with
income level, with the difference between the incomes of the two spouses,
and with the method of claiming deductions. In general, married couples
with a single earner are treated more favorably than unmarried individuals, who in turn are better off than two-earner married couples. Many
wives who work face higher marginal tax rates on their earnings than they

[3]More precisely, each spouse has an undivided present equal interest. No right to
participation during the ongoing marriage exists under traditional community-property law.
Under management and control of community-property statutes (which have been adopted
recently in all community-property states), each spouse has a right to manage and control
100% of the community property, subject to a duty to manage in good faith on behalf of the
community. Before the adoption of the statutes, there was only one person who had
management and control rights over the entire community property and that was the
husband.

[4]In some community-property states, the court has equitable power to divide the
community property at divorce and that power in some instances extends to the separate
property of a spouse as well as the community property.

[5]The federal tax law has no effect on a state's property system. It permits couples in
common-law states to treat their income as if earned under community property for purposes
of tax calculations only. No property rights or rights to management and control are affected.

would as single individuals. These perceived inequities have led some proponents of women's rights to advocate the abolition of the community-property type of income splitting in the federal income tax.[6] On the other hand, women in some non-community-property states have lobbied for adaptations of divorce and inheritance laws to embody community-property concepts.

The New Home Economics

An interesting halfway house between the notion that market income belongs to the one who contracts for it and the notion that it should be assigned 50–50 by marital status is that the marital unit may be viewed as a partnership producing market and nonmarket goods. According to "the *new home economics*," the marital "firm" aims at joint utility maximization over the life cycle and accomplishes this by specialization of labor. A spouse who specializes in nonmarket production, or who finances the education of the other partner, may be said to add nonmarket income and also to contribute to the earning power of the market producer. However, no one has yet developed an objective way to evaluate the combined market and nonmarket income of such a firm, nor a way to identify the share of total income attributable to each partner.

Some critics of the new home economics assert that it supports the traditional concept of the family, in which homemakers play a dependent and subservient role. In their view, the gains from specialization promoted by marriage primarily benefit the male breadwinner while homemakers lose the opportunity to obtain the market skills necessary to provide adequate self-insurance against divorce or the death of a husband. Indeed, some feminists want to abolish OASI spouse and widow benefits and AFDC benefits as well, because they believe these benefits contribute to women's dependency by distorting their choices toward work in the home and away from market work.

DEFINING THE BENEFIT UNIT

Many of the issues that arise with respect to the treatment of women under social security involve the appropriate definition of the benefit unit.

***

[6] A study by the Organisation for Economic Cooperation and Development (1977) reports that among member countries "Increasingly, the individual is taken as the tax unit rather than the married couple or the family. . . . Help for families with children increasingly takes the form of tax credits or, more frequently, of cash transfers, in place of allowances against taxable income [pp. 9, 15]."

On this question, it is clear that a familist orientation leads to the choice of the family as the relevant unit. Policymakers must then decide on whether the appropriate unit is the nuclear family or the extended family.[7]

The guiding principle for the familist is that units with greater consumption needs ought to receive greater benefits. This principle is followed in most welfare programs. However, in some programs that provide benefits in exchange for contributions for or on behalf of specific individuals (e.g., unemployment insurance), the individual contributor is the filing unit.

We noted earlier that OASI benefits go not only to the contributing worker but also to his or her dependents. The family benefits are also often justified as encouraging people to marry (and remarry) and to have children. In the case of a marriage broken by the death of a working man, such benefits may make it possible for the widow to keep the children rather than give them up for adoption. Similar incentives for marriage and family unity are found in the several versions of property law reviewed above. (AFDC, by restricting benefits to female-headed families, is under fire because it is suspected of contributing to family instability.)

Another reason why the family rather than the individual is often selected as the beneficiary unit is that the calculation of benefits against total family resources is a way to limit benefits and hence to save taxpayers' money. Consider the case of cash benefits for children. It costs less to pay AFDC benefits and surviving-children benefits under OASI than it would cost to fund a universal child allowance which takes no account of family status or income.

There is, of course, a case to be made for benefits that are not family-based. Some argue that government should not encourage marriage over nonmarriage and that it should be neutral with respect to fertility. Further, the individualist will point out that some family-based benefits, while offering economic security to a woman, will discourage her from working. This can be said of community-property law. It can also be said of the features of OASI that tie a spouse's benefit to her husband's work record and ignore her payroll tax contributions. (This is the case for a wife whose benefit based on her own work record is smaller than her spouse benefit.)

Thus, there is a conflict between incentives to encourage family security on the one hand, and incentives to encourage women to adopt a full-time, full-life career in the labor force.

---

[7]It is interesting to note that the Food Stamp program adopts neither the individual nor the family. Instead, the filing unit for stamps is the household, defined as the unit that buys, cooks, and eats food together.

SCALING THE SIZE OF BENEFITS

After the appropriate beneficiary unit for a social welfare program is determined, the issue of selecting the method for scaling the size of benefits remains. These methods include

1. Per capita benefits, as in public school benefits. Here a family benefit varies with the number of children attending school.

2. Means-tested benefits, wherein the size of the benefit varies both with an estimate of the unit's needs and a count of variable income and assets. This method is followed in public-assistance programs.

3. Contribution-related benefits, wherein loss of income by the contributor is offset without regard to demonstrated need. Examples of this are found in social insurance against accident, unemployment, and disability, and for retirement. However, social insurance benefits are not always related solely to contributions. Some are related both to contributions and to presumed need as indicated by family size. One social insurance program, Medicare, features benefits that do not vary with the level of contribution.

The field of social insurance is marked by continuing controversy about how much it should be "social" in character and how much it should be like private insurance. It is like insurance in that it relates contributions, variously called premiums and taxes, to the sharing of definable financial risks. It is social in that participation is compulsory and contributions are often designed to be out of alignment with benefits for special groups of contributors.

In social insurance, "insurance equity" is often at odds with broader social purposes related to "fairness." The former requires classification of people according to their exposure to the risk which is being insured against. Thus, term life insurance reasonably may group its clients by age. Further, insurance equity requires that all persons in a risk class (e.g., age group), pay the same dollar premium for a given level of financial protection, and that the combined total of premiums paid plus interest accrued by the risk class must equal the expected benefits.

An application of this principle to retirement insurance is the reduction of the monthly benefit for people who retire early. Insurance equity also dictates that if one group is to have a higher level of retirement income than another, then that group should pay enough, but no more than enough, to cover the additional cost of the higher benefits. Social security now deliberately violates this principle by giving low-wage workers more benefit per dollar of contribution than high-wage workers. The resulting variation in replacement rates is aimed at redistributing income from rich to poor. This redistribution via benefits is somewhat offset by the regressive pattern of social security taxes.

It is interesting that the controversy about fair treatment of women in social security has come to the fore at the same time that a quite separate "movement," led by economists, is calling for more insurance equity in social security. These enthusiasts for insurance principles have concentrated mainly on the lack of "equity" in OASI between wage-earners in different income categories. (They have given little attention to similar equity issues which can be found in disability insurance. One can argue that contributions for this form of insurance should be varied among workers by likelihood of disability.)

However, the proponents of insurance equity are quick to point out the lack of equity in allowing two workers who make the same contribution to receive different total benefits on the grounds that one has a spouse and dependent children and the other does not.[8] This nonconformity with insurance principles could be remedied either by abolishing the family benefits or by reducing the contributions required of workers who have no families. It would, of course, be difficult to classify youthful workers by the likelihood that they will have spouses or dependent children when they reach retirement age or die. At any rate, those who favor insurance principles are quite right in identifying the family benefits as justifiable only by reference to the "social" part of social insurance.

Changing the Social Security System

REDESIGNING THE SOCIAL INSURANCE ASPECTS OF THE SYSTEM

We now turn to a discussion of three of the possible ways to revise the social insurance part of social security. These include abolishing spouse and dependent benefits, and substituting earnings sharing or homemaker credits for the present method of calculating spouse and dependent benefits.

Abolishing Benefits for Spouses and Survivors

Social insurance could, of course, be changed to make it more like private insurance. Benefits could be related more closely to contributions

---

[8]For an estimate of how family benefits tend to swamp out insurance equity see Bennett (1979). While these benefits may vary within earnings classes, they may not in fact vary a great deal as a percentage of earnings across earnings classes. Hence, the issue is one of horizontal rather than vertical equity, to use the jargon of redistribution.

by going to a strictly individualistic system, with no benefits for spouses or widows or survivors. All other income redistribution could be taken out of social insurance and assigned to other public programs. OASI could be made more "efficient" (i.e., it could encourage rather than discourage work effort and private saving), by eliminating the retirement test, which has no actuarial basis and which is an incentive to early retirement. The same claim of efficiency could be made for lowering the high replacement rates associated with low earnings and spouse benefits. Other efficiency reforms include the proposal that the ceiling for taxable earnings be kept low to leave room for (fully funded) private pensions so that funds will accumulate for investment in the private capital stock.

Women can qualify for OASI benefits by their own contributions; they may claim a spouse benefit or widow benefit; and their children may claim survivors' benefits. Divorced women may claim spouse and widow benefits if they were married to an insured man for ten or more years. Because of these dependent benefits and also because of their longer life expectancy, women receive over half of all OASI benefits.[9] Despite this relatively generous treatment of women as a group, OASI is criticized by individualists and, for different reasons, by familists as well.

Individualists are dissatisfied because a married woman who does market work for a number of years but whose earnings record qualifies her for a benefit which is smaller than her spouse benefit has contributed taxes to the system that yield no increase in benefits for her. These "redundant" taxes are viewed as a penalty on working wives. Some two-earner couples also complain because a married couple consisting of two earners may get less in combined benefits than a couple in which there is a single earner, even though both couples have the same combined lifetime earnings. Some redistributionists criticize the current system because spouses of high-wage earners receive what may be considered as unnecessarily high spouse benefits. These may offset the progressive structure of benefits with respect to preretirement wages and increase income inequality among retired persons.[10] Some would abolish spouse and widow benefits entirely, on the ground that they see such benefits as an unjustified subsidy for a socially undesirable role, namely, that of home-

---

[9]See the paper by Alicia H. Munnell and Laura E. Stiglin, Chapter 5 in this volume.

[10]See footnote 8. This seems to be a sore point with some critics. It is true that the big losers from a move to abolish spouse benefits would be the nonworking wives of high-wage earners. These high benefits are hard to justify either on the basis of need or as a replacement of income loss. One possible remedy for this would be to go to a flat dollar amount for all spouse benefits.

maker.[11] Hence, critics of different persuasions share a desire to gear insurance benefits exclusively to market work contributions.

Familists, on the other hand, object to the current social security system because it doesn't provide adequate protection from the economic risks of working in the home. Specifically, they focus on four deficiencies:

1. A divorced woman who was not married 10 years may find that her retirement benefit is low because she spent years outside the market work force and received no social security credit for her work in the home.

2. Disability benefits are not available to homemakers.

3. A surviving widow of divorcée under age 60 who has no dependent children is not entitled to any benefit.

4. There are especially needy aged widows who have inadequate benefits.

The current system does tilt the burden of divorce prior to the tenth year of marriage to women without strong labor force attachments. It also presumes a breadwinner spouse will be able to handle the loss of services from a homemaker who becomes disabled. The nonaged homemaker with no dependent children is not insured against a likely inability to compete in the labor market, which stems from caring for children before they become independent. And aged widows complain about inadequate benefits because they receive only their deceased husband's benefit, whereas before his death they shared one-and-a-half times that benefit with him.

Individualists place a high priority on realigning social insurance benefits with contributions. One step in this direction would be to refund the payroll taxes paid by working wives at the time they accept a spouse or widow benefit. Another would be to simply abolish all benefits for spouses, widows, and children. Two widely recognized proposals to replace the spouse and widow benefits are earnings sharing and homemaker credits.[12]

---

[11]This seems to be the position of "radical feminists." See Barbara Bergmann's paper, Chapter 9 in this volume, for a fuller discussion of this view.

[12]A less ambitious approach would involve incremental changes that increase some women's benefits. The 1979 Advisory Council on Social Security recommended earnings sharing only by divorced spouses. Others have advocated reducing the number of quarters required for coverage, to permit more wives to generate their own earnings records. The equity and adequacy concepts that underlie these incremental changes are hard to identify. Increased benefits for particular groups of women would be financed at the expense of all payroll taxpayers, including these women, who would continue to pay "redundant" taxes.

Earnings Sharing and Homemaker Credits

Homemaker credits would introduce into spouses' earnings records some arbitrary amount of covered wages per year spent in nonmarket work. These credits would enable a married or divorced woman to qualify for a more reasonable benefit on her own record than she might under present rules. Homemaker credits could be financed by general revenues or across-the-board payroll tax increases or increases in the payroll taxes of one-earner couples. It can be argued that two-earner couples should be exempt from any new tax to pay for these credits. These credits seem to be based on a view of marriage akin to that of the "new home economics."

Earnings sharing would combine the market earnings of husband and wife and assign at time of divorce or retirement—again on an arbitrary basis—a share to each spouse. The community-property principle would indicate a 50–50 division as the appropriate intrafamily redistribution. Unlike homemaker credits, earnings sharing would finance itself in part by reducing the retirement benefit of the higher-earning spouse. It may be said to realign women's benefits with women's contributions; the variations in benefits among nonworking spouses might be justified on the somewhat unlikely ground that persons married to high-earning spouses produce more that is of social value than do persons married to low-earning spouses.

Earnings sharing would need to be carefully designed so as not to penalize certain beneficiaries, namely, divorced primary earners, widows under 60 and surviving children of a deceased worker, and wives and children of disabled workers. Continuing the *status quo* for widows and for dependents of disabled workers would deal with concerns about benefit adequacy that pure earnings sharing ignores. There are certain "rough spots" involved. For example, instituting earnings sharing at divorce might seem unfair to primary earners who would have preferred that the marriage continue and who are not at fault for the divorce. The view of marriage as a partnership that justifies earnings sharing may not be acceptable in such circumstances.

Homemaker credits and earnings sharing would tie benefits more closely to payroll tax contributions. Hence, they would increase the insurance equity in social security. However, neither of these proposals adopts a purely individualistic approach, because they both recognize marriage as a resource-sharing institution and take marital status into account in assigning benefits.

From a familist perspective it seems odd to take any account of marriage without further recognizing that marital unions are the basis for the important social functions that families perform. Because marriage ordinarily fosters commitments to childbearing and parenting, a familist views marital status as a convenient tag for ascribing benefits based on all contributions of family members, including home work as well as market production. In this view, earnings sharing and self-financed homemaker credits are undesirable because they are tied exclusively to market work contributions. And the fact that these proposals force market workers to share a work-related benefit with their spouses would not override the familist concern that other family products are not rewarded. For a familist, rewarding these other contributions requires that benefits exceed those that are generated from market work. Hence, a familist tends to favor the present system or other than self-financed homemaker credits.

Feminist positions straddle individualist and familist concerns. Bergmann states, "the disadvantages of the role of housewife are so great that it would be better if the 'option' to assume the role were to disappear."[13] Hence, she favors eliminating the spouse and widow benefits, although, in "solidarity with all women," she speaks favorably of earnings sharing as a second-best remedy. Other feminist leaders support homemaker credits.

REDESIGNING THE REDISTRIBUTIVE ASPECTS
OF THE SYSTEM

The Two-Tier and Double-Decker Systems and the Negative Income Tax

Other ways to respond to calls for benefits that are not based on a family relationship to a payroll tax contributor involve redesigning the redistributional features of social security (the tilt in the benefit formula and the family benefits) and SSI and AFDC. The redistributive features of OASI could be eliminated, with the means-tested SSI and AFDC programs remaining to provide adequate income for those in need.[14] This two-tier system is discussed by Alicia Munnell and Laura Stiglin.[15] Solutions to the problem of redistribution that would respond to women's rights and needs are a demogrant and a *negative income tax* (NIT) for the aged and disabled that would modify some of the harsher aspects of SSI.

Under a double-decker system, all men and women, including those

---

[13]Barbara R. Bergmann, Chapter 9 in this volume. We note that Professor Bergmann seems to call for social security reform as a way to accelerate change in the role of women.

[14]AFDC would automatically pick up some of the burden carried by the survivors portion of OASI.

[15]Chapter 5 in this volume.

receiving social insurance benefits, who reach retirement age or who become disabled at any age would be eligible for a flat monthly benefit without any admission of or test for dependency (a demogrant). Other flat benefits could be designed for children of retired workers and young spouses caring for these children, and for surviving children. As noted before, an individualized structure of this type avoids incentives to choose one form of living arrangement over another. To provide the same benefit under a demogrant that the means-tested program of SSI provides would require massive additional funding. It has been argued that this could be accomplished by increasing the income taxes of higher-income persons.

Proponents of demogrants allege that SSI participants are stigmatized because receipt of these benefits is associated with failure. They argue that SSI does not actually deliver benefits to needy persons who feel strongly about stigma. SSI is also said to accentuate class distinctions, and there is concern that recipients of SSI have so little political power that their benefits will erode. Another objection to SSI is that it imposes a benefit-reduction rate on earnings, which discourages work. A demogrant, by definition, has no benefit-reduction rate.

A NIT could be restricted to those age 65 or older and to those who are disabled. A sliding scale would confine benefits to those who are judged to have inadequate income. To be responsive to women's sensitivity about being categorized as dependents, the receiving unit could be defined as the individual rather than the married couple (the individual is the unit in SSI), and the resources to be counted could be those of the individual rather than of the couple (SSI counts the resources of the couples). To make this NIT for aged and disabled persons less stigmatizing and less restrictive than SSI, the asset test could be eliminated and the benefit-reduction rate for all types of income, including "unearned" income, could be standardized at 50%. Depending on how the social insurance part of OASI is revised, special provisions might be needed in a NIT for children of retired, disabled, and deceased workers.

All of the remedies for the problems we have discussed are motivated in part by a preference for individualistic as opposed to familistic tax–transfer devices. They would move us further away from relatives' responsibility for meeting income needs of family members. Earnings sharing and homemaker credits offer benefits related to recognized albeit presumed producer contributions as opposed to benefits that are forthrightly redistributive and justified by family status. On the other hand, a demogrant would break the link between benefit and contribution, as well as the link between benefit and family status. The NIT sketched here would go further than SSI toward making the individual the beneficiary unit.

PRECEDENTS FOR RECENT PROPOSALS

Some of the proposals discussed here have been considered before and rejected. In the early thirties, Dr. Francis E. Townsend proposed an Old Age Revolving Pension Plan with a flat payment of $200 per month for every citizen 60 years of age and over, to be financed with a 2% sales tax. This popular approach to a demogrant for the aged remained topical until the early fifties, but never was favored by any congressional committee. Similarly, there are children's allowances in over sixty countries, but the United States Congress has never seriously considered them.

The NIT idea has been embodied in the structure of important income-conditioned programs, yet we have not embraced it wholeheartedly. The Family Assistance Plan (FAP) was proposed as a NIT alternative to AFDC in 1969. This began as an elegantly simple approach to income transfer, was successively modified as unforeseen issues developed, but was never adopted by Congress. However, the SSI program was proposed as part of a package that included FAP, and it succeeded. At about the same time, food stamp benefits were increased, and this NIT-like program began its dramatic growth.

Pension plans for private and government employees offer some precedent for abolishing social security benefits for spouses and children. These plans generally assign pension rights on an individualistic basis, whereby earnings-replacement rates do not vary with marital status or family size. Most plans have provisions for paying vested pensions to survivors. The value of the survivor benefit does not depend on the number of the deceased's dependents. King documents that most plans do not permit collection of death benefits prior to the time at which the worker would have retired.[16] The courts in community-property states have consistently ruled that vested pension benefits are accessible to the divorced spouse of the worker.

The community-property method of income taxation, which was adopted in 1948, is a precedent for earnings sharing. However, this tax provision has continued to be a matter of contention. It imposes high marginal tax rates on wives' earnings, and this has led some women's advocates to argue for an end to the community-property provision. These persons want the option to file combined or separate income tax returns without penalty. It seems anomalous that there is a movement to end the community-property provision at a time when earnings sharing is proposed for OASI purposes.

Homemaker credits have no precedent, although there is some similar-

---

[16]Francis P. King, Chapter 8 in this volume.

ity to the credits for military service granted by social security during
World War II.

Precedents for some of the proposals we have discussed are to be found
in the social security systems of other nations. The majority of systems
add supplements to the pension if the recipient is supporting a wife or
young children and also provide pensions for survivors of insured persons
or pensioners. However, a number of nations do treat family members
quite differently from the United States (see Table 2.1). Some have gone
to a two-tier system. For example, Canada has a demogrant for all persons
at age 65 but has no spouse benefit in its earnings-related pension.
Sweden and the United Kingdom also have spouse benefits in the social-
adequacy component but none in the earnings-related component. Some
nations (e.g., the Netherlands and Japan) have flat benefits for dependent
spouses and children. France and the Federal Republic of Germany have
neither a demogrant nor a spouse benefit.

Table 2.1
Spouse and Dependent Benefits in the Social Security Systems of Selected Countries

Country	Cash Benefits for Insured Workers and Family Members	Survivor Benefits
Australia	Only income-tested benefits from age 65 to age 70; flat benefit after age 70. Wife's supplement.	Widow's pension same as old-age pension. Income-tested benefit for orphans.
Canada	Universal old-age pension for persons at age 65. Earnings-related pension has no spouse benefit. Income-tested pension for old-age pensioner's spouse age 60 to 64.	Universal pension has no survivor benefit. Earnings-related pension pays 60% of insured pension and a flat benefit to orphans.
France	Old-age pension has no spouse benefit. Dependent's supplement is means tested.	50% of insured's pension for widows.
Germany, Federal Republic of	No spouse benefit.	60% of insured's pension for widow or dependent widower. 10% to orphans.
Japan	Employee's pension insurance has flat benefit for dependent spouse and children. National pension has no spouse benefit, but spouse may claim pension at age 65 if contributor.	Employee's pension insurance pays 50% of insured's pension to widow or widower, flat benefits to children. National pension has flat benefits for widows and orphans.

(continued)

Table 2.1 (Continued)

Country	Cash Benefits for Insured Workers and Family Members	Survivor Benefits
Netherlands	Old-age pension has flat supplement for wife of any age.	Flat benefits for widows and orphans.
New Zealand	Flat-rate pension for aged couple is 166% of pension for single person. Flat benefits for children.	Income-tested benefits for widows and orphans.
Sweden	Universal old-age pension for aged couple is 160% of pension for single person, with supplements for children and for wife aged 60. Earnings-related pension has no spouse benefit.	Universal survivor benefits for widows and orphans of specified ages. Earnings-related pensions pay widow 40% and orphans 15% of pension of insured.
USSR	Old-age pension has supplement of 10% of pension for one dependent, 15% for two or more.	Eligible survivors include widows and children. Benefits vary by earnings and number of survivors.
United Kingdom	Flat-rate old-age pension has supplements for wife and children. Earnings-related component has no spouse benefit.	Flat-rate and earnings-related benefits payable to widow and children.
United States	Earnings-related old-age pension pays 50% of worker's pension to wife or dependent husband (reduced for ages 62–64) or to wife at any age caring for child, and 50% to each child.	Widow's or dependent widower's benefit is 100% of insured worker's pension at age 65. Orphan's benefit is 75% of above.

Source: U.S. Department of Health and Human Services (1980).

Summary

Having started in the individualist model, OASI was converted in 1939 to the familist model, wherein spouse and children and parents could qualify for benefits by virtue of a family relationship to a contributor. The family model is not unusual for tax and transfer programs. The income tax also takes account of the income and needs of family members other than the principal earner, and so do most public-assistance programs, but there have been challenges to the appropriateness of this model in recent decades. Most recently, women's advocates have questioned the appropriateness of OASI's collecting contributions from individuals but of making benefits contingent upon a marital relationship.

A similar controversy rages around the related issue of scaling benefits. Assuming that there are to be spouse and family benefits, should they be flat per capita amounts, should they be variable and means tested, or should they be (as they now are in OASI) variable and directly related to the contributions of the wage earner to the insurance fund? There is, of course, a rationale for each of these options, and there are arguments against each of them. With respect to the present law, it can be claimed that it departs from the principle of insurance equity in that two workers with the same earnings record may draw very different total benefits if one has family dependents and the other does not. This departure is justified by its proponents as a form of redistributive justice.

Critics seem to have quite different reasons for wanting to redesign the present social insurance component of our social security retirement system, namely OASI, and the social adequacy component, namely SSI. One of the reasons is to eliminate what some call a demeaning condition under which a woman (or a man) qualifies for a benefit simply because she (he) is or was married to a contributor. To circumvent this situation, the social insurance component could be revised in one of three ways: (*a*) benefits for spouses and dependents could be abolished; (*b*) the present spouse benefits could be replaced by benefits based on a 50–50 sharing of the combined earnings records of spouses; or (*c*) the present spouse benefit could be replaced by one based on a spouse's earnings record supplemented by credit for each year spent out of the labor market in the role of homemaker. Further, to get away from the condition cited, the social adequacy component could be modified by introducing either a demogrant (a flat per person grant) for everyone age 65 or over, or an individualized NIT, which takes no account of marital status.

There are precedents for each of these proposed revisions of the social security system. They are to be found in the history of American practice and debate with respect to tax–transfer programs, in the field of private pensions, and in the current social security systems of other countries. However, it should be noted that any of these changes will open or renew a conflict between those who hold familist and those who hold individualist values, and a conflict between those who want social insurance to emphasize pure insurance equity and those who want it to emphasize a version of redistributive justice. Moreover, a change to any one or to a combination of the proposed schemes would cause some persons to gain and some to lose in reference to the status quo. The losers will be found among those who receive benefits as well as among those who contribute to the system. The conflict between rationales for qualifying conditions for benefits, and the disagreement over who should give up benefits or pay more taxes are not altogether new in the history of social security, but a new compact is not easy to come by and is likely to require compromises and trade-offs among the parties and the principles.

ACKNOWLEDGMENTS

The authors want to thank Barbara R. Bergmann, Robert J. Myers, June Weisberger, and the editors for valuable comments on an earlier version of this paper.

3

Supplemental OASI Benefits to Homemakers through Current Spouse Benefits, a Homemaker Credit, and Child-Care Drop-Out Years

KAREN C. HOLDEN

The focus by the HEW report on ways to eliminate dependency as a factor in entitlement to social security benefits (U.S. Department of Health, Education, and Welfare, 1979a), and the amount of time spent by the Advisory Council on Social Security on this same issue (U.S. Department of Health, Education, and Welfare, 1979b) are indications of the considerable stress placed on the social security system by the changing roles of men and women in work and marriage. The change is not that entirely new roles have been adopted, for some women have always worked and some marriages have always shared child-care and market-work obligations, but that a rapidly growing percentage of women and men are moving in and out of paid work during their working-age years. One of the consequences of this change is that the effects of noncontributory benefits paid to aged wives and widows may no longer be consistent either with their original goals or with current views of marriage, dependency, and social needs. Discontent over benefits to wives and widows arises in part from the fact that eligibility for these noncontributory benefits and the amount paid are not consistently related to current income, past earnings, or time spent out of the work force by beneficiary women. Proposed changes in these benefits to wives and widows seek to establish

41

a more consistent relationship between eligibility for benefits and the current income or preretirement work experience of these women.

This paper discusses two proposed changes in benefits for women who have spent some years out of the paid work force—the posting of a homemaker credit to the covered-earnings records of homemakers during periods when no earnings are reported, and the reduction in the earnings averaging period by some number of years spent caring for one's children at home. Both of these proposals are judged on (a) their ability to redistribute income to the poor; (b) their ability to compensate retirees for past low earnings or time spent in work at home; and (c) their consistency with the underlying value judgments of the social security programs and society about the economic role of women in marriage.

The Dual Entitlement Provision:
An Implicit Means Test

That the Old Age and Survivors Insurance program (OASI) provides some "reasonable" level of income has always been a major objective shaping eligibility rules and provisions for calculating benefits. Unfortunately, the basic principles upon which "adequacy" of benefits is determined and the relative importance of adequacy and equity considerations in determining program regulations have never been clearly articulated. The recommendation by the 1937–1939 Advisory Council that supplemental, noncontributory benefits be granted to wives and widows of insured workers had the goal of providing income adequacy to a needy group. These benefits, together with the progressive benefit structure (made more progressive in 1939) and lack of differentiation in benefit calculations between men and women despite a difference in lifespan, were explicit recognition that strict conformance with actuarial practices of private insurance, especially during the early years of the program, was likely to result in unacceptably low benefits for retirees and their wives (Brown, 1977).[1] The Advisory Council predicted quite correctly that over time benefits based on longer earnings records would rise and that more

---

[1]The political and economic climate out of which these recommendations grew is interesting. OAI was considered a program which could be manipulated to achieve social goals. In 1939 social security contributions exceeded benefit disbursements. The projected size of the trust fund led many to question the social appropriateness of a rapidly accumulating trust fund when benefits were low and unemployment high. In addition, there was some sympathy expressed in Congress and the administration for the use of social security benefits as a countercyclical program raising and lowering benefits depending upon economic conditions (Altmeyer, 1966, pp. 108 ff.).

women would enter the work force, thereby becoming eligible for their own retired-worker benefits. With less accuracy they predicted that under these conditions dependent benefits for wives and aged widows would diminish in size and in number granted. They had no way of predicting the controversy which would be created as working wives "lost" or duplicated these benefits for dependents with their own retired-worker benefits.

In assuring higher old-age benefits to the needy, an alternative available to the 1937–1939 council was to increase benefits and the number of elderly eligible for the means-tested Old Age Assistance (OAA) program.[2] The decision to raise social security benefits was in part a political decision, since support for the program was expected to erode, especially among current workers, if few beneficiaries were better off than they would have been with only public assistance.[3] On the other hand, raising all retired-worker benefits would have been a costly alternative. Benefits to wives and widows were designed to target a particular needy group, with the method of determining eligibility for these benefits—the dual entitlement provision—functioning as a type of means test to screen out the relatively better-off aged.

The assumption that women were less likely to work than men and that men typically worked throughout their working-age years determined the different treatment of dependent husbands. Until 1950 no benefits were provided for dependent husbands or widowers. In that year an explicit dependency test was required for a husband applying for benefits on his covered-earnings record, although the dependency of a wife continued to be determined only on the basis of marriage and the relative size of her own retired-worker benefit.

If the dual entitlement provision is considered a type of means test, the discrepancy between the treatment of dependent wives and husbands is easily understood. Because it was assumed that few women would have long working careers, few women applying for a spouse benefit would in fact have other work-related income. The cost of paying benefits to the

---

[2]Federal–state public assistance programs were also established by the 1935 Social Security Act and were administered under the auspices of the Social Security Board. The 1939 council did recommend an increase in the federal share of public assistance payments. The joint state–federal administration of public assistance programs made across-the-board improvements in benefits to old-age assistance clients administratively more difficult to achieve.

[3]In 1940 the average OASI retired-worker benefit was $22.10 per month ($22.80 for retired males) or $265.20 per year. The average OAA benefit was $20.25 *per recipient* in 1940, with an additional amount for dependents. The maximum OASI benefit for those retiring in 1940 at age 65 was $41.20, or $494.40 per year. This compares with the median earnings of males working four quarters in 1940 of $1353.

few women with other pensions would be low compared to the cost of administering a dependency test, which would require proof of dependency from all wives and widows. On the other hand, the high percentage of workers not covered by OASI in 1939 meant that a sizable number of husbands could claim dependency benefits if a simple dual entitlement provision were applied to both sexes.[4]

When, in 1950, a dependency test was adopted for men, it reflected the assumption that few men were dependent on their wives, and therefore the total cost of administering a more complex dependency test for dependent men would be small compared to the potential program costs of allowing husbands who had worked in noncovered jobs to receive a dependent benefit.

It can be seen then that the dependency tests finally adopted (both for women and for men) were attempts to combine administrative ease with low net program costs—two criteria which have been major factors determining final policy recommendations made by all advisory councils, including the most recent. Administrative ease is maximized when decisions can be made on the basis of records readily available to the Social Security Administration. Cost is minimized when decisions can be made without high personnel costs or large increases in benefits.

The Distribution of Dependent Benefits among the Aged

Forty years after OASI dependent benefits were enacted, it is necessary to evaluate how well these supplemental benefits are *now* achieving the original goal of meeting "the greatest social need with the minimum increase in cost." Do benefits to wives and widows reach otherwise poor aged beneficiaries?[5] Because a wife or widow can receive only the higher of her spouse or retired-worker benefit, an important distinction is made in this paper between the dependent benefit a women is eligible for based on her husband's benefit (i.e., her spouse benefit) and the *additional* amount

---

[4]In 1939 only slightly more than half (57.8%) of all workers were in work covered by social secutiry. By 1951 this percentage had increased to 79.5%. However, 20% of all workers were still in noncovered employment.

[5]The eligibility of husbands and widowers for dependent benefits is now determined in the same way as is that of wives and widows. However, 99.7% of all benefits to dependents are paid to wives (*Social Security Bulletin, Annual Statistical Supplement, 1975,* Table 70). Thus, for ease of exposition, the rest of the paper discusses benefits to aged wives and widows only.

a woman will receive as a spouse above her own retired-worker benefit. This additional amount, defined for the purposes of this paper as the *supplemental spouse benefit* (SSB), is the difference between a woman's dependent-spouse benefit and her retired-worker benefit.[6]

The original goal of paying supplemental benefits was clearly to raise incomes of OASI beneficiaries in greatest need—those whose incomes would otherwise be unacceptably low if they were to receive only retired-worker benefits. The Social Security Administration's definition of poverty income provides a convenient and frequently used benchmark by which to classify the relative income status of a population group. Thus we examine the distribution of benefits first among beneficiary couples and then among formerly married women (those separated, widowed, or divorced) who are beneficiaries, classified by relative poverty status. If SSBs are granted largely to otherwise poor beneficiaries, the goal of increasing incomes of beneficiaries most in need is at least partially fulfilled. If, on the other hand, SSBs are received largely by couples and women with relatively high incomes from other sources (including OASI retired-worker benefits), while other beneficiaries remain poor, the redistribution goals are not being met. Failure of these benefits to satisfy income redistribution goals implies the need for changes either in eligibility requirements, or in the underlying rationale for these benefits—or in both.

Data from the 1973 Exact Match Study are used. This joint study by the Bureau of the Census and the Social Security Administration (U.S. Department of Health, Education, and Welfare, 1975) matches selected items from the March 1973 Current Population Survey with data on social security earnings and benefits. Records of husband and wife were matched for this paper in order to estimate retired-worker benefits of husband and wife and the SSBs for which each wife was eligible.

The sample from the Exact Match Study that was selected for analysis included couples of which (*a*) both were at least 65 years of age; (*b*) the husband was eligible for OASI retired-worker benefits; and (*c*) neither

---

[6]For example, a married woman eligible for a spouse benefit of half her husband's $400 monthly benefit, and also eligible for her own retired-worker benefit of $150, will be eligible for an SSB of $50.00 (1/2 × $400 − $150). Her SSB is zero if her own retired-worker benefit is $200 or more. It is useful to consider only these supplemental benefits rather than the entire spouse benefit, since it is the total of these supplements which are the budgetary cost to the social security system of providing spouse benefits, and it is these supplements which determine whether the incomes of couples are indeed raised by the existence of benefits for dependents.

husband nor wife, if younger than 72, earned more than $1680 in 1972.[7] Formerly married women had to meet the age and earnings requirements for inclusion in the selected sample. These criteria identify beneficiary couples and aged women, the groups which the 1937–1939 Advisory Council identified as legitimate recipients of higher benefits through social security.

The earnings test cutoff selects only those aged who have reduced their labor market work sufficiently to be retired by SSA definitions and be in probable need of additional retirement income. The earnings test ensures that benefits are targeted on the retired population.[8] The effectiveness of benefits for dependents in raising incomes of the poor within this target population is the issue addressed here. Thus, the application of the earnings test criterion to select the target population is appropriate. An age limit was imposed, since couples in which either wife or husband was younger than 64 are eligible for actuarially reduced benefits only. Because the actuarial reduction for early acceptance depends on benefit type, the SSB for younger wives and widows could not be accurately calculated.

SUPPLEMENTAL SPOUSE BENEFITS

Table 3.1 shows the 1972 distribution of income of couples (A, cols. 1–3) and the distribution of beneficiary couples (B, cols. 5–7), by relative poverty status. Net personal income, the distribution of which is given in column 1, is defined as total personal income received in 1972 by both the husband and wife, net of OASI benefits received. Column 2 shows the percentage of all retired-worker benefits for which couples in each pretransfer income group are entitled without reductions for early retirement. Column 3 indicates the percentage of SSBs accruing to each group after retired-worker benefits are included in the income measure, and column 4 gives the average size of SSBs for each income group. Columns 5, 6, and 7 show the percentage of couples in each income group when

[7]The 1972 earnings test applied to all OASI beneficiaries less than 72 years of age. It required that for every $2 earned between $1680 and $2880, $1 in OASI benefits be withheld. Aged persons with annual earnings below $1681 were not subject to a loss of benefits. A husband's earnings could result in a loss both of his own retired-worker benefits and of dependent benefits to his wife. A woman's earnings could reduce her own retired-worker benefits and her dependent benefits from her husband.

There was also a monthly earnings limit. Because data in the file were provided on annual incomes only, the monthly test could not be incorporated in the sample selection.

[8]Because the earnings test reduces the benefits of wage earners, beneficiaries with earnings below this limit tend to have lower incomes from non-OASI sources than do all aged (Appendix, Table 3.9). Thus, the sample analyzed is biased towards the pretransfer poor.

Table 3.1
Distributions of Income of Couples (A), and Couples by Income (B),
Relative to the Poverty Line, 1972

	A. Income			
	(1)	(2)	(3)	(4)
		Own	Supplemental	
	Net Personal	Retired-Worker	Spouse Benefits	Average Annual
Income Level	Income (NPI)	Benefits (RWB)	(SSB)	SSB
Below poverty line	17.7%	62.0%	15.6%	$520
1.0–1.5 × poverty line	9.3	9.8	26.6	782
1.5–2.0 × poverty line	10.0	8.2	20.3	663
Above 2.0 × poverty line	63.0	20.1	37.4	610
Average amount	$3,353	$2,470		640

	B. Couples		
	(5)	(6)	(7)
			NPI + RWB
Income Level	NPI	NPI + RWB	+ SSB
Below poverty line	64.0%	19.3%	11.4%
1.0–1.5 × poverty line	10.2	21.8	16.6
1.5–2.0 × poverty line	7.7	19.6	22.4
Above 2.0 × poverty line	18.1	39.3	49.7

Source and notes: Reprinted with permission from "Spouse and Survivor Benefits: Distribution among Aged Women" by Karen C. Holden, p. 311 in *Research on Aging*, Vol. 1, © Sage Publications, Beverly Hills. Couples are those in which both husband and wife are at least 65 years old and not subject to OASI earnings test. Net personal income is income net of OASI benefits in 1972. Own retired-worker benefits are benefits for which husband and wife are eligible based on their own earnings records. The distribution of supplemental spouse benefits among couples depends upon their NPI and their own RWB.

income includes pre-OASI income only (net personal income), retired-worker benefits plus net personal income, and retired-worker benefits plus both net personal income and SSBs respectively. All benefits are not reduced for early retirement.

Table 3.1 shows a highly skewed income distribution when OASI benefits are excluded from income—18% of aged couples (col. 5) receive 63.0% of all non-OASI income (col. 1). Over 60% of all retired-worker benefits for which aged couples are eligible (col. 2) accrue to the 64% of aged beneficiary couples who would otherwise have annual incomes below the poverty line (col. 5). These benefits alone could move two-thirds of all prebenefit poor aged couples out of poverty. Only 15.6% of SSBs (col. 3) are available to the 19.3% of couples (col. 6) who would be below the poverty line based on their full retired-worker benefits and net personal incomes. These SSBs would raise incomes of less than half of those in pre-SSB poverty above the official poverty level. Even if the SSBs were paid to all women eligible for these benefits, 11.4% of beneficiary couples would remain poor (col. 7).

Several conclusions may be drawn from Table 3.1. Prior to the consideration of SSBs, relatively few couples would be below the poverty level. If paid in full, over 37% of these benefits would be paid to the 39% of couples with incomes more than twice the poverty level. Although an average SSB of $520 per year is available to couples below the official poverty level, couples in the highest income group are eligible for an average, unreduced benefit of $610. There does appear to be a slight redistribution of income toward couples with incomes above the poverty level but less than twice that level. The major point, however, is that SSBs are not paid primarily to beneficiary couples most in need of additional income. Poor couples receive less than their expected share of these benefits based on the percentage of couples who are poor. The distribution of income among couples, which is altered greatly by the progressive nature of the retired-worker benefit formula and the average size of this benefit, is not much changed by the availability of spouse benefits.

SUPPLEMENTAL WIDOW BENEFITS

The same techniques used for SSBs may be applied in evaluating the income redistributional impact of benefits paid to separated, divorced, and widowed women. Again, the relevant benefit is the additional amount paid to a woman above that which she would receive as her own retired-worker benefit, since she may receive only the larger of her retired worker or dependent benefit. This amount, defined here as the *supplemental widow benefit* (SWB)[9] is equal to the difference between the benefits she is eligible for based on her own work record (if she were to receive them unreduced for early retirement) and the amount she receives. Actual benefits rather than full retired-worker and SWB were used (the latter for a widow is equal to her deceased husband's PIA) because information on

[9] Although the term "supplemental widow benefit" is used, some women eligible for SWBs are divorced or separated.

covered earnings of husbands are not uniformly available for women not living with husbands.[10] Because it is not possible to identify the amount of each benefit type received by women entitled to both a retired-worker and dependent benefit, any actuarial reductions in benefits were assumed to apply to the SWB. This reduces the size of the estimated SWB below the amount paid if a woman's retired-worker benefits were reduced for early acceptance. Because Thompson (1977) finds no difference among widows by income level in the probability of an actuarial reduction in retired-worker benefits, this should not bias the distribution of SWBs, although it will reduce their absolute size.[11]

Table 3.2 presents the distribution of income of formerly married women (A), and the distribution of those women, by relative poverty level (B), as was done for couples in Table 3.1. Prior to the payment of OASI benefits, virtually all formerly married women (82.0%) have income below the poverty line compared to less than two-thirds (64.0%) of couples. Because of this concentration of formerly married women in the pre-transfer poor income group, a larger percentage (78.8%) of retired-worker benefits are paid to poor, formerly married women than was true in the case of couples. However, the small average size of retired-worker benefits ($757 versus $2470 for couples) raises only 22.3% of the pretransfer poor, formerly marrieds out of poverty. Almost 64% of these women would remain poor even if full retired-worker benefits were paid. For these women, SWBs represent an income source at least as important as retired-worker benefits. The SWBs raise another 29% out of poverty, although almost half of women continue to have incomes below the SSA poverty level. The SWBs to appear to target poor, formerly married women, paying 79.4% of these benefits to the 63.6% of women who otherwise would be poor.

[10]The absence of data of benefits on husbands of separated and divorced women is not critical. Retired-worker benefits to ex-husbands are a source of income only if transferred privately, a transfer which will increase reported net personal income. If not transferred, his benefits do not represent a source of personal income to the woman. Dependent's benefits will be based, of course, on his PIA, but her receipt is constrained by his age and earnings—earnings which may not be reflected in her income. Although poor, she may be ineligible for spouse benefits because of her husband's continued activity in paid work. The inability of such a woman to receive dependent's benefits despite her age and despite earnings below the earnings limit is an indication of the failure of OASI to provide benefits to nonmarried women in need of additional income transfers.

[11]Dependent and retired-worker benefits are reduced by a different fraction per month of acceptance prior to age 65. The total actuarial reduction also depends upon the timing of entitlement to each benefit received by a woman. Thus, information on total benefit amount received in 1972, and whether benefits were actuarially reduced, does not allow an estimate of the amount by which a woman eligible for both a retired-worker and survivor benefit had each benefit reduced.

Table 3.2
Distributions of Income of Formerly Married Women (A),
and Formerly Married Women by Income (B), Relative to the Poverty Line, 1972

	A. Income			
	(1)	(2)	(3)	(4)
		Own	Supplemental	
	Net Personal	Retired-Worker	Widow Benefits	Average Annual
Income Level	Income (NPI)	Benefits (RWB)	(SWB)	SWB
Below poverty line	30.5%	78.8%	79.4%	$898
1.0–1.5 × poverty line	11.3	7.6	7.2	313
1.5–2.0 × poverty line	8.2	4.2	3.8	383
Above 2.0 × poverty line	50.0	9.3	9.5	528
Average income	$1,386	$757		719

	B. Formerly Married Women		
	(5)	(6)	(7)
			NPI + RWB
Income Level	NPI	NPI + RWB	+ SWB
Below poverty line	82.0%	63.6%	45.2%
1.0–1.5 × poverty line	6.6	16.4	28.0
1.5–2.0 × poverty line	3.4	7.0	10.7
Above 2.0 × poverty line	8.0	13.0	16.1

Notes: Formerly married women are separated, divorced, and widowed women who are not subject to the earnings test. Net personal income is personal income net of OASI benefits in 1972. Own retired-worker benefits are benefits for which the women are eligible based on their own earnings records. Their distribution is determined by NPI. The distribution of supplemental widow benefits depends on NPI and own RWB. Supplemental widow benefits are the difference between a woman's actual OASI benefits and her own PIA.

The large proportion of SWBs paid to otherwise poor women is in part an artifact of the concentration of formerly married women in low-income groups and of these older women being less likely than are couples to be eligible for their own retired-worker benefits. Recall that the largest drop in poverty among couples was due to their eligibility for retired-worker benefits. The SWBs represent an important income source for formerly married women only because of low pretransfer incomes even after retired-worker benefits are paid.

Because SWBs are not on the average large, almost half of the women who receive them remain in poverty after these benefits are paid. While the distribution of SWBs does favor poor women, the size of SWBs is not sufficient to raise most out of poverty. Other income transfers are required to accomplish the antipoverty goals of SWBs.

Substituting an Explicit Credit for Spouse Benefits

The above discussion indicates that supplemental benefits to wives and widows of OASI beneficiaries do not effectively do what they were intended to do—provide additional income to those beneficiaries in greatest need. This is due primarily to the dual entitlement provision itself, which, rather than determining need for additional income on the basis of the combined earnings (and thus OASI benefits) of a couple, does so on the basis of the preretirement division of earnings. Thus, one- and two-earner couples with identical combined retired-worker benefits are treated differently, with the former more likely to receive a supplemental spouse benefit. Likewise, the receipt of a survivor's benefit depends on the split of retired-worker benefits between the deceased husband and widow prior to his death. The different treatment of one- and two-earner couples has been a feature of OASI ever since the enactment of supplemental benefits. Recent changes in the pattern of work among men and women has increased the number of couples who split earnings over their lifetime in nontraditional ways.[12] As the number of such couples has grown, the dual entitlement provision has become an increasingly less satisfactory means of identifying those beneficiaries most in need of additional benefits.

In view of the original purpose of supplemental benefits to wives and widows, it is surprising that there has been little public discussion about the discrepancy between the originally expected and the actual income redistribution effects of these benefits. That some proposed changes in dependent benefits would grant more liberal benefits to dually entitled women, suggests the degree to which these benefits are no longer considered a supplemental transfer to more needy beneficiaries, but a benefit to which all married women and widows are entitled. This

---

[12]In 1975 22.3% of all women eligible for spouse benefits because of age were dually entitled (i.e., entitled to retired-worker benefits which were less than their spouse benefits). In 1952 this was true for only 2.0% of eligible wives (*Social Security Bulletin, Annual Statistical Supplement, 1975,* Table 91).

perception may well be the result of the fact that the dual entitlement provision identifies as dependent beneficiaries, not the poor aged, but those women who have spent some years out of covered work.[13] Because OASI provisions are not neutral with respect to the preretirement division of earnings, SSBs are most likely to be paid to those women who did not work during marriage. Thus, these benefits provide to these women protection against the drop in old-age benefits which would otherwise result from years spent not working in covered employment. An explicit homemaker credit or child-care drop-out years would merely formalize what the current system already does for most homemakers.

The extent to which married women are protected by the current provision of supplemental benefits, and differences among women in the protection provided, can be estimated with data for all married women 65 and older in the Exact Match Sample.[14] Almost all women (84.3%) who had some zero-earning quarters included in their own covered-earnings averaging period were eligible for spouse benefits larger than their own retired-worker benefits. Of those homemakers not eligible for an SSB, half were married to men who themselves were not eligible for retired-worker benefits and thus belonged to a group which the Social Security Administration has traditionally considered the responsibility of other income transfer programs. Conversely, of those wives who were eligible for an SSB, 94.4% had some quarters with no reported covered earnings included in this average (Holden, 1979b). The average homemaker credit which would have had to be posted to the covered-earnings record of each woman in order for her to be eligible for an equivalent increase in her retired-worker benefit can be calculated for each woman eligible for an SSB who had spent some quarters of work not in covered work.[15] For the 59.8% of married women in the Exact Match Sample for whom an implicit homemaker credit was calculated (i.e., those with an SSB and some nonearning quarters) their SSB was equivalent to an average monthly wage when not working of $106. To gain some perspective on the relative

[13]Public perception of the dependent benefit as a benefit to which all women should be entitled probably was reinforced by the Social Security Administration's emphasis on the insurance nature of OASI and neglect in stressing to the public the welfare basis of much of the program's benefit structure.

[14]All married women are included whether or not their spouses were fully insured, or whether current earnings by either were above the earnings limit. Thus, the calculation is for the implicit credit which could have been realized in 1972 if beneficiary status had been elected. The same calculation could not be done for formerly married women, since the earnings records of their husbands were not available.

[15]For some women of course this meant a credit in every quarter, if they had never worked in covered employment.

size of this implicit homemaker credit, it should be compared to the average monthly covered earnings of the husbands of these women ($316) and the average earnings for women in this group who did some covered work ($89 per month) during quarters worked. Whether this amount is too low a wage for home work will not be discussed here. The key point is that the OASI program operates as if married women had an average home wage of approximately $106 per month credited to their earnings records for each quarter in which no earnings were otherwise recorded. This credit is somewhat higher than the actual monthly covered earnings received by these women while working.

The variation in the implicit-earnings supplement and the homemaker credit is indicated by Table 3.3, which shows the distribution of wives by the size of the implicit homemaker credit. Excluded are those wives eligible for an SSB, but who had worked all relevant quarters. The SSBs of almost one-half of wives eligible for a homemaker credit is equivalent to a credit of $75–110. However, almost 10% of wives are rewarded for time spent out of the work force with a monthly credit of less than $50, and 27.3% were credited with an implicit homemaker credit of more than $110 per month. Although the current SSB program does provide the protection intended by an explicit homemaker credit system, it does so without uniformity and somewhat unpredictably, since the eligibility for this credit is based upon marital status, husband's retirement, and the average earnings of the spouse upon whose record the woman's SSB is based.

Table 3.3
Distribution of Wives by Implicit Homemaker Credit
(Percentage of Eligible Wives)

Implicit Monthly Amount	Homemaker Credit
$1.00–49.00	9.2%
50.00–74.00	17.0
75.00–110.00	46.5
111.00–174.00	21.1
175.00 and over	6.2
Average	$106.00
N	1,114

Source and notes: Holden (1979b), reprinted with permission from the *Gerontologist,* Vol. *19*, No. 3, 250–256. Eligible wives are those eligible for a supplemental spouse benefit and having some quarters with no covered earnings included in the accounting period. The homemaker credit is calculated over quarters in which there were no covered earnings.

THE HOMEMAKER CREDIT

Bills which would provide social security credits to homemakers have been proposed in the past by former Representatives Barbara Jordan (Texas), Bella Abzug (N.Y.), and Martha Griffiths (Mich.). Under each proposal an imputed dollar value would be assigned to home work and would be credited for each period during which no covered earnings were posted.[16] The advantage of such a system is that it would allow a married woman to build up her own earnings record upon which OASI benefits would be based independent of changes in marital status and her husband's own earnings. A credit would allow homemakers to accumulate sufficient earnings credits to become entitled to their own benefits, would compensate in part for the loss of earnings due to work in the home, and, under the more generous proposals, would provide disability protection. A uniform credit would alleviate but not compensate entirely for declines in retired-worker benefits because of time spent out of paid work. It would not of course compensate for subsequent lower earnings which are due to shorter and interrupted labor market careers of homemakers.

The posting to covered-earnings records of an earnings credit for time spent out of covered work is not a fundamental change either in the public's perception of who should receive supplemental benefits or in the risk against which the current program provides protection. An explicit credit would formalize what the current system does informally by specifying a uniform credit granted under specified conditions.

To investigate what changes in income distribution and program costs would result if a homemaker credit were substituted for spouse and survivor benefits, retirement benefits under such a system were simulated for all married and formerly married women in the Exact Match Sample. These women are those for whom SSBs and SWBs were estimated in Tables 3.1 and 3.2. This is equivalent to the assumption that a credit would be available only to those women whose husbands were covered by OASI. An unresolved issue of all proposed systems is, Would all women be eligible for such a credit, whether or not they or their husbands had ever worked in covered employment? If such women were eligible for a credit, the cost of the program would be higher than estimated below.

Several alternative credits were investigated: the median earnings of females working four quarters in the year during which the credit was posted, the OASI earnings base in that year, and the value which the

---

[16]These bills would replace spouse and survivor benefits with a homemaker credit. It is, of course, possible, as has also been proposed, to add a homemaker credit to current benefits. Only a credit which replaces spouse and survivor benefits is considered in this paper.

market, through the payment of full-time household workers, places on the services provided by homemakers. Tables 3.4 and 3.5 present estimates using median earnings of women working four quarters, the most conservative of the proposed credits, for couples and formerly married women, respectively. These tables show the distribution by income group of the additional benefits for which fully insured women would qualify above the benefits based on their actual covered earnings. The method used to compute the marginal benefit is identical to that described earlier for supplemental spouse and widow benefits—i.e., the difference between the hypothetical benefit when their covered-earnings record includes the homemaker credit relevant to each year and either their benefit based on actual earnings (col. 3) or their benefit under the current system, including supplemental benefits (col. 4). In column 3 beneficiaries are arrayed by income level including retired-worker benefits under the current system, in column 4 by income including both retired-worker and SSB or SWB. Column 7 shows the income distribution which would result with a homemaker credit.

Interestingly, for both couples and formerly married women, the distribution of additional benefits above retired-worker benefits under a credit system (col. 3) would differ only slightly from that of present SSBs and SWBs respectively (compare with col. 3 in Tables 3.1 and 3.2). Only the larger size of this credit than is implicitly provided by current supplemental benefits assures that a larger proportion of couples and women would be moved out of poverty than is true under the current system. Only 12.6% of couples would have incomes below or just above the poverty line compared to 28.0% under the current system. Among formerly married women, over half of those who remained in poverty after SWBs would be raised out of poverty by a homemaker credit system. This last is an interesting result. Although it was expected that wives, eligible for total spouse benefits of only half their husbands', would do better under a homemaker credit, it was not expected that surviving spouses, eligible for a benefit equal to 100% of their deceased spouses', would notice an improvement in benefits when the credit was based on median female earnings. This implies that in many cases the homemaker credit of the wife is higher than the covered earnings of the husband, upon which the SWB is based. Virtually all women would benefit from a system in which the credit was generous compared to the implicit credit provided by the current system. Since the distribution of benefits is identical under both the current and the hypothetical system, the degree of improvement is determined by the size of the credit. Proposals to provide a smaller independent credit to women may do little to improve the economic position of poorer beneficiaries. It should be further noted that almost half

Table 3.4
Distributions of Income of Couples (A) and Couples by Income (B),
Relative to the Poverty Line, with Hypothetical Homemaker Credit, 1972

A. Income

| | (1) | (2) | Additional Benefit/Credit from Homemaker Credit | |
| | | | (3) | (4) |
Income Level	Net Personal Income (NPI)	Own Retired-Worker Benefits (RWB)	Above Own RWB	Above Current System
Below poverty line	17.7%	62.0%	24.7%	14.2%
1.0–1.5 × poverty line	9.3	9.8	24.6	18.0
1.5–2.0 × poverty line	10.0	8.2	18.1	21.9
Above 2.0 × poverty line	63.0	20.1	32.6	45.9
Average income	$3,353	$2,470	$1,461	$820

B. Couples

| | (5) | (6) | (7) |
Income Level	NPI	NPI + RWB	NPI + RWB + Change
Below poverty line	64.0%	19.3%	2.8%
1.0–1.5 × poverty line	10.2	21.8	9.8
1.5–2.0 × poverty line	7.7	19.6	25.5
Above 2.0 × poverty line	18.1	39.3	61.9

Notes: Couples are those in which both husband and wife are at least 65 years old and not subject to OASI earnings test. Homemaker credit is equal to the median average monthly earnings of women working 4 quarters during a year in which earnings credit was applicable. Net personal income is income net of OASI benefits in 1972. Own retired-worker benefits are benefits for which husband and wife are eligible based on their own earnings records. The distribution of their RWB depends upon their NPI. The distribution of the change in RWB among couples depends upon their NPI plus RWB under the current system. The distribution of the difference between the benefit under a homemaker credit system and the current system is determined by NPI, RWB, and supplemental spouse' benefit under the current system.

Table 3.5
Distributions of Income of Formerly Married Women (A),
and Formerly Married Women by Income (B), Relative to the Poverty Line,
with Hypothetical Homemaker Credit, 1972

	A. Income		Additional Benefits/Credit from Homemaker Credit	
	(1)	(2) Own	(3)	(4)
Income Level	Net Personal Income (NPI)	Retired-Worker Benefits (RWB)	Above Own RWB	Above Current System
Below poverty line	30.5%	78.8%	77.7%	50.1%
1.0–1.5 × poverty line	11.3	7.6	8.9	26.7
1.5–2.0 × poverty line	8.2	4.2	4.2	9.3
More than 2.0 × poverty line	50.0	9.3	9.1	13.9
Average income	$1,386	$757	$1,062	$344

	B. Formerly Married Women		
	(5)	(6)	(7) NPI + RWB
Income Level	NPI	NPI + RWB	+Change
Below poverty line	82.0%	63.6%	26.1%
1.0–1.5 × poverty line	6.6	16.4	39.2
1.5–2.0 × poverty line	3.4	7.0	16.0
Above 2.0 × poverty line	8.0	13.0	18.7

Source and notes: Reprinted with permission from "Spouse and Survivor Benefits: Distribution among Aged Women" by Karen C. Holden, p. 314 in *Research on Aging*, Vol. 1, © Sage Publications, Beverly Hills. Formerly married women are separated, divorced, and widowed women who are not subject to the earnings test. Homemaker credit is equal to the median average monthly earnings of women working 4 quarters during a year in which earnings credit was applicable. Net personal income is personal income net of OASI benefits in 1972. Own retired-worker benefits are benefits for which the women are eligible on their own earnings records. Their distribution is determined by NPI. The distribution of the change in total benefits among women depends on their NPI and RWB under the current system. The distribution of the difference between the benefit under a homemaker credit and the current system is determined by NPI, RWB, and the supplemental widow benefit under the current system.

of the additional benefits paid (Table 3.4, col. 4) in the case of married women would be paid to relatively well-off couples. While half of those paid to formerly married women (Table 3.5, col. 4) would go to those who are below the poverty line under the current system, over half of the formerly married women would still have incomes below or close to the poverty level.

Two major policy decisions had to be made in simulating a homemaker credit system. The decision to exclude women with husbands not insured for retired-worker benefits was mentioned earlier. In addition, because the simulated credit is equal to median earnings of female workers over four quarters, some part-time and full-time earners had actual covered earnings less than this credit. In the simulation, women with lower earnings were granted a credit equal to the difference between actual covered earnings and the maximum credit. This supplemental credit thus increased the covered earnings of some women who were not eligible for a spouse benefit under the current program.

Because of the large average credit allowed and the increase in the number of women eligible for this credit, the incidence of poverty among the aged is substantially reduced. However, this reduction in poverty among OASI beneficiaries would come at a high cost to the system, with OASI benefits to couples and formerly married women almost one-quarter larger than under the current system. Lower credit amounts would of course reduce this cost, but would also imply a smaller reduction in the incidence of poverty among beneficiaries. As under the current system, married women fare better than the formerly married, mainly because the older age of the latter would mean less recent credits and consequent lower credits.[17] Although married women account for only 28% of all married and formerly married women, almost one-half of additional benefits above the current system (including current SSBs) would be paid to them.

What would a homemaker credit system accomplish? It would provide an independent earnings record to women who remained at home during some period of their working life upon which retired-worker benefits would be based, independent of whether they remained married or whether their spouse actually retired. The size of this credit would determine the actual increase in OASI benefits afforded by such a system, with a lower credit causing less reduction in poverty among women. The different treatment of single- and two-earner couples would remain. Women who worked would have actual covered earnings posted, while

---

[17]Indexed earnings and credits would change this somewhat, since past credits would increase with the average wage up to retirement.

women who did not would be eligible for a credit which could exceed the actual earnings of the former. If women with low earnings were also eligible for a credit, the charge that they are no better off in terms of retired-worker benefits because they had worked could still be made.[18] A crucial issue would be whether these credits would be noncontributory or whether a tax would be imposed on women receiving the credit. The large increase in total benefits implied by the credit simulated in this paper suggests an increase in the tax on both homemakers and current workers which may be unacceptable at a time when increases already proposed have created considerable controversy.

CHILD-CARE DROP-OUT YEARS

A homemaker credit, as proposed under several alternative plans, would be granted to any married woman who, during some calendar period, had low enough earnings to suggest complete or partial withdrawal from work in order to carry out responsibilities at home. An alternative method of dealing with the decline in earnings due to labor force withdrawal of this nature is to allow women to drop a year from the period over which earnings are averaged, for every year spent out of the work force. Such a proposal (*child-care drop-out years*) has been offered to deal with a specific group of homemakers, those who reduce earnings in order to care for young children. Although a homemaker credit is usually proposed for all homemakers, and drop-out years for parents with young children remaining at home, there is no reason why a homemaker credit could not be restricted to parents of young children only, or why drop-out years could not be allowed for all homemakers, whether or not children were present. Projected costs would depend upon which combination of credit type and eligible group were adopted. The following discussion will focus on the proposal for drop-out years for parents of young children, although objections—which might be alleviated by either expanding the credit to all homemakers or providing a uniform credit to all parents—will be noted.

Proposals to partially compensate parents for the loss of earnings due to child-care responsibilities are based on the assumption that society in some way should explicitly recognize the economic value of parents raising future generations of producers and consumers. Because actual care of children by the parent would be administratively difficult to

---

[18]If the earnings posted to the records of all workers had to be at least equal to some set credit for every year, the system would duplicate a double-decker system, since the minimum earnings would generate a minimum guaranteed benefit for all retirees.

determine, each plan examined by the 1979 Advisory Council would assume child-care responsibilities based on the presence of a child (e.g., a birth certificate) and earnings of the parent below some maximum amount. The most conservative proposal would grant a credit for years in which no earnings by a parent were reported. Other options were examined by the 1979 Advisory Council: (a) annual earnings less than the amount needed to earn four quarters of coverage during each child-care year; (b) earnings less than one-third of the average earnings of all workers; (c) indexed earnings at least 60% below the parents' average earnings during those years when she/he had no qualifying child; or (d) a "child-care freeze," by which these years could be excluded if their exclusion resulted in higher benefits. Under the plan examined by the council, parents with children less than seven years of age would qualify for a drop-out year, with the number of years dropped out not to exceed a maximum of ten (in addition to the five years of lowest earnings currently allowed). Absolute earnings limits would assume reduced earnings from low earnings, thereby enabling parents with low earnings to qualify even though no decline actually occurred. The last two options would grant the drop-out privilege only to those parents whose earnings were actually lower than average during the child-rearing period. Those parents whose lifetime average earnings were low but who suffered no decline in earnings would not qualify, even though their low earnings were the result of child responsibilities. Such parents might be those whose child-care responsibilities extended over a period longer than the maximum allowed, or whose low earnings during child-rearing years limited subsequent job options and earnings.

Estimating the effect of child-care drop-out years on OASI benefits requires information on the future work and covered earnings of parents. This is difficult to obtain for parents now caring for young children. However, data on women with young children allow us to analyze the characteristics of women who would qualify for a child-care drop-out year in the future calculation of social security benefits. For this purpose we use data on women aged 18–39 from the 1976 Survey of Income and Education of the Bureau of the Census.

Under each of the options for a child-care drop-out year, some parents would be compensated for the loss in earnings due to child-care responsibilities while others would not be compensated, either because their annual earnings exceeded an allowed maximum or because prior child-care responsibilities equal to a maximum number of years had already been allowed. Tables 3.6–3.8 provide some evidence on the characteristics of parents of young children who in 1975 would not have qualified for a drop-out year if such a system had been in place. The first two tables

Table 3.6
Percentage of Married Women 18–39 with Work Experience, by Husbands' Incomes in 1975 and Ages of Children

Income of Husband		2+ Children under 18	
	(1) 1 Child under 7	(2) All under 7	(3) 1+ under 7 and 1+ older
None	49.1%	44.2%	50.0%
Under 3,000	52.0	40.8	51.1
3–4,000	46.8	45.0	45.6
5–6,000	50.8	42.2	46.5
7–9,000	52.7	40.7	50.6
10–12,000	50.1	38.1	44.4
13–14,000	44.5	33.8	42.9
15–19,000	44.1	27.1	36.2
20–24,000	40.5	21.7	33.7
25–34,000	38.2	19.2	24.7
35–49,000	30.9	22.6	27.8
50,000+	29.4	26.1	15.7
All	48.4	35.0	41.2

Source and notes: Microdata from the Survey of Income and Education, Data Access Descriptions No. 42, Bureau of the Census, Jan. 1978. Married women are women whose spouses are present.

Table 3.7
Percentage of Women 18–39 with Work Experience in 1975 by Marital Status and Ages of Children

Marital Status		2+ Children under 18	
	(1) 1 Child under 7	(2) All under 7	(3) 1+ under 7 and 1+ older
Married, spouse present	48.4%	35.0%	41.2%
Divorced	76.0	58.1	66.6
Separated	62.0	43.3	47.5
Widowed	51.2	28.0	44.5
Never married	56.4	32.9	42.6

Source: Microdata from the Survey of Income and Education, Data Access Descriptions No. 42, Bureau of the Census, Jan. 1978.

Table 3.8
Percentage of Women 18–39 with Work Experience in 1975 Earning More Than
$1,000 (A) and $2,615 (B), by Marital Status and Ages of Children

	A. 1975 Earnings > $1,000		
		2+ Children under 18	
Marital Status	(1) 1 Child under 7	(2) All under 7	(3) 1+ under 7 and 1+ older
Married, spouse present	73.2%	60.8%	64.8%
Divorced	80.9	70.2	79.0
Separated	65.6	65.6	63.8
Never married	63.4	44.2	59.0
	B. 1975 Earnings > $2,615		
Married, spouse present	57.9%	42.9%	48.3%
Divorced	68.8	50.9	65.4
Separated	50.0	42.6	51.3
Never married	47.8	23.4	51.8

Source and note: Microdata from the Survey of Income and Education, Data Access
Descriptions No. 42, Bureau of the Census, Jan. 1978. Widows are excluded from this table
because of small sample size in each category.

show the percentage of women who had some work experience in 1976.
These women would not have been eligible for a drop-out year under a
system providing for a reduction in the earnings averaging period only
when no earnings were reported. Table 3.8 gives the percentage of women
with work experience in 1975 who earned in that year more than $1000,
the amount needed for four quarters of coverage (panel A), and, in the
lower panel (B), those who earned more than one-third of the average
1975 annual earnings of all workers ($2615).[19]

Under each of the three child-care drop-out options illustrated in these
tables, large numbers of women with young children would not be eligible
for a reduction in the earnings averaging period, even though some decline
in earnings may have resulted from parenting responsibilities. Women in

[19]Earnings are all earnings in 1975 whether covered by OASI or not. The Advisory
Council recognized that all earnings would have to be considered in determining whether a
year should be dropped. The obtaining of information on all earnings would be difficult
without universal coverage.

the first two columns of each table would not be eligible, since their earnings exceeded the proposed maximums despite the presence of a young child. Women in column (3) in the tables would not be eligible even without a binding earnings limit, if the maximum number of drop-out years had already been used caring for older children. Variations among women of similar parity in the number of years they spent out of the labor market are also found by Kestenbaum (1979), who used data from the Exact Match File to estimate differences in covered-work experience and parity among women first married between 1950 and 1957. He reports that while mothers with children were less likely to have covered earnings reported during all 20 years since marriage, there was considerable variation in the number of years out of covered work among mothers of like parity. Table 3.6 also presents work experience rates of married women by husbands' incomes, which suggest that women with high-earning husbands would be more likely to benefit from this proposal, since women married to low earners are more likely to work.

In simulating the effect of child-care drop-out years the Advisory Council found no losers—a not surprising result, since at worst a woman's earnings record and AMW would remain unchanged. However, the change in benefits varied considerably among women, in part due to differences in the number of years dropped out, but also because the estimated increase in AMW depends directly on the average earnings of those years not dropped from the earnings average. Drop-out years will have the largest effect on women who actually do experience sharp drops in earnings, with high-earning women receiving the largest absolute increase in benefits. Thus women showing the greatest increase in retired-worker benefits compared to the current system will be those with high earnings prior to childbearing, who leave the work force for no more than the maximum years allowed, after which they return to full-time work. Women who choose to spread earnings and child care more evenly over their working-age life would show smaller benefit increases.

Evaluation of Alternative Systems

The major factor reducing the effectiveness of current supplemental benefits in targeting poor beneficiaries has been the growth in the number of couples who divide preretirement earnings in nontraditional ways. The current system, based on a presumption that the earning and homemaker roles are performed by different members of a couple, treats couples (and surviving members) differently, depending on the preretirement division of earnings. The two proposed changes examined in this paper are also based on this presumption. Under neither proposal are earnings of a spouse viewed as the product of the joint effort of husband and wife. Under each proposal, the earning spouse would retain all rights to the benefits based on his or her own earnings, while the nonearning or lower-earning spouse would be compensated for a decline in earnings by a system-provided change in average earnings. Neither proposed system deals well with cases in which there is a somewhat even division of child care and earning responsibilities. Conforming to the traditional view of a couple with one member having major earning responsibilities, the 1979 Advisory Council conceded that the homemaker credit or child-care drop-out years would have to be granted to the lower-paid spouse. Thus in cases where a couple jointly reduced earnings, only one would be compensated. Once again, total OASI benefits of a couple would vary, based on the preretirement division of earnings. In addition, both a credit and drop-out-year system would compensate women for lost earnings by substituting a credit in some way related to her own average earnings or those of other workers. In either case the earnings implied would be low relative to those of many full-time earning husbands, denying the wife a share in the higher earnings of her husband. The lower earner would bear the greater risk of earnings declines, and subsequent loss in retired-worker benefits, as a result of child rearing, a risk which need not be shared by the higher-earning spouse.

The original intent of supplemental benefits was to increase benefits of those beneficiaries most in need. It has been shown that neither the current system nor a homemaker credit would target poor beneficiaries. Data on the characteristics of women with young children in 1976 suggest that child-care drop-out years would also fail to target poor women to the extent that low earnings of husbands and separation, divorce, and widow-hood induce women to work. Both proposed systems, as does the current program, would favor those couples who were able to divide total earnings such that the highest share was earned by one spouse.

The actual incidence of the receipt of SSBs among women has rein-forced the belief that women—regardless of income status—are rightful recipients of supplemental benefits, and that a legitimate goal of OASI is to protect women against the loss of income resulting from home and child-care responsibilities. The proposed systems would provide this protection. However, under both systems, a noncontributory benefit increase would result in some working wives being no better off than if they had not worked. Although homemakers could be taxed on the credit provided at either the employee or self-employed rate, child-care drop-out years would grant higher benefits without an equivalent increase in OASI contributions.

The proposed systems would target a particular type of activity as worthy of social compensation. However, neither homemaking nor child care requires total labor force withdrawal, nor are these the only activities which may lead to earning reductions. Those working women who still have primary responsibility for child care may argue that they deserve the compensation provided to nonworking parents. This is particularly likely for parents who may have reduced earnings because of child-care responsibilities, but whose earnings are not sufficiently low to entitle them to the credit or to have a year dropped. While it may long continue to be true that child care and work in the home will be performed by women, the narrow focus on lost earnings as a "women's" issue has led to the neglect of other reasons for years spent out of the work force, such as time in school, caring for sick, disabled, or aged relatives, or because of periods of unemployment.

The current debate over OASI may lead to program changes that take account of the different ways in which husbands and wives can share child care and market work. Systems providing an explicit homemaker credit or child-care drop-out years would favor a particular division of earnings between spouses as does the current system. Such proposals would not reflect the growing public perception that, as labor economists have long known, the labor force decisions of a couple are a joint decision determined by the interaction of a variety of economic and noneconomic factors (Boskin, 1973; Cain, 1966). Reforms in the social security system that are not neutral with respect to the sharing of home responsibilities and earnings between husband and wife are not likely to eliminate the inequalities of the current system.

Appendix

Table 3.9
Distributions of Aged Couples and Formerly Married Women in Sample Compared with All Aged

Income Level (Net of OASI)	Aged Couples		Formerly Married Women[a]	
	All[b]	With Earnings below Earnings Test	All	With Earnings below Earnings Test
Below poverty line	58.4%	64.0%	77.6%	82.0%
1.0–1.5 × poverty line	11.0	10.2	7.3	6.6
1.5–2.0 × poverty line	8.3	7.7	3.8	3.4
Above 2.0 × poverty line	22.3	18.1	11.3	8.0
All incomes	100.0	100.0	100.0	100.0

[a]Widows and divorcées.
[b]Each age 65+ and husband fully insured.

Discussion

EDITH U. FIERST

Karen Holden's paper on (*a*) current spouse benefits under the dual entitlement rule; (*b*) homemaker credits; and (*c*) child-care drop-out years contains an excellent economic analysis of how these benefits are or would be distributed, and who is or would be helped. Her results confirm my own biases—which are against all these approaches and in favor of earnings sharing. For that reason, I may be the wrong person to discuss her paper. You may prefer to hear from someone who would take sharp issue with Holden's conclusions.

However, in another sense I am a good person to discuss the paper because I care deeply about the purpose of all these provisions; namely, to assure that women who choose to be homemakers not pay the steep price of poverty during old age.

In my opinion the pressures on women, especially the mothers of young children, to work for money are currently too great. Having said this I must add that changes in social security will not relieve these pressures significantly. When women make the decision to stay home to care for young children or to take paid employment, they are not worrying about retirement income. Most are under 40 and probably have only the vaguest notion that they will someday need social security or that their years at home might affect their benefits. The mothers of young children have more immediate problems to engage their attention. Society must therefore assume the responsibility of making certain those who decide to stay home to meet family needs will not be impoverished as a result when they are aged.

There are many reasons why the present system with its dual entitlement rule does not fill this need equitably and adequately, and why homemaker credits or increased child-care drop-out years would not do so either. Holden has discussed a number of them, and I will add to and elaborate on her views.

First, the Holden paper demonstrates that the dual entitlement rule does not target benefits on the most needy. Instead the rule causes benefits to be paid primarily to the wives of those men who earn significantly more than their wives do, and these men are likely to be highly paid. The working wives of the poor are not helped. These data support what other analysis has already told us.

Indeed, despite the original intent of the dual entitlement rule to benefit homemakers, spouse benefits are not payable only to women who have taken time out from paid employment for homemaking. Some of the recipients of supplemental spouse benefits (SSB)—to use Holden's descriptive term—have worked a full career for earnings that are so much lower than those of their husbands that half his primary insurance amount (PIA) is greater than their own PIA. This is the sure result if her earnings are one-sixth or less of the couple's earnings (within the taxable maximum), and the possible result if she earns less than two-sixths. Only when she earns one-third or more of the couple's income will her worker benefit be reliably higher than the spouse benefit during retirement. (Of course it remains higher in survivorship so long as he earned more than she did, however small the difference in their earnings.)

Since women on average earn less than 60% of men's earnings, the percentage who are entitled to an SSB is likely to remain substantial in the future, despite the massive entry of women into the labor force. It will be a long time before the earnings of husband and wife are so close in amount that the dual entitlement rule would exclude payment of spouse benefits to all working wives. Nevertheless, fewer working women should be entitled to an SSB in the years ahead, for two reasons. One is that women's average earnings are unusually low today because during recent years so many middle-aged women have joined the labor force in entry level positions, part of a big social change. This entering group is likely to taper off, and those already employed will get pay raises. The other reason is the movement of women into nontraditional occupations which are better paid, although this development is still in an early phase.

Table 3.10
Percentage of Women 65 and Older Entitled to Social Security

Year	Dependent Only	Dually Entitled	Worker Only	Total
1980	38%	12%	41%	92%
2000	31	17	46	94
2020	20	19	56	95
2040	15	22	60	97

Source: Unpublished estimate from the Office of the Actuary of Social Security.

Taking into consideration these factors plus the public pension offset,[1] which will eliminate many wives who are eligible for public pensions from entitlement for social security spouse benefits, the Office of the Actuary of Social Security in an unpublished estimate has predicted the trends in the benefit entitlement of women (Table 3.10).

As women's earnings increase compared to those of men, we may even see more men who are eligible for spouse benefits larger than their worker benefits. At present less than one percent of men have such entitlement. This figure should increase as women earn more and also because of a change in men's eligibility. The Supreme Court's decision in *Califano* v. *Goldfarb*[2] invalidated the previous rule that men could qualify for spouse benefits only if they were dependent upon their wives. To be "dependent" before that decision, a man had to earn less than one-quarter of the couple's income. Since the Court's decision, husbands may qualify on the same basis as their wives.[3] Thus, the *Goldfarb* case, together with the anticipated gradual increase in women's earnings, should result in a greater number of men becoming entitled to SSBs. This would be a further drift away from the original intent for the spouse benefit to compensate women for years at home.

HOMEMAKER CREDITS

A major difficulty with the proposal to give credits to homemakers based on noncompensated and therefore nontaxable service at home is that someone must pay for them. I don't anticipate there being many

[1] It reduces the spouse benefit by the amount of public pension (of federal and state employees not covered by social security) which is payable to the same individual.

[2] 430 U.S. 199, 1977.

[3] There is an exception: The public pension offset has been in effect for nondependent husbands and certain divorced women since 1977, but will not apply to other women or dependent husbands until December 1982.

volunteers. Taxpayers generally would certainly resent having to contribute more for nontaxpayers. A recent letter to Ann Landers from a working wife put it this way: "I read recently that housewives are trying to get Social Security benefits because their husbands work. I'm sick and tired of people leeching off my paycheck. I am supporting enough welfare people now without adding a group of women who can work but prefer to sit at home. Staying at home is their privilege, but they should not expect the same benefits as a working person [*Washington Post*, January 3, 1980]."

Many proponents of homemaker credits think the homemakers would pay the additional cost. In my view they and their husbands (whose earnings would be the real source) would usually be unwilling to do so. If the plan were made voluntary, they (except perhaps for the well-to-do) would be unlikely to enter it. If it were mandatory, couples would oppose its passage by the Congress, arguing that husbands of homemakers are already burdened with family support. Martha Derthick has cogently explained to us the politics of changing social security.[4] A political fight will inevitably arise when an effort is made to reduce benefits, either directly or by raising the costs for a particular group. Now homemakers get spouse benefits free. They will not voluntarily pay for them, even if their benefits were increased as a result.

I would like to give two examples of this principle in operation, taken from recent related experience. One is what happened when a proposal was made by the Carter administration to eliminate the mother's (not the child's) benefit on her youngest child's 16th birthday. Today she gets benefits until her youngest is 18. There was so much opposition to the proposal—although there is no apparent reason why the mother of a 16-year-old with no younger children cannot work—that the proposal was dropped.[5]

The other affects divorced Foreign Service wives. Divorce makes them ineligible for a survivor annuity from the Foreign Service Retirement System, and they are unlikely to qualify for social security. Those who served abroad were generally prohibited by the law of the country in which they were stationed from obtaining paid employment. Moreover the Foreign Service made demands upon their time and energies: They were often expected to help in representational activities such as entertaining, visiting foreign schools, etc., and they had additional homemaking responsibilities, such as frequent moves and problems in helping children adjust to living abroad. Many of these women have been divorced after 20 or 30 years of marriage by a husband who then marries a much younger woman.

---

[4]Derthick gave an opening speech at the conference which is not included in this volume.

[5]It was later enacted as part of the 1981 Budget Reconciliation Act.

If ever there was a group that deserved compassionate consideration, I believe this group of divorced wives is it. Congresswoman Patricia Schroeder (Colorado) introduced a bill that would qualify a former wife whose marriage lasted 10 or more years to a share of the survivor benefit that an employee can elect proportionate to the period of marriage. The bill—now P.L. 96-465—was passed in late 1980. This sounds like a reasonable suggestion (although not necessarily the best way of taking care of the divorced Foreign Service wives), but it is being opposed by the second wives. Now they receive the entire survivor annuity, and naturally they don't want to give it up.

A second major problem with homemaker credits is how to identify the group that should benefit. The most popular suggestion is to select married women with young children whose incomes drop significantly in the early years, perhaps from two to five, of their children's lives. But what about unmarried mothers? How about someone who is staying home to care for aged parents or a sick husband? Obviously, "househusbands" would have to be eligible too. What about the involuntarily unemployed receiving unemployment insurance who had children in the right age bracket? And should we be equally willing to compensate a woman who stays home and doesn't care for her family? I believe it would be impossible for the government to distinguish fairly between those who stayed home for good reason and should be compensated, and those whose reasons were insufficient.

The third major problem is how to value the services of a homemaker in monetary terms. Is a homemaker worth more or less than the going wage for a cleaning woman, chauffeur, nurse, etc.? Suppose she employs domestic help to perform these chores; then what? The wife of a poor man may or may not work harder than the wife of a rich one, but can we consider such factors?

Some suggest use of an entirely different standard, namely the average wage of working women. This would surely be the roughest justice and would result in some homemakers getting more credit than some full-time workers (many of whom are mothers of young children and cannot afford the luxury of staying home to care for them), while in other cases homemaker credits would not compensate fully for the time lost from work.

In my view these problems are so difficult to solve that they rule out homemaker credits as a practical solution.

CHILD-CARE DROP-OUT YEARS

The proposal regarding child-care drop-out years is to disregard appropriate years of nonwork when computing the lifetime average earnings for purposes of setting the level of social security benefits. This too raises problems.

First, how do we select the persons to benefit? Many of the same problems arise as with homemaker credits. Would any unemployed parent of a young child be eligible? Why exclude a person who is taking care of an aged or sick person? Etc.

Child-care drop-out years are not of equal value to everyone. They wouldn't help a woman who doesn't go to work after the children are in school, because she still would lack credits to average. Similarly they wouldn't help a woman whose work pattern deviates substantially from the supposed norm, for example, one who works part time for many years as a way of accommodating to home responsibilities. On the other hand, they would give a big boost to women whose incomes rise rapidly over the years, including those who never stop working, because increasing drop-out years would enable these women to disregard years of lowest earnings. These women tend to be the highly educated and well-to-do.

A fairer approach for everyone would be to add all earnings over a lifetime and divide them by the applicable number of benefit computation years, thus giving credit for more years worked rather than fewer. This would also help fathers who may work shorter hours or less intensively in order to help bring up their children.

Most important, child-care drop-out years wouldn't remedy the disadvantage in today's system for a mother who continues to work throughout the early years of her child's life. Frequently these are the women who are poorest and work because they must. Sometimes they are divorced, widowed, or abandoned by the father of their children, and have no option but to work. While it is argued that they would be no worse off because others got child-care drop-out years, they would be in a worse relative position, and this seems inequitable to me.

CONCLUSION

Finally, I am offended philosophically by both the homemaker credits and increased child-care drop-out years because they increase the rewards of not being employed. Fair play requires that the woman who works and pays taxes should get more for her efforts than the one who does not. Much as I want the homemaker to be secure in old age, I do not want to give her preference over the working woman. The problem with the dual entitlement system today is that it gives preference to the nonworker, and these proposals would perpetuate that inequity.

Only earnings sharing provides security to the homemaker without being unfair to the working wife. Under it the husband who supports his wife during homemaking years would share his earnings credits with her during retirement years also. The couple is free to decide without inappropriate government incentives how many years the wife should spend homemaking. It is up to the couple whether the wife's use of time at home increases their well-being adequately to compensate for the loss in income she would otherwise earn. After the children are grown, when she and her husband are likely to begin thinking about retirement years, there would be time under an earnings-sharing system for her to go to work in covered employment and thus increase social security benefits for both partners in the marriage, if that is their wish.

9150
9170
U.S.

4

Earnings Sharing: Incremental and Fundamental Reform

RICHARD V. BURKHAUSER

Old Age and Survivors Insurance (OASI), from its inception, has attempted to satisfy the requirements of both social adequacy and social insurance. Originally conceived primarily as a means of providing a safe financial instrument for those retiring from the labor force, it nevertheless had a limited commitment to social adequacy. The 1939 amendments to the Social Security Act however expanded the social adequacy goal by providing additional income to aged workers and their spouses, independent of their earnings records.

Included in the 1939 amendments was a spouse benefit. In an era when few women worked in the labor market, the spouse benefit was conceived as a means of providing the family of a married worker with an additional benefit over and above that provided to a single worker with the same earnings record.[1] But significantly the right of a nonworking wife to a benefit was not direct; it was based on her husband's earnings record, and so was its value.

---

[1] As the Social Security amendments were originally conceived, only a nonworking wife was eligible to receive a spouse benefit. Today both women and men can receive such benefits, based on the earnings record of their spouses. However, a working husband with a homemaker wife is still the dominant case, and for clarity of discussion, it is the example used throughout the paper.

In the past few years several government commissions, including the 1979 Advisory Council on Social Security, have argued that this system of providing benefits to women should be changed. Of the many principles on which reform of the system could be based, the most frequently discussed has been earnings sharing. It was not officially recommended by the 1979 Advisory Council, but the members of the council concluded that some form of earnings sharing was the most reasonable of all possible reform alternatives (U.S. Department of Health, Education, and Welfare, 1979b).

This paper explores the potential impact of establishing earnings sharing as the base for distributing OASI benefits. Two major aspects are seen as important: (a) the impact of this change in the assignment of within-household property rights on the dependency of women within the family; (b) its impact on the dual nature of the system—serving both social insurance and social adequacy—across the families of different types of women.

In the first instance, it is argued that the present system of assigning benefits on the basis of individual earnings streams is *not* preferable to a system based on equal sharing of the household earnings stream by a married couple. In the second case, it is argued that the redistributive effectiveness of the current spouse benefit can be seriously questioned on grounds of both equity and efficiency. From a pragmatic policy perspective, furthermore, it is demonstrated that even the strictest adherence to an earnings-sharing principle, one which included a complete end to the spouse benefit, would neither seriously decrease benefits to the great majority of traditional one-earner families, nor increase benefits to the great majority of two-earner families. The principal losers of such a change would be relatively high-income, one-earner families who over time are most capable of adjusting to this change and who, on income-adequacy grounds, have the weakest case for its continuance.

Spouse Benefit versus Earnings Sharing

WITHIN-HOUSEHOLD PROPERTY RIGHTS

Between our current system of providing protection for women and an earnings-sharing system, there is a fundamental difference in the method used to assign benefit rights within a household. OASI now follows the English common-law procedure of assigning rights to an earnings stream to each individual earner. Earnings sharing, in contrast, uses the household as the relevant unit and assigns an equal share of total household earnings to each spouse. In so doing it follows the Roman law tradition, which is used in community-property states to determine ownership of most family-generated assets. An OASI system based on earnings sharing would continue to make the family the unit of protection, but would differ from our present system, which provides rights to a spouse only as a derivative of the earnings of the primary earner, by giving each partner a direct right to benefits.

The changing nature of marriage has strained the ability of OASI to protect homemakers. Because a homemaker has no direct right to OASI benefits, she may lose her claim to a spouse benefit in the event of divorce—a problem of major consideration today. The present system now guarantees such a homemaker a spouse benefit after 10 years of marriage, but because she has no direct right to her husband's earning stream, the worker benefit going to her ex-husband will be twice the spouse benefit she receives.[2] While consistent with the common law, this method of within-household distribution of property rights, which views homemakers as dependent on their spouses, is seriously questioned by those who view marriage as an equal partnership.

In a pure insurance system, changes in the method of assigning within-household property rights would have no effect on the distribution of benefits across households. A pure insurance system, like any private insurance system, would be actuarially fair, relating contributions to the expected value of benefits. For instance, fire insurance purchased by a family is equal to the value of their insured property multiplied by the risk of a fire. If their house burns down, the payment is the same to the household regardless of whether the husband, the wife, or both, jointly own the house.

If earnings sharing were introduced in an actuarially fair, OASI system, a one-earner family in which the husband earned $15,000 per year would continue to receive benefits derived from taxes on those earnings. The difference would be that two checks would be sent, one to the husband based on his $7500 per year earnings record and one to the wife based on her $7500 per year earnings record. In a two-earner family where the husband made $10,000 per year and the wife $5000, each would be credited with a $7500 earnings record. Such a system avoids the need for a spouse benefit, since both spouses are entitled directly to one-half the earnings of the household.

The merits of applying the earnings-sharing principle to an actuarially

---

[2]Until 1977, a couple had to be married for 20 years before the nonworking spouse had a vested right to a spouse benefit. The 1977 amendment to the Social Security Act reduced this to 10 years.

fair social insurance system are relatively clear-cut. It would avoid placing homemakers in a dependency role; it would provide them with direct protection; and it would be portable in the case of divorce.

EQUITY AND EFFICIENCY

Unlike Supplemental Security Income (SSI), which provides benefits based solely on need, contributions made into the OASI system at younger ages are linked to benefits received at older ages. Recognition of this link provides a mechanism for judging the appropriateness of benefits. Those benefits which are the result of previous contributions are justified on insurance grounds. Pure transfers must be justified on social adequacy grounds. Within this framework, we can measure the impact of spouse benefits on the insurance-adequacy mix across families and the reasonableness of the distributional impact that would result from earnings sharing.

In a world filled with single people and one-earner families in which divorce is virtually unknown, a spouse benefit based on the earnings of the male simply redistributes income from single people to married people, since single people effectively pay for uncollectable spouse benefits.[3] Since its inception in 1939, this dependent-spouse model of the family has become less and less realistic. In 1940, only one woman in four actively participated in the labor market and in only 3 out of 20 households were both the husband and wife in the labor force at the same time. By 1980, over one-half of all women were actively in the work force, and in over one-half of all households in the country, both the wife and husband performed market work in the same year. This movement of women, particularly married women, into the labor force is an important aspect of the changing roles of women and men in marriage. One consequence has been a significant change in the redistribution impact of the spouse benefit.

Since the system is based on individual earnings records, contributions by the wife into the OASI system go toward creating her own separate earnings record rather than toward a joint family record. The net result is that second earners, in effect, purchase redundant insurance. For instance, a wife eligible for an $1800 spouse benefit based on her husband's earnings record receives no additional benefits from her contributions until her separate earnings record produces a benefit in excess of $1800.

[3]If both the husband and wife in a household are alive and eligible for OASI in any one period, the family receives a monthly benefit of 1.5 PIA. If one spouse is alive and the other dead, the benefit equals two-thirds of 1.5 PIA or PIA. Since single people by definition have no spouse, they at most receive PIA in any period.

In Burkhauser (1979), I show that the dependent-spouse family model used in OASI has put both single people and two-earner families at a disadvantage relative to traditional one-earner families. Using data from the 1973 Social Security Exact Match File, I found that at each OASI benefit level, single people contributed more into the system, per dollar received, than their married counterparts, and two-earner families contributed more than their one-earner counterparts.

Over the entire population, however, the across-generational transfers were sufficient to make all families better off than they would have been in an actuarially fair system. That is, up to 1973 taxes paid by younger generations were sufficient to more than compensate current OASI recipients for the taxes they paid into the system over their work lives. Although one-earner families did better than both two-earner families and single workers, all received more than would have been the case in a pure insurance system. Only when the marginal contribution of second earners is examined do OASI contributions yield less than an actuarially fair return. That is, the net increase in total household benefits gained as a result of the second earner's contributions into the system is less than would have been received from a fair annuity, because for the most part these contributions purchase insurance that would be available through the spouse benefit of the first earner. Thus the current spouse-benefit system affects women—and the families of different types of women— differently. In effect, it reduces the marginal return from contributions made into OASI at younger ages by both single women and most married women.[4]

On equity grounds, it can be argued that, holding total family income constant, families with two earners should pay the same amount of OASI contributions as one-earner families. On efficiency grounds, it can be argued that a negative marginal return on OASI contributions will negatively affect the work effort of married women. Replacing the spouse benefit with an earnings-sharing principle would comply with both these criteria. Adopting this principle would strengthen the social insurance aspect of OASI by more closely relating benefits to contributions.

---

[4]As was pointed out in our Introduction, taxes paid by younger generations have been sufficient to allow all OASI beneficiaries to receive a greater than actuarially fair return on their contributions into OASI. However, this is changing. Those aged 65 in 1972 were receiving a 50% intergenerational transfer compared to the age cohort 80 and older, who were receiving a 90% intergenerational transfer. The maturing nature of the system together with the fall in fertility rates makes it impossible to continue to provide everyone with a positive OASI transfer without significantly raising OASI taxes (see Burkhauser and Warlick, 1981).

IMPACT OF EARNINGS SHARING ACROSS FAMILIES

In addition to the spouse benefit, two other income adequacy provisions—a minimum benefit and a decreasing marginal benefit adjustment—were included in the 1939 amendments that established the framework for the OASI system. The distributional impact of replacing the current dependent-spouse model of the family with the equal-partner model of earnings sharing is significantly affected by these two characteristics of OASI.

OASI benefits are derived by first calculating a worker's *average monthly wage* (AMW), based on yearly earnings up to a taxable maximum on which workers and employers paid OASI taxes. For a worker aged 65 in 1973, the calculation was based on his highest 18 earnings years. Then, on the basis of some multiple of AMW, a worker's Primary Insurance Amount (PIA) is calculated. On income adequacy grounds, this PIA coefficient (r) decreases as AMW increases. Table 4.1 shows the relationship between AMW and PIA for both 1973 and 1979. Note than in 1973 a minimum PIA of $84.50 per month was given to any worker eligible for benefits but with an AMW less than $78. For single workers who accepted benefits at age 65 in that year, actual monthly benefits equaled the PIA. For married couples in which both husband and wife were aged 65 in 1973, monthly

Table 4.1
Old Age and Survivors Benefit Calculations, 1973 and 1979

Year	Average Monthly Wage (AMW)	r	1.5 r	Primary Insurance Amount (PIA)	PIA + Spouse Benefit
1973	$ 0–78			$ 84.50[a]	$126.75[b]
	78–110	1.08	1.62	85–119	127–179
	110–400	.39	.59	119–233	179–350
	400–550	.37	.56	233–288	350–432
	550–650	.43	.65	288–331	432–497
1979	$ 0–134			$121.00[a]	$181.50[b]
	134–180	.9	1.35	121–162	182–243
	180–1,085	.32	.48	162–452	243–678
	1,085+	.15	.23	452+	678+

Sources and notes: Social Security Bulletin, Annual Statistical Supplement, 1977–1979, p. 18. The marginal PIA coefficient, r, is the % of the increase in AMW that is added to PIA. After 1979, bend points will automatically adjust with inflation, but the minimum benefit will remain constant.

[a] Minimum benefit for a single person.

[b] Minimum benefit for a married couple.

benefits equaled the larger of two amounts: 150% of the higher earner's PIA or the sum of each spouse's PIA.

It is important to recognize the relationship between an additional dollar of AMW and its impact on total family benefits. For any worker, single or married, the marginal benefit of increases in AMW are zero up to the minimum benefit. Thereafter, for single workers and two-earner couples marginal increases in AMW yield benefits equal to the marginal PIA coefficient (r). For one-earner couples the benefit yield is 150% of (r).

We can best comprehend this relationship and its effect on the distributional consequences of substituting earnings sharing for spouse benefits by first looking at the impact of substituting earnings sharing for spouse benefits in a much simpler system, one with no minimum benefit and $(r) = 1$. In such a case, the change to earnings sharing would have no impact on single people or two-earner families regardless of AMW level. For instance, a two-earner family where the husband had an AMW of $200 and the wife had an AMW of $100 would have total benefits of $300. Under earnings sharing, total AMW would be $300 and each member of the family would receive $150 in benefits. Thus within-family benefits would change, but total benefits would remain the same.

This is not the case for one-earner families. Shifting to earnings sharing means that such families could no longer multiply their (r) by 150% and total benefits would fall by one-third at every AMW level—that is, at a constant rate of $.50 per dollar of AMW (Figure 4.1). In a one-earner

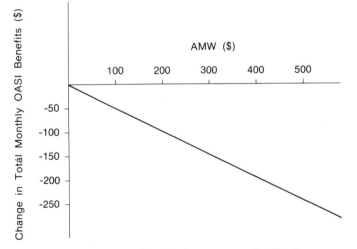

Figure 4.1. Change in total family benefits for one-earner families in a system with no minimum benefit and PIA coefficient equal to 1. (Figure by University of Wisconsin Cartographic Laboratory.)

family where the spouse had no work record and the husband's AMW was $200, total benefits would fall from $300 to $200, since each spouse receives $100 in benefits from sharing the family AMW equally, but the spouse benefit disappears. As long as (r) is constant across AMW, alternative (r) values will alter the slope between AMW and the difference in total benefits, but not the one-third loss in total benefits.

Given rules similar to the current OASI system, which contains both a minimum benefit and a variable PIA coefficient, the distributional impact of earnings sharing is not so clear-cut. Not only would the slope vary across AMW levels, but it would in fact be positive at some points. Figure 4.2 plots the change in total OASI benefits of one-earner families that would occur across all AMW levels if the family AMW were shared equally and the spouse benefit removed. The slope of the curve is a result of the change in total benefits caused by removing a dollar of AMW recorded in a husband's name and assigning it to his wife's AMW. The net impact of ending the spouse benefit system and sharing total family AMW is the sum of the husband's marginal loss of 150% of the relevant (r) (see Table 4.1), and the wife's gain in AMW based on her higher (r). A positive slope is possible, since (r) falls almost continuously as AMW increases. The

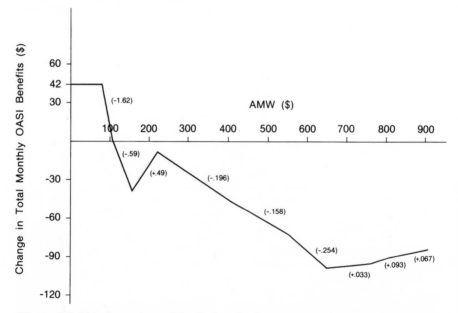

Figure 4.2. Net change in total family benefits for one-earner families under earnings sharing (1973). (Slopes in parentheses.) (Figure by University of Wisconsin Cartographic Laboratoy.)

AMW values at which (r) changes—*bend points*—are shown in Table 4.1 for both 1973 and 1979. Thus over some range the negative impact of losing a dollar of AMW, even when multiplied by 150%, is offset, since the new shared AMW is multiplied by a higher (r) at the lower mean AMW level.

Not only can the slope be positive in Figure 4.2, but one-earner families currently receiving a minimum benefit might actually experience a gain in net total benefits: They would now be eligible for two minimum benefits, which exceed the 150% of a single minimum benefit they now receive. In addition, because no one-earner family can fall below a benefit level that is twice the minimum, those families with an AMW below $104 gain from earnings sharing. From that point until $156.50 (twice the minimum benefit), one-earner families lose at the rate of 1.5 r in husband-related AMW, with no marginal gain in shared benefits to offset it. But from this point until $220 (twice the initial AMW bend point), the gain from the wife's higher (r) offsets the husband's loss.

For example, look at a family where the husband's AMW is $200 and the wife's AMW is zero. In 1973 total benefits for this family under OASI as currently constituted would be $231: $154 for the husband, $77 (.5 PIA) for the wife. In a Figure 4.1 system, total benefits would fall by $77, or by one-third. But as can be seen in Figure 4.2, which uses actual 1973 OASI rules, at the $200 level (r) equals .39, whereas at the $100 level it is 1.08. Because of the higher (r), the loss of the $100 spouse benefit is cushioned by the fact that each spouse now receives $108 in his or her own right, for a family total of $216. Because of the change in (r), their total loss is $15 or 6.5%. Beyond $220, however, the slope is negative, although at a much smaller rate. It is not until AMW is $370 that the absolute loss once again reaches $37 per month. It should be noted that even these reduced losses overstate the impact on many families receiving a spouse benefit. Figure 4.2 assumes that the wife's AMW is zero. This need not be the case, for redundant contributions could have been made by a wife whose earnings record was not sufficient to provide benefits greater than the spouse benefit. In an earnings-sharing system, such contributions are not redundant, and will be included in total AMW. In the previous example, where a wife was receiving a spouse benefit based on her husband's $200 AMW, earnings sharing would increase total family benefits if her AMW were over $7.

Beneficiaries who are single continue to be unaffected by a shift to earnings sharing, under the assumptions of Figure 4.2, but now two-earner families are affected. Because earnings sharing allows total AMW to be split, some two-earner families can increase total benefits. In general, the greater the difference between the AMW of wife and husband, the more

Table 4.2
Distributional Impact on Couples of Replacing the Dependent-Spouse System with Earnings Sharing across Average Monthly Wages, 1973

Status of Husbands	(1) Ineligible	(2) Minimum Benefit	(3) AMW $78–110	(4) AMW $110–220	(5) AMW $220–400	(6) AMW $400–550	(7) All Eligible Wives (2–6)	All Wives
Ineligible								
Current system		$1,521	$1,820	$2,476	$3,693	$4,537	$2,746	$2,746
Earnings sharing		2,028	2,028	2,218	3,369	3,948	2,614	2,614
Percentage of couples in category		5%	4%	8%	6%	6%	6%	3%
Minimum benefit								
Current system	$1,521	2,028	2,159	2,730	3,401	4,269	2,889	2,013
Earnings sharing	2,028	2,028	2,071	2,838	3,455	4,096	2,870	2,331
Percentage of couples in category	5	3	7	3	4	2	4	4
AMW $78–110								
Current system	1,820	2,294	2,513	2,909	3,598	4,487	3,068	2,182
Earnings sharing	2,028	2,038	2,513	2,996	3,680	4,374	3,073	2,331
Percentage of couples in category	5	3	2	3	4	2	3	5
AMW $110–220								
Current system	2,511	2,734	2,884	3,403	3,993	4,642	3,358	2,812
Earnings sharing	2,259	2,833	2,999	3,403	3,993	4,650	3,401	2,665
Percentage of couples in category	18	20	16	16	10	15	15	16
AMW $220–400								
Current system	3,678	3,620	3,766	4,139	4,768	5,469	4,263	3,912
Earnings sharing	3,359	3,591	3,820	4,139	4,768	5,480	4,262	3,721
Percentage of couples in category	48	45	46	51	52	35	49	48

AMW $400–550								
Current system	4,515	4,572	4,566	4,621	5,387	6,152	5,046	4,717
Earnings sharing	3,932	4,220	4,401	4,614	5,401	6,152	4,961	4,323
Percentage of couples in category	21	21	17	16	21	35	20	21
AMW $550 and over								
Current system	5,622	*a*	*a*	*a*	*a*	*a*	6,207	5,856
Earnings sharing	4,681	*a*	*a*	*a*	*a*	*a*	5,959	5,192
Percentage of couples in category	3						3	3
All eligible husbands								
Current system	3,507	3,604	3,702	4,024	4,754	5,657	4,263	3,795
Earnings sharing	3,192	3,509	3,682	4,028	4,760	5,657	4,220	3,584
Percentage of couples in category	100	95	96	92	94	94	37	97
All husbands								
Current system	3,507	3,501	3,627	3,900	4,690	5,590	4,150	3,764
Earnings sharing	3,192	3,434	3,616	3,883	4,677	5,554	4,117	3,562
Percentage of couples in category	60	8	5	12	11	4	40	100

Sources and notes: Social Security Exact Match File (1973). This is a subsample of all married couples covered by OASI. It includes all married couples in which both the husband and the wife are aged 65 or older and in which at least one member is eligible to receive OASI benefits on her or his own earnings record. No women were in the $550 and over AMW range in 1973. The total OASI-covered population (married couples eligible to receive benefits) is 3.59 million couples, with total OASI benefits under our current system equal to $12.6 billion and equal to $11.9 billion under earnings sharing. Benefits going to one-earner families would fall from $7.3 billion to $6.7 billion or 8%. Benefits going to two-earner families would fall from $5.3 billion to $5.2 billion or 2%.

a Less than 1%.

83

likely it is that they will be in different (r) ranges and will thus gain from the change. For those two-earner families in the same (r) range, total benefits do not change—only within-family distribution of personal benefits. One group of two-earner families, however, could be negatively affected. If the wife is receiving a minimum benefit and her husband has an AMW above the minimum, total family benefits may fall, since the marginal gains from shifting benefits to the lower AMW are zero until average AMW equals $78. At this bend point, (r) increases to 1.08, and the negative impact is quickly reversed.

The creation of the 1973 Social Security Exact Match File makes it possible to simulate the impact across the entire OASI beneficiary population of replacing the dependent-spouse system with a pure earnings-sharing system. The 1973 Social Security Exact Match File merges individual records from the Current Population Survey of that year with actual OASI earnings and benefit records. Using the OASI rules relating contributions to benefits in 1973 (Table 4.1), we can measure the marginal impact of the change not only for one- and two-earner families but also across AMW levels of these families.

Table 4.2 uses the actual AMW records of married couples eligible to receive OASI benefits in 1973 to examine the distribution of those benefits across families with different AMW combinations. Couples are grouped within AMW bend points for 1973, defined in Table 4.1. As expected, on average, low-AMW, one-earner families actually gain from earnings sharing. Those at the minimum level would increase yearly benefits from $1521 to $2028, that is by $507, or 33%. Those between the minimum and $110 would increase benefits by $208, or 11%. The great majority of one-earner families, however, would lose total benefits. Those between $110 and $220 would average losses of $252 per year, or 10%. The losses for those between $220 and $400 would average $319, or 9%. For those between $400 and $550, losses would average $583, or 13%. At the highest range, $550 and above, losses would be $941, or 17%. There is a similar result for one-earner households in which the wife is the earner. Over all, total benefits for one-earner families fall from $7.3 billion to $6.7 billion, or 8%.

For two-earner families, average benefits fall slightly, from $4263 to $4220, and total payments from $5.3 billion to $5.2 billion. As predicted, the principal losers among two-earner families are those where one spouse is at the minimum level. When both spouses are at the minimum, benefits are unchanged. However, if the husband has an AMW between $78 and $110, total benefits fall from $2294 to $2038, or 11%. For those between $110 and $220, this changes to a gain of $99, or 4%. Across all families, the effect of earnings sharing is to reduce total benefits from $12.6 billion to $11.9 billion, or 5%.

In examining these figures, it is important to bear in mind that our current dependent-spouse system, in the presence of a minimum benefit and a decreasing PIA coefficient, redistributes income to only certain types of one-earner families. Table 4.2 shows that the principal gainers of this system are families with high-wage, male workers. It is these families who would be most seriously affected by earnings sharing. However even for the great majority of this subset of high-wage, one-earner families, benefits would fall at most by 13%.

THE IMPACT OF EARNINGS SHARING IN 1980

The 1977 amendments to the Social Security Act have significantly changed the AMW bend points, the PIA coefficients, and the minimum benefit level (see Table 4.1); but these changes do not affect the 1973 results. Figure 4.3 shows the net change in total benefits under 1979 OASI regulations for a one-earner family where the wife has a zero AMW. The minimum AMW level is now $134.44. Thus under earnings sharing an AMW below this point would yield net gains of $60.50 per month. The break-even point is $180, which is by coincidence a bend point. Total benefits fall with a slope of −.45 until $268.88 (twice the minimum), then, as in 1973, marginal benefits increase. For this reason, the total benefit

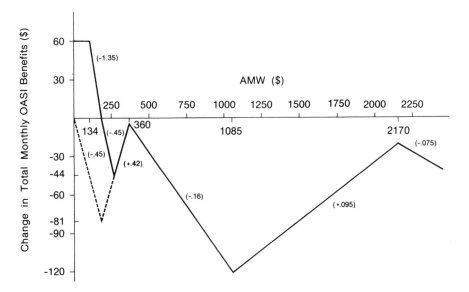

Figure 4.3. Net change in total family benefits for one-earner families under earnings sharing (1979). No-minimum-benefit case is shown by dotted line. (Slopes in parentheses.) (Figure by University of Wisconsin Cartographic Laboratory.)

loss at an AMW of $360 is only $4.39, and it is not until an AMW of $640 is reached that benefits once again fall as much as $42.66. The maximum fall in total benefits is at $1085, the final AMW bend point. At this AMW level the slope is once again positive, so that at $2170 losses equal only $18.

It is possible to approximate the impact of moving to earnings sharing under the 1979 rules both now and in the future. Table 4.3 shows the impact on one-earner families across average yearly earnings (AMW multiplied by 12). As was the case in 1973, not all one-earner families lose. Those below $2160 gain. Few one-earner families would lose more than 10% of current benefits. The greatest losses (10% or more) are clustered within the $9000 to $15,000 range, which encompasses the highest 25% of previous wage earners. The other area where losses are above 10% is among the 9% of beneficiaries with average earnings between $3000 and $4000, whose OASI benefits could in most cases be supplemented by federal Supplemental Security Income (SSI).

Legislation to end the minimum benefit has been proposed in the 97th Congress. Such a change would reduce the redistributive nature of OASI for low-wage earners and put more pressure on SSI to provide a socially adequate level of income for the aged poor. In Figure 4.3 a dotted line shows what the effect of moving to earnings sharing in 1979 would have been with no minimum benefit. Because spouse benefits are lost and are not cushioned by a variation in r until the $180 AMW level, benefits are lost from the first dollar of AMW up to a maximum loss of $81. As discussed above, however, SSI will completely make up this loss for those eligible for this income-tested program.

Since there is no relationship between contributions made into the system and the marginal benefits generated by the spouse benefit, such benefits must be justified on grounds of need—social adequacy. It is difficult to argue that the highest 25% of the previous wage-earning population should receive additional benefits on redistributive grounds. The redistribution case is more appealing for lower-wage earners, although here, too, it is difficult to support the argument that one-earner families with a total AMW equal to their identical two-earner counterparts deserve higher benefits.[5]

[5]This argument is made even more untenable when other means of achieving income adequacy goals are considered. The SSI program would completely cushion any losses sustained by aged married couples whose average yearly earnings had been $3000–$4000. Alternatively, redistribution within OASI is possible by simply increasing either the range to the first bend point or increasing (r). Both of these solutions would aid low-income aged people in a more systematic manner than the current dependent-spouse system. It should be noted that in essence the first solution is the two-tier approach to income support, and the second solution is a form of the double-decker approach.

Table 4.3
Impact of Earnings Sharing on One-Earner Families under Present OASI Benefit Rules (1979 Dollars)

OASI Covered Earnings (AMW × 12)	Total OASI Benefits	Change in Total OASI Benefits		Cumulative Distribution of Men Age 65 in 1979 and Eligible for OASI Benefits[a]
		Dollar Amounts	Percentage of Change	
$ 0	$ 2,178[b]	$ 726	+33.3%	—
1,613	2,178[b]	726	+33.3	10.1%
2,160	2,916[b]	0	0.0	16.7
3,000	3,320[b]	−416	−12.5	23.5
3,227	3,428[b]	−512	−14.9	25.4
4,000	3,800	−200	−5.3	32.0
4,320	3,953	−52	−1.3	34.6
5,000	4,280	−174	−4.1	39.8
7,000	5,240	−494	−9.4	54.2
9,000	6,200	−814	−13.1	72.1
11,000	7,160	−1,134	−15.8	88.4
13,020	8,129	−1,430	−17.6	95.9
15,000	8,575	−1,269	−14.8	97.6
18,000	9,250	−984	−10.6	100.0
21,000	9,925	−699	−7.0	100
24,000	10,600	−414	−3.9	100
26,040	11,058	−193	−1.7	100
30,000	11,950	−490	−4.1	100

Notes: Total OASI benefits include both a retired-worker benefit and a spouse benefit for a couple both eligible and retiring at age 65. Benefits are estimated for various hypothetical AMWs, based on 1979 Primary Insurance Amount (PIA) formula (see Table 4.1).

Change in total OASI benefits measures the difference between current total benefits and benefits received in an earnings-sharing system in which AMW was equally shared and spouse benefit removed.

[a] The distribution of the eligible male population (regardless of marital status) is based on the actual distribution of the eligible male population at the end of 1977 (*Social Security Bulletin, Annual Statistical Supplement, 1977–1979*, p. 146) adjusted for inflation. While inflation adjustment in the bend points should make the distribution neutral with respect to inflation, the distribution will move toward the upper end owing to the increase in real AMW of new beneficiaries.

[b] In 1979 all OASI payments below $3748 for married couples could be supplemented by federal SSI payments.

The Current Earnings-Sharing Proposals

WHO PAYS AND WHO COLLECTS

The earnings-sharing proposal simulated in the previous section shows that the redistributional impact across beneficiaries is much less than might be expected. Those who lose from removing the spouse benefit are cushioned to a large degree by the tilt in the PIA coefficient. This would be true for most people currently retired or nearing retirement age. As was seen in the 1973 simulations (Table 4.2), average benefits to male-headed one-earner families fell from $3507 to $3192, that is, they would receive 9% less than under the current system, and the major losses would occur at the upper end of the wage distribution. Two-earner family benefits would remain virtually the same. Going to an earnings-sharing system in 1973 would have reduced total benefits to all married couples by $0.7 billion, or 5%. Clearly such a change would have only a minor impact on most individual families or on the size of the system's liabilities.

Although the 1979 Advisory Council suggested that earnings sharing was a possible solution to the current unequal treatment of women, it did not recommend its implementation at this time. Rather, it used the principle of earnings sharing to recommend two specific changes in the current system. The first addressed the issue of divorce. The council here recognized the equal-partner principle of the family and recommended that each divorced spouse should be entitled to one-half of the total earnings record accumulated during the marriage, but only if the marriage lasted 10 years. For the first 10 years of marriage, a homemaker would remain dependent on her husband and would have no vested right to any part of his earnings stream. It is notable that this is one of the first proposals ever made by the Advisory Council which would explicitly increase the benefits of one group of beneficiaries—divorced home-makers—at the expense of another group of beneficiaries—divorced workers. This is in sharp contrast to the usual method of increasing the benefits of some group by enlarging the liabilities of the system, and thus increasing the taxes paid by the current generation. The reluctance to decrease benefits regardless of the justification for doing so is one major impediment to a fuller earnings-sharing system, even when these decreases are minor.

The second proposal—an *inherited credit*—is much more in keeping with the traditional method of increasing benefits to one group by simply increasing the size of OASI expenditures. The council recommended that survivor benefits no longer be based on the joint and two-thirds to survivor formulation.[6] In keeping with the equal-partner concept of the family, they recommended that survivor benefits should be based on an AMW that was the sum of all previous earnings by the couple. This increase in survivor benefits would not, however, be offset by a reduction in benefits to another group—in this case, the same couple when both spouses are alive. Rather, it would be financed by increased taxes raised from the current generation.

It is important to note that an earnings-sharing system can be compatible with our current joint and two-thirds to survivor system. Earnings sharing need not result in a joint and one-half annuity system—one in which the shared AMW yields two equal PIAs to husband and wife when both are alive, but falls to one PIA at the death of one or the other. It is a simple matter to reset the benefit schedule so that when both spouses are alive they each get 3/4 PIA or 1.5 PIA for the family. At the death of one spouse, the survivor will continue to get his or her 3/4 PIA but will also receive a 1/4 survivor PIA from the deceased spouse's benefit. Hence total benefit equals PIA. Earnings sharing need only change the method by which PIA is initially estimated, not the joint and two-thirds method of allocating income across the lifetime of both spouses within a family. More important, from a policy standpoint, recognition of this flexibility allows the earnings-sharing issue to be separated from the issue of whether some survivors should receive higher benefits through an increase in the size of the OASI tax bill.

THE ROLE OF WOMEN

Table 4.2 suggests that earnings sharing will have only a minor impact on income distribution or on the total costs of the system. In these dimensions, it can be classified as simply an incremental change, especially when it is compared with alternatives such as a two-tier benefit structure or a double-decker system, which would significantly alter the social insurance/social adequacy nature of OASI.[7] However, adoption of

[6]In the dependent-spouse model of social security, if both spouses are alive, benefits include a worker benefit (PIA) and a spouse benefit (.5 PIA). At the death of one member, the survivor receives (PIA) in benefits. Hence benefits are reduced to two-thirds of the amount received when both spouses were alive. This is also a standard form of private annuity payment.

[7]A two-tier system would resemble Figure 4.1 with a constant (r) relating contributions to benefits in an actuarially fair manner. All attempts to provide a socially adequate income would be done through SSI. A double-decker system would make the minimum benefit of Figure 4.3 a demogrant, but would significantly enlarge its value, with some constant (r) thereafter. Both these systems would have redistributional impacts far in excess of earnings sharing.

the principle of earnings sharing would signal a fundamental change in the perception of the family and the roles of women and men within the family. And it would require significant change in the kind of insurance social security would provide. This includes disability insurance (DI), as well as old age and survivors insurance (OASI). It is the reasonableness of this new perception of the role of women and men within a family on which the decision to implement earnings sharing must be made.

Clearly, earnings sharing treats men and women as equal partners in the maintenance of the family. In doing so, it frees a woman to choose to work at home, with no fear that an unforeseen marital split will leave her with reduced or no OASI protection in old age. It also rewards women who choose to go into the labor market, by more closely relating future OASI benefits to taxes paid into the system while in the labor market. But it no longer provides extra benefits to the families of women who choose not to work in the labor market. As Holden (1979b) points out, the spouse benefit was an implicit return to homemakers for which no payments were necessary on their part. Its removal ends one method of redistributing income from single people and two-earner families to traditional one-earner families. Because such transfers go primarily to high-income households, it is difficult, on income adequacy grounds, to fault their replacement by earnings sharings.

More difficult to justify is the presumption implicit in earnings sharing that married women could and should be able to move in and out of the labor market as easily as men. Clearly the steady increase in the labor force participation of married women suggests that such movement is occurring. But just as clearly many women still remain completely out of the labor force.

In a one-earner family, when an older husband retires, his benefits under earnings sharing would be based on only one-half his AMW until his wife was also eligible to retire. Under the present system, the wife is not, of course, eligible to receive a spouse benefit either, until she is at retirement age, but the worker's benefit that the husband receives is larger than it would be under earnings sharing. The equal-partner presumption in earnings sharing is that in such households a younger wife is capable of entering the work force and should, if necessary, do so to supplement her husband's retirement benefits. In like manner the husband could and should, if necessary, take on more of the homemaking responsibilities.

A potentially more serious problem exists with respect to disability insurance. If the earner in a one-earner household becomes disabled, benefits are based on his share of AMW. Once again, the presumption is that additional income could and should be provided by his able-bodied wife. There is yet another problem with respect to the care of dependent children. All of these problems and special cases, however, can be handled under earnings sharing. But their solutions are sensitive to the reasonableness of the basic proposition that men and women should and could move between work in the house and work in the labor market.

Conclusion

The changes involved in a move to earnings sharing can, in summary, be viewed as incremental in some respects, fundamental in others.

They are incremental in that their impact on the benefits of current beneficiaries or on those nearing beneficiary age would be relatively minor. Most two-earner families would gain slightly or be unaffected; most middle-income, one-earner families would lose slightly, and higher-income, one-earner families would lose moderately. Low-income, one-earner families would actually gain. The impact on the total expenditures of the OASI system would be very small. Married women would have added incentives to enter the labor force, and OASI would more closely follow the horizontal-equity proposition that equal contributions yield equal benefits.

Earnings sharing would require a fundamental change in the social security system's perception of the family and the roles of women and men within the family. An earnings-sharing system would treat women and men as equal partners in maintaining and supporting their family and would provide old age, survivors, and disability insurance in accordance with these principles.

Clearly, such a change would recognize the changing nature of the family and the role of women in the labor force, but equally clearly, it would put an added responsibility on both women and men to shift between home and labor market work. Support for earnings sharing depends on the reasonableness of this proposition.

Discussion

VIRGINIA P. RENO

I'd like to discuss four topics in commenting on Rich Burkhauser's paper: first, the general role of the social security program; second, some specific issues posed by the earnings-sharing proposal; third, some alternatives to earnings sharing; and finally, a comment on the survivor option suggested by Burkhauser.

ROLE OF SOCIAL SECURITY

In his opening sentence, Burkhauser refers to two goals of social security—one being "social adequacy" and the other being "social insurance." In this context, it appears that "social insurance" is akin to "pure insurance," which, according to Burkhauser, "like any private insurance system, would be actuarially fair, relating contributions to the expected value of benefits." This definition is similar to what is sometimes called the "individual equity" goal of social security—that individuals should be assured of getting out at least as much as they put in. Opinions may differ on whether this idea should be labeled "individual equity" or "social insurance," or something else. I prefer to call it the return-on-taxes or the rate-of-return concept of social security. And, I question whether this idea—that each individual should expect to get his taxes back from social security—is a necessary or desirable goal.

The system is not now designed to relate an individual's taxes to the expected value of his benefits. If this were an explicit goal, we would see a very different benefit computation procedure: one in which individuals' benefits are directly related to the present value of their past taxes; or alternatively, one in which each individual's tax rate is set according to his "risk" of getting a certain amount of benefits. The system is not now set up this way. Instead, benefits are based on average *earnings* from which social security taxes were paid.

Within this basic structure, the purpose is to pay monthly benefits to people who lose earnings because of retirement, disability, or death of a family member. The purpose is related to earnings replacement, and the goals are to provide that earnings replacement in a fair and adequate way.

If we look at social security as an earnings-replacement system, then it is quite possible that the system can be designed to replace earnings in a way that is both equitable and adequate, given whatever resources we are willing to devote to the purpose. But the hard choices remain in answering the basic question: What constitutes fair and adequate earnings replacement for people in different circumstances? For example, what is fair and adequate for high-earners vis-à-vis low earners? long-service workers vis-à-vis short-service workers? individuals vis-à-vis couples and families? individuals within families vis-à-vis each other? It is on these questions, particularly the last two, that earnings sharing brings new perspectives on questions of fairness and adequacy within the earnings-replacement framework.

EARNINGS SHARING

Three attributes of the earnings-sharing proposal seem to underlie its appeal. These are the concept; the consequences between retired couples; and the consequences between spouses at divorce.

The Concept

Earnings sharing is based on the principle that marriage is a partnership of equals. This is an appealing concept. Few want to categorically refute it.

Consequences for One-Earner Couples and Dual-Earner Couples

Earnings sharing equalizes replacement rates between dual-earner couples and one-earner couples who have had similar past earnings.

Under present law, the 50% spouse benefit brings somewhat higher benefits (and replacement rates) to one-earner couples.

In terms of fairness, paying equal benefits to couples with equal earnings seems reasonable. As Burkhauser demonstrates, earnings sharing achieves this by lowering somewhat the benefits for one-earner couples.

In terms of adequacy, this change may also be appropriate. If one compares the income needs of aged individuals with those of aged couples, it is the unmarried aged who have the greater unmet needs. In 1976 only 9% of aged couples were poor, whereas 38% of unmarried women and 27% of unmarried men had individual incomes below the official poverty threshold.

The measure of equivalent need used in the official poverty threshold indicates that an individual needs about 80% as much as a couple (Orshansky, 1965). In the original near-poor threshold, the ratio was 72%. These ratios imply that couples need 25–39% more than an aged individual alone. Earnings sharing brings the couple's benefit to about 130–135% of the individual's benefit.

Thus earnings sharing provides equal benefits to couples with equal earnings; and it brings the relationship between couples' and individuals' benefits closer to our best estimates of their relative needs.

Consequences at Divorce

The earnings-sharing plan provides a 50/50 division of earnings credits at divorce. On the theory that both parties had relied on those earnings prior to the divorce, a 50/50 sharing of those credits for computing future earnings-replacement benefits has appeal on grounds of fairness.

The approach may also have appeal on adequacy grounds, because it raises incomes of a low-income group—retired divorced women. The U.S. Department of Health, Education, and Welfare report, *Social Security and the Changing Roles of Men and Women* (1979a), presents estimates of benefits for a simulated cohort of retirees in the year 2000. Those data show that divorced women, as a group, fare far less well than divorced men under the present social security system. The average benefit for divorced women under present law is projected to be about 60% of the average for divorced men. Under earnings sharing it is about 83%. In these projections, earnings sharing narrows the gap between divorced women's and divorced men's benefits through a 10% reduction in the average for men and a 24% increase in the average for women.

Thus, the appeal of earnings sharing relates to the concept—of marriage as a partnership of equals—and to two types of distributional results: between retired couples; and between parties within couples at divorce.

A key problem with earnings sharing occurs for married couples when only one spouse is eligible for benefits: that is, when only one member is retired or disabled. In this case, earnings sharing is in conflict with the concept of earnings replacement. This is illustrated in Table 4.4. Each panel compares two couples with identical past earnings: couple 1, in which only the husband is retired or disabled, and couple 2, in which only the wife is retired or disabled.

In panel A the husband is the sole earner. In panel B he is the primary earner. In both cases, benefits (and replacement rates) for the family are considerably reduced if the husband is the one who is retired or disabled. And benefits are increased—or paid where none are now paid—if the wife is the one who is retired or disabled.

Judged by earnings-replacement criteria, earnings sharing poses problems of both fairness and adequacy in these cases. Is it fair to pay identical benefits to couple 1 and couple 2 when their earnings loss is so vastly different? Does it meet our standards of social adequacy to pay the same amount to couple 1—when most or all their earnings are lost—as to couple 2—when little or none of their earnings are lost?

This table illustrates an inherent conflict between earnings sharing and earnings replacement for intact couples when only one spouse is retired or disabled. We must choose between earnings replacement, in which benefits are related to earnings loss, and earnings sharing, in which benefits are based on half of family earnings, regardless of whose earnings are lost.

Burkhauser points out that earnings sharing would work best under these circumstances if we could expect husbands and wives to have equal earning potential. That would minimize the conflict between earnings replacement and earnings sharing. If, however, husbands and wives actually had equal earning potential and equal earning behavior, then the problems that earnings sharing is designed to solve would also disappear.

What are the prospects that husbands and wives will have similar earning potential? Clearly more wives are in the labor force than in the past, and their participation is projected to increase in the future. Yet the employment rates of wives are projected to remain below those of husbands. The difference between husbands' and wives' earnings remains wide (U.S. Department of Commerce, 1979a, Table 28). In 1977, the median earnings of married men was $13,880 while the median for married women was $5070, only about one-third as much. Of all couples with any earnings in 1977, in only 10% did the wife earn more than the husband. The remaining 90% include 40% in which only the husband had earnings and 50% in which the husband earned more than the wife.

Given the wide difference between husbands' and wives' labor market

Table 4.4
Comparison of Present System with Earnings Sharing When Only One Spouse Is Eligible

A. Husband as Sole Earner
(Couple's total prior earnings = $24,000;
husband's = $24,000; wife's = 0)

	Present System	Earnings Sharing
	Couple 1: Only Husband Entitled	
Benefits	$ 7,339	$ 5,190
Earnings	0	0
Total income	7,339	5,190
Income as a percentage of prior earnings	31%	22%
	Couple 2: Only Wife Entitled	
Benefits	$ 0	$ 5,190
Earnings	24,000	24,000
Total income	24,000	29,190
Income as a percentage of prior earnings	100%	122%

B. Husband as Primary Earner
(Couple's total prior earnings = $24,000;
husband's = $18,000; wife's = $6,000)

	Present System	Earnings Sharing
	Couple 1: Only Husband Entitled	
Benefits	$ 6,439	$ 5,190
Earnings	6,000	6,000
Total income	12,439	11,190
Income as a percentage of prior earnings	52%	47%
Benefit as a percentage of earnings lost	36%	29%
	Couple 2: Only Wife Entitled	
Benefits	$ 3,270	$ 5,190
Earnings	18,000	18,000
Total income	21,270	23,190
Income as a percentage of prior earnings	89%	97%
Benefit as a percentage of earnings lost	54%	86%

behavior, problems in applying earnings sharing to couples when only one partner receives benefits are important.

Ways to avoid these problems have been explored. One way is *not* to divide earnings credits between spouses when only one is retired or disabled, but to wait until both are retired, or until the marriage ends in divorce. This modification achieves the same desired results between couples and between divorced spouses. And, it avoids the problem illustrated in Table 4.4. However, it may create a new one. That is, that the system is no longer "neutral" with regard to divorce. Under the present system nobody gains higher benefits as a result of divorce. Under this modified earnings sharing, some would gain. Thus, we must choose between three desirable goals—only two of which can be met at once: (*a*) earnings-related individual benefits for members of intact couples; (*b*) 50/50 sharing at divorce; (*c*) no change in individuals' benefits because of divorce. To implement earnings sharing one must choose which of these goals can be set aside.

ALTERNATIVES TO EARNINGS SHARING

It may be that the two distributional effects of earnings sharing that make it attractive can be achieved in other ways.

Retired Couples

On the question of replacement rates between one- and two-earner couples, more nearly equal benefits could be achieved by lowering the rate of the spouse benefit from 50% to, say, 35 or 33%. In reality, that may affect relatively few retired couples. Relatively few spouse benefits are paid, and even fewer are paid at the full 50%. In 1976 spouse benefits were paid on the accounts of only 17% of all retired workers—representing about 40% of retired married men. Most wives who receive the spouse benefit take an actuarial reduction. If the wife's benefit is claimed at age 62, it is reduced to 37.5% of the worker's full benefit. If the spouse benefit were set at 35% and not reduced for early retirement, more nearly equal benefits would be payable to one-earner and dual-earner couples with the same earnings.

Divorced Women

On the question of benefit adequacy for divorced women, or of recognizing the work of women in the home generally, there are alternatives to earnings sharing. One option is to allow child-care drop-out years in the benefit calculation. Estimates for a cohort of retirees in the year

2000 show that divorced women are the group most likely to benefit from child-care drop-out years. Married women benefit to a lesser extent.

Child-care drop-out years represent a conceptual alternative earnings sharing. The added protection would be linked, not to a marriage license, but to the responsibilities of parenthood and the low earnings that may accompany that job. We have a choice between two appealing concepts:

1. Earnings-Sharing, built on the principle that marriage is a partnership of equals. As Burkhauser points out, this works best if the equality in earning power between husbands and wives already exists.
2. Child-Care Drop-out Years, built on the principle that parenthood is a job of sufficient value to not be penalized in the benefit calculation.

AGED WIDOWS AND WIDOWERS: THE SURVIVOR OPTION

My final point in commenting on Burkhauser's paper relates to provisions for aged widows and widowers. Burkhauser discusses the inherited-credit proposal for survivor benefits that was recommended by the 1979 Advisory Council on Social Security. Under that proposal a surviving spouse would receive a benefit based on her (or his) own earnings record combined with that of the deceased spouse. The total of combined annual earnings on the survivor's record would be limited to the annual maximum earnings creditable to an individual. Burkhauser notes that this proposal is in keeping with the past practice of addressing problems of fairness by raising rather than lowering benefits. He suggests an alternative, built on the return-on-taxes perspective on social security. Under that approach, a couple would take a cut in their retirement benefits in order to provide a benefit for the survivor. This kind of survivor option would significantly reduce the appeal of earnings sharing for couples, particularly for one-earner couples. Burkhauser's results show that earnings sharing lowers benefits for one-earner couples by an average of 10%. Average benefits for other couples don't change much. His survivor option, however, would lower benefits for the one-earner couples still further and would lower benefits for many dual-earner couples as well. Even if the money saved were redistributed across the beneficiary population, it would be a major shift away from couples and their survivors.

This concept of survivor benefits—in contrast to the Advisory Council recommendation—illustrates the difference between the rate-of-return perspective and the earnings-replacement perspective on the role of social security. Under the rate-of-return perspective, a retired couple has to spread their benefits thin in order to span the remaining life of the survivor and still keep the relationship between benefits and taxes the same.

Under the earnings-replacement perspective, the Advisory Council approach becomes more reasonable. The inherited-credit proposal simply changes the definition of which earnings should be replaced when a person is both widowed and retired. The present system allows a benefit that either replaces the survivor's earnings or replaces the deceased spouse's earnings, but not the sum of family earnings. The Advisory Council plan allows the survivor's benefit to be based on the family's earnings.

The inherited-credit proposal is expected to raise benefits for survivors of low-earning dual-earner couples. Under the weighted benefit formula, the survivor benefit for most low-earning dual-earner couples would be about three-fourths of their combined benefits as a couple, which is about what the poverty thresholds indicate that an individual needs to maintain the couple's standard of living.

My main point is that the conclusions one reaches about the fairness and the adequacy of social security differ markedly depending on which perspective one takes. Under the rate-of-return perspective one can establish a specified relationship between lifetime benefits and taxes, but the results may fail when judged by earnings-replacement criteria. Or, one can design the system to achieve the desired results in terms of earnings-replacement and end up with some winners and some losers by the rate-of-return criterion.

5

Women and a Two-Tier
Social Security System

ALICIA H. MUNNELL
LAURA E. STIGLIN

In the past the trade-off between individual equity and social adequacy within the social security system was practicable and desirable. Tax revenues supplied by a growing work force provided ample resources to guarantee a generous return on contributions and an adequate level of income support to the low-income retired population. Moreover, the adequacy components of social security were necessary in the absence of any federal welfare program. Although most states provided for the needy aged and disabled through federally supported public assistance programs, the benefit levels and eligibility requirements among state programs varied significantly, and these programs did not relieve social security of its social adequacy burden.

Today, however, the inherent conflict between adequacy and equity goals within social security has potentially destructive consequences. First, the real rate of return on social security contributions will decline markedly in the future, since coverage is no longer expanding and labor force growth is expected to cease. In this setting, the goals of income support and a fair return on contributions will come into direct conflict: High returns for low-income workers may dictate zero or negative returns for high-wage workers, thus undermining support for the program. Second, adequacy provisions have created serious inequities between one-earner and two-earner couples, and married and single individuals. Third, the provision of income support through social security is ineffi- cient. A means-tested program such as the Supplemental Security Income program, established in 1974, is a more effective mechanism for chan- neling money to the elderly and disabled poor. Finally, although the payroll tax is already viewed as a burdensome levy, rates will continue to rise in the future as the ratio of workers to retirees declines.

Two proposals have emerged which would separate the income ade- quacy and individual equity provisions into two distinct programs. The double-decker system, discussed extensively in the HEW Report, *Social Security and the Changing Roles of Men and Women* (1979a), would provide a strictly wage-related benefit on top of a flat pension payable without a means test to all elderly and disabled. The second proposal, a two-tier system, would include a similar wage-related system but would provide additional benefits through a means-tested program such as SSI. The introduction of either of these proposals would require a major restucturing of the entire social security program with many far-reaching implications.

This paper examines one facet of these implications by exploring the impact on women of a two-tier benefit system with an earnings-sharing provision for married couples. First we shall summarize the major prob- lems surrounding the treatment of women under today's social security program. Next, we shall present a more detailed description of the major provisions of the proposed two-tier system, with a discussion of the budgetary and administrative implications. Earnings sharing is included as an integral part of this two-tier system in order to insure protection for homemakers within the wage-related benefit structure. Finally we shall analyze the benefit implications of this two-tier system for aged and disabled women.

Major Problems Surrounding the Treatment of Women under Social Security

The increased labor force participation of women and the rising divorce rate have exacerbated both equity and adequacy problems under the current social security system. Moreover, because the system attempts to combine the goals of income maintenance and earnings replacement, it is an inefficient mechanism for targeting funds to low-income individuals.

This section reviews the major adequacy, equity, and efficiency prob- lems for which the social security system is commonly criticized. While these criticisms are valid for the most part, they often have been exaggerated and interpreted as proof that women are treated unfairly under social security. In an effort to reassess the importance of these women's issues in the context of the broader range of social programs and to clarify those areas which do require reform, an alternative perspective on the treatment of women under social security is provided.

COMMONLY CITED ADEQUACY, EQUITY, AND EFFICIENCY PROBLEMS UNDER THE CURRENT SYSTEM

Adequacy

The adequacy problems under the present system stem primarily from inadequate benefits and gaps in protection for women who spend a significant portion of their lives as homemakers. The three major adequacy problems are (a) lack of protection for women divorced after less than 10 years of marriage; (b) inadequate benefit levels for aged divorced women; and (c) gaps in protection for women whose spouses die before retirement.

Divorced women married less than 10 years are not entitled to any retirement or disability benefits based on their husbands' earnings records. Since two-thirds of all divorces occur after less than 10 years of marriage, a majority of divorced women receive no benefit protection based on their husbands' earnings (U.S. Department of Health, Education, and Welfare, 1979b, p. 90). This creates serious problems for homemakers divorced later in life, since it is often difficult for these women to enter the labor force. Moreover, the provision is arbitrary and discontinuous, since a woman married 9 years and 11 months receives no benefits on the basis of her husband's earnings and a woman divorced after 10 years of marriage is eligible for a spouse benefit based on her husband's entire earnings record.

Although an aged divorced woman married 10 years is eligible for a spouse benefit equal to 50% of her former husband's primary insurance amount (PIA), this benefit is often inadequate for women with separate households and no other income, since it was originally designed as a supplement for married couples. Furthermore, benefit eligibility for the divorced spouse is determined by her husband's retirement date rather than by her own age and needs. Disabled divorced women are eligible for disability benefits at age 50, but these benefits are actuarially reduced and therefore tend to be quite low.

Among widows, the major gap in protection occurs for the woman who has been married for a long time and has spent most of her life as a homemaker. If she is widowed after age 45 or 50 and has never worked, she often finds it difficult to enter the labor force, yet is not eligible for a widow's benefit until age 60. At this time, the benefit she receives will be based on her husband's average indexed monthly earnings (AIME) indexed only for price increases since his death, and she thereby will be denied the productivity growth which his wages would have reflected had he survived until retirement. Young widows who were predominantly homemakers also are unprotected if their husbands die, but these women are in a less serious situation, since their youth should facilitate entry into the labor market. Disability protection for widows is available at age 50, but again the benefit is actuarially reduced to 50% of the husband's AIME and therefore is usually inadequate.

Equity

Those provisions which are generally criticized for being inadequate are also the source of inequities within the social security program. The provision of these spouse and survivor benefits generates inequities both between one-earner and two-earner couples and between married couples and single individuals. Dissatisfaction over these inequities has intensified as the labor force participation rate of women has increased and a growing number have qualified for social security benefits in their own right as well as dependents of their husbands. In 1978, 41% of the women who became entitled to social security benefits did so on the basis of their own earnings and an additional 13% were receiving benefits both on the basis of their own earnings and as dependent spouses (U.S. Department of Health, Education, and Welfare, 1979b, p. 89). Because wives are automatically entitled to spouse benefits on the basis of their husbands' earnings, the additional benefits which they can earn by working are not perceived as being worth the extra taxes paid.[1]

Another inequity exists between the aged survivors of one- and two-earner couples. Since a widow's benefit equals 100% of the PIA of the spouse with the higher AIME, the larger the proportion of the couple's earnings that was earned by one spouse, the higher the benefit for the aged survivor. Thus, the survivor of a two-earner couple generally receives a lower benefit than the survivor of a one-earner couple with the same total AIME. In addition, the survivor of a one-earner couple receives as much as two-thirds of the total benefits that the couple was receiving, while the survivor of a two-earner couple may receive as little as half of the couple's benefit.

The inequity which exists between single and married workers is

---

[1]In fact, working wives do gain protection not available to nonemployed spouses. Employed women are eligible for benefits when they reach retirement age, rather than being dependent on their husband's decision to retire. Insured women also have disability protection as well as protection for their survivors.

straightforward. A single and married worker with equal earnings will be entitled to equivalent social security benefits. However, the married worker's dependent spouse will also receive a spouse benefit, and, should the worker die, a widow benefit. In short, the married worker's contributions will generate substantially greater benefits than will contributions made by the single worker.

Efficiency

Despite the inclusion of social adequacy components in social security, the current system is an inefficient mechanism for providing income support to retired and disabled workers and their families. Because social security is viewed as a social insurance plan, benefits are not subject to a means test. Yet, when benefits are provided on social adequacy grounds, means testing is the only way to efficiently target them to the low-income individuals for whom they are intended. The two most flagrant examples of inefficiency under the present system result from the progressive benefit structure and the provision of dependent and survivor benefits.

The weighted benefit formula is designed to replace a greater portion of preretirement earnings for a low-wage worker than for a high-wage worker. However, many of the progressive benefits are inappropriately awarded to workers with short earnings histories in covered employment, such as public employees, rather than to those with a career of low wages.

Dependent and survivor benefits are also distributed inefficiently under the present social security system. Because they are not means tested, they are provided for all dependents and survivors rather than only to those who would qualify for them on social adequacy grounds.

CRITICISMS OF THE CURRENT SYSTEM—
AN ALTERNATIVE PERSPECTIVE

The aforementioned criticisms of the treatment of women under social security are misleading for two reasons. First, while these arguments indicate that women are treated unfairly and inadequately under social security, closer examination reveals that women workers as a group are actually favored under the present system. Second, adequacy analyses typically examine the benefits provided by the social security program alone and therefore tend to exaggerate gaps in protection. Because the adequacy goal for the aged and disabled is currently pursued by SSI as well as social security, a more appropriate method of measuring benefit adequacy would be to examine the combined benefits distributed through the two programs.

Women and Social Security

The conventional discussion of the "women's issue" in social security has created the unwarranted impression that women as a group receive less from social security than men do, or, at least, that women workers get less protection for their contributions than do men workers. In fact, women workers and men workers are treated alike under the present system. Moreover, once it is considered that women have a longer life expectancy, tend not to work beyond age 65, and receive greater advantage from the progressive benefit formula because of their lower earnings, it becomes clear that the current social security program actually treats women workers more favorably than men workers. These extra benefits enjoyed by women workers more than offset the greater number of secondary benefits generated by men workers' accounts. Were separate contribution rates established to cover the cost of cash benefits derived from wage records, the rates for women workers would be about one-fourth higher than for men workers (Ball, 1979).

When aggregate benefits received by women (based both on their own wage records and those of their husbands) are compared to the total contributions that women pay, this benefit-contribution ratio is shown to be considerably higher than the same ratio for men. According to the Office of the Actuary of the Social Security Administration, contributions from women account for about 28% of the payments into the system, while about 54% of benefits are paid to female beneficiaries (Ball, 1979). Several factors contribute to this result, but the two most important are the greater life expectancy of women and the dependent and survivor benefits which are paid to spouses and widowed spouses, most of whom are women, without any required contributions. Thus, women are not discriminated against under the social security system; in fact, as a group they gain through the provision of dependent benefits and from the fact that contribution rates are not actuarially determined on the basis of life expectancy. It is important that these advantages be emphasized, because one possible outcome of reform is an equalization in the treatment of men and women, which would subsequently reduce the proportion of benefits received by women.

The Relevance of SSI

In analyzing gaps in protection, it is necessary to decide whether one is concerned about all divorced and widowed homemakers who become aged or disabled or only members of this group who are poor. In this connection it is difficult to provide a strong rationale for the distribution of government-administered benefits to middle- and high-income women who have chosen to spend most of their lives outside the labor force. Life and disability insurance is readily available in the private sector to provide protection for these women. Rather, our concern is with protection for those aged or disabled homemakers who are left without any source of income.

The appropriate method of analyzing benefit adequacy for poor aged and disabled women is to consider the protection they receive from SSI as well as from social security. It would be misleading to evaluate benefit adequacy for this group on the basis of social security benefits alone, since SSI was designed specifically to meet the needs of those low-income aged and disabled persons not adequately protected by social security. While SSI by no means provides perfect protection in terms of coverage or benefit levels, an analysis which ignores these benefits will exaggerate the gaps in protection under the current system. For instance, widows and divorced women who are disabled or over age 65 are currently guaranteed SSI benefits of $208 per month regardless of their employment history. Once both this SSI benefit and social security benefits are considered, the only major group which remains unprotected is that of widowed or divorced homemakers between the ages of 45 and 65 who, while not aged or disabled, may find it difficult to enter the labor force.

The Two-Tier System with Earnings Sharing

The two-tier social security system with earnings sharing would differ from the present system in several fundamental ways. First, it would increase equity between one-earner and two-earner couples and between married and single individuals. Second, it would eliminate the danger of high-income workers receiving negative rates of return on their contributions as the social security system matures. Third, it would alleviate pressure on the payroll tax by reallocating the income maintenance burden to general revenues. Finally, the means-tested first benefit tier would provide an efficient mechanism for the distribution of funds to low-income individuals. This section will describe the proposed two-tier system, its budgetary and administrative implications, and the ways it differs from a double-decker approach.

Design

The two-tier system with earnings sharing would assign the pursuit of the goal of social adequacy to the first benefit tier and the element of individual equity to the second tier in order that each play a specific role, distinct from but integrated rationally with the other. Tier I would consist of an expanded version of the means-tested SSI program and would guarantee a minimum monthly income to each U.S. resident at age 62 or upon disability, regardless of labor force participation. The second benefit tier would relate benefits to earnings, awarding each worker over age 65 or disabled a monthly benefit directly proportional to his AIME in covered employment. Reduced tier II benefits would be available at age 62. In addition, the second benefit tier would include an earnings-sharing provision for married couples according to which each spouse would be credited with 50% of the couple's earnings from the marriage. These earnings would be divided at divorce or when one spouse became disabled, or died, or reached age 62. A person's tier II benefit, then, would be based on his or her own earnings record while unmarried and one-half of the total earnings of the couple. This provision would create an earnings record for each individual, according to which he or she would become eligible for tier II retirement and disability benefits in his or her own right.

The concept of earnings sharing is intended to highlight both the needs of the homemaker and the contention that responsibility for the home-maker's support should rest with the couple. Despite the increased labor force participation rate of women, there are still many households in which the wife assumes the responsibilities of a full-time homemaker. Even those women who do enter the labor force are likely to devote at least part time to homemaking activities, particularly when their children are young. However, given the increased opportunities available to women, there is an element of choice involved in their decisions to have children and either to remain in the home or to enter the labor force. Since both spouses participate in these decisions, it is appropriate that the burden of support for the homemaker be placed on the couple through the earnings-sharing provision.

Because the death of one spouse (and consequently the termination of his tier II benefit) can be a source of economic hardship for the surviving spouse, a joint–survivor annuity option, such as that provided by private pension plans, is also included in this version of the two-tier system. Through this provision an individual could elect to receive actuarially reduced tier II benefits in order that his spouse receive additional retirement income at the time of his death. A reduction of approximately 12% in an individual's benefit would purchase this joint–survivor annuity for his spouse.[2] In effect, the individual would be able to purchase

---

[2]Teachers Insurance and Annuity Association of America (1979, p. 4). This reduction applies to a man retiring at age 65 with a wife age 63 and would vary according to the spouses' ages.

protection in the same manner as through an insurance plan in the private sector.

One additional provision would be contained in the proposed two-tier system—a benefit for nonaged widows, consisting of a lump sum equal to the accumulated contributions of the deceased worker and his employer, plus accrued interest. This benefit is similar in intent to the 100% of the worker's PIA awarded for one year to young widows under the earnings-sharing option in the HEW report. Of course these women would not later qualify for retirement benefits based on their deceased spouses' earnings.

Budgetary Implications

The long-range cost of a two-tier system with earnings sharing would depend upon both the income level which the first benefit tier guarantees and the percentage of the worker's AIME awarded by the second benefit tier. Although precise cost figures are not available, it is possible to generalize about the short-run cost implications of the introduction of the proposed two-tier system by comparing it with present law and the double-decker proposal.

Because tier I would provide means-tested, government-administered benefits on the grounds of social adequacy, a strong rationale exists for the establishment of the minimum income guarantee at the poverty level defined by the federal government. Table 5.1 shows the poverty level calculated by the Bureau of the Census, comparing it with SSI benefit levels. As indicated, in order for SSI to guarantee each aged and disabled person at least a poverty-level income in 1979, monthly benefits would have had to be increased by $82 for an individual and $54 for a married couple. Tier I benefits therefore would have cost approximately $12

Table 5.1
Poverty Level Thresholds and SSI Benefit Levels, 1979

	Poverty Level Income	SSI Benefits[a]
Annual income		
Married couple	$4,390	$3,748
Individual	3,480	2,498
Monthly income		
Married couple	366	312
Individual	290	208

Sources: Estimates of poverty thresholds from the Bureau of the Census. SSI benefit levels from the Social Security Administration.

[a]Does not include additional SSI supplements which may be awarded by individual states.

billion in 1979 as opposed to actual SSI expenditures of $5.4 billion (see Table 5.4).

Once tier I benefits have been set at the poverty threshold, the level of cost desired for the entire system would determine the percentage of a worker's AIME provided by the second benefit tier. Tables 5.2 and 5.3 illustrate a two-tier scheme designed so that costs would equal those under the present system. Tier II benefits are set at 48.2% of a worker's AIME and tier I insures a poverty-level income—$290 a month per individual and $366 a month per couple. Furthermore, tier I benefits are reduced by only 75¢ for every $1 of unearned income as opposed to the present dollar-for-dollar reduction. This partial offset of tier I benefits for tier II unearned income should eliminate some of the work disincentive caused by the current offset procedure.

Introduction of the two-tier system with earnings sharing would alter the distribution of benefits found under the present system (see Tables 5.2 and 5.3). First, replacement rates—ratios of benefits to preretirement earnings—for one-earner couples would be reduced substantially owing to the elimination of the spouse benefit. Second, because the two-tier system would efficiently target benefits to low-income individuals, it would increase replacement rates for low-income workers significantly while approximating present-law replacement rates for most average- and high-wage workers.[3] In contrast, the double-decker system shown in Tables 5.2 and 5.3 would yield replacement rates closely resembling those under present law for single individuals and two-earner couples at all earnings levels.

As shown in Table 5.4, the two-tier system described in Tables 5.2 and 5.3 would maintain short-run costs equal to the combined present costs of social security and SSI. This result should not be surprising, since the proposed system eliminates inefficiencies created by the provision of dependents' benefits, reducing benefits substantially for one-earner couples. Thus, the two-tier earnings-sharing system need not involve increased expenditures for social security but rather a reallocation of funds among groups of beneficiaries.

Administrative Implications

The introduction of a two-tier system with earnings sharing would necessarily complicate the administration of social security. First, the two-tier proposal would alter the entire method by which benefits are

[3]Replacement rates would be reduced slightly for two-earner couples except where both spouses earn either very low wages or wages near the taxable maximum. Benefits for this group could be increased by increasing overall tier II benefits.

Table 5.2

Social Security and SSI Monthly Benefits and Replacement Rates for a Single Individual under Present Law and Double-Decker and Two-Tier Earnings-Sharing Proposals, 1979

Earnings History	AIME	*Present Law* Social Security	SSI	Total	Replacement Rate
Minimum wage	$ 441	$246	$ 0	$246	0.533
Average wage	815	365	0	365	0.415
Taxable maximum	1,096	455	0	455	0.308

Earnings History	AIME	*Double Decker* Deck II	Deck I	Total	Replacement Rate
Minimum wage	$ 441	$132	$122	$254	0.553
Average wage	815	245	122	367	0.417
Taxable maximum	1,096	329	122	451	0.306

Earnings History	AIME	*Two-Tier with Earnings Sharing* Tier II	Tier I	Total	Replacement Rate
Minimum wage	$ 441	$213	$131	$344	0.749
Average wage	815	393	0	393	0.447
Taxable maximum	1,096	528	0	528	0.358

Source and notes: Authors' calculations. The single individual is one who retires at age 62 in 1979. Benefit amounts do not include reduction for early retirement.

   The earnings history was calculated using minimum wage data from U.S. Department of Commerce (1979b, p. 423); average wage data from Office of the Federal Register (*Federal Register*, 1978, p. 61016); and data on social security payroll tax maximum from Board of Trustees of the Federal Old-Age and Survivors Insurance and Disability Insurance Trust Funds (*Annual Report*, 1979).

   Deck I pays a flat $122 to each aged and disabled U.S. resident. Deck II benefit equals 30% of individual's AIME in covered employment.

   Tier I pays a means-tested benefit which guarantees a minimum income of $290/individual. Tier II benefit equals 48.2% of individual's AIME in covered employment. Tier I benefits are reduced by 75¢ for every $1 of unearned income, which includes the tier II benefits.

computed. Second, inclusion of the earnings-sharing provision for married couples would further complicate administration.[4]

   Since the first benefit tier essentially would be an expanded version of the SSI program, it would not undergo any structural alterations. How-

[4]The following discussion closely parallels the description of the administrative effects of the earnings-sharing and double-decker options in the HEW *Report* (1979a).

Table 5.3
Social Security and SSI Monthly Benefits and Replacement Rates for One- and Two-Earner Couples under Present Law and Double-Decker and Two-Tier Earnings-Sharing Proposals, 1979

		Present Law: One-Earner Couple			
Earnings History	AIME	Social Security	SSI	Total	Replacement Rate
Minimum wage	$ 441	$ 368	0	$ 368	0.801
Average wage	815	548	0	548	0.623
Taxable maximum	1,096	683	0	683	0.463

		Present Law: Two-Earner Couple			
Combined Earnings History	AIME	Social Security	SSI	Total	Replacement Rate
Minimum wage	$ 441	$ 350	0	$ 350	0.762
Average wage	815	470	0	470	0.534
Taxable maximum	1,096	560	0	560	0.380
Each spouse at taxable maximum	2,192	910	0	910	0.308

		Double-Decker			
Combined Earnings History	AIME	Deck II	Deck I	Total	Replacement Rate
Minimum wage	$ 441	$ 132	$244	$ 376	0.819
Average wage	815	245	244	489	0.556
Taxable maximum	1,096	329	244	573	0.388
Each spouse at taxable maximum[a]	2,192	658	244	902	0.306

		Two-Tier with Earnings Sharing			
Combined Earnings History	AIME	Tier II	Tier I	Total	Replacement Rate
Minimum wage	$ 441	$ 213	$207	$ 420	0.914
Average wage	815	393	71	464	0.527
Taxable maximum	1,096	528	0	528	0.358
Each spouse at taxable maximum[a]	2,192	1,057	0	1,057	0.358

Source and notes. Authors' calculations. The benefits are for individuals retiring at age 62 in 1979. These calculations assume that each spouse in a two-earner couple earns one-half of AIME. The benefit amounts do not include reduction for early retirement. Replacement rate is the ratio of the total monthly benefit at award to monthly taxable earnings in the year just before retirement.

Earnings history was calculated using minimum wage data from the U.S. Department of Commerce (1979b, p. 423); average wage data from the Office of the Federal Register (*Federal Register*, 1978, p. 61016); and data on social security payroll tax maximum from Board of Trustees of the Federal Old-Age and Survivors Insurance and Disability Insurance Trust Funds (*Annual Report*, 1979).

(continued)

Table 5.4
Estimated Costs under Present Law and Double-Decker and Two-Tier Earnings-Sharing Proposals, 1979 (in Billions)

Present Law		Double Decker		Two-Tier Earnings Sharing	
OASI	$107.6	Deck II	$ 63.0	Tier II	$101.2
		Deck I	47.3		
SSI	5.4	SSI	2.7	Tier I	11.8
Total	113.0		113.0		113.0

Sources and notes: Present law estimates from Board of Trustees of the Federal Old-Age Survivors Insurance and Disability Trust Funds (1979, p. 53) and Social Security Administration; double-decker and two-tier earnings-sharing estimates are authors' calculations.

According to the U.S. Department of Health, Education and Welfare (1979b), under the double-decker approach annual general revenue costs, including an offset for reduced SSI costs, would be roughly $50 billion. Since the HEW report does not describe the interaction of deck I benefits and SSI, we assume that SSI disbursements would be reduced to approximately one-half of present levels and the remainder of general revenue appropriations, $47.3 billion, would be used to pay deck I benefits.

The estimated long-range cost of the double-decker plan in the HEW report would range in 1979 from $5 billion above present law to a savings of $19 billion. Here we adopt the intermediate assumption that the total cost of the double-decker plan would equal costs under the present system. Deck II benefits are therefore estimated as $63.0 billion ($113.0 billion − $50.0 billion).

Because deck II under the double-decker approach provides 30% and tier II under two-tier earnings sharing provides 48.2% of a worker's AIME, tier II cost is estimated as .482/.3 ($63.0 billion) = $101.2 billion.

Sum of 1979 SSI expenditures ($5.4 billion) and estimates of expenditures needed to bring all persons aged 62 and over up to the poverty threshold defined by the Bureau of the Census (see Table 5.1):

Total expenditure for persons 65+ (Bureau of the Census)	=	$4.2 billion
Total expenditures for persons 62–64 (Assumes that the average benefit and the percentage of poor persons in this group are the same as for the 65+ age group; authors' calculations)	=	$2.2 billion

---

Deck I pays a flat $122 to each aged and disabled U.S. resident. Deck II benefit equals 30% of worker's AIME in covered employment. Benefit amounts are equal for one- and two-earner couples.

Tier I guarantee equals $290/individual and $366/married couple. Tier II benefit equals 48.2% of worker's AIME in covered employment. Tier I benefits are reduced by 75¢ for every $1 of unearned income which includes the tier II benefits. Benefit amounts are equal for one- and two-earner couples.

[a]Not applicable to one-earner couple.

ever, the number of SSI beneficiaries would be increased substantially for two reasons. First, the aged would become eligible for tier I benefits at age 62, as opposed to age 65 under the present system. Second, because the social adequacy components currently found in both SSI and social security would be consolidated in the first benefit tier, the minimum income guarantee would be significantly higher than the present SSI guarantee. Thus, most individuals with earnings up to the average wage would receive some portion of their benefit from the first benefit tier. The anticipated growth in the number of SSI beneficiaries would require computer programming changes, increased record keeping, retraining of employees, and distribution of updated public information materials.

The implementation of a wage-related benefit structure in the second tier would necessitate significant administrative changes. In order to effect a transition from the present progressive benefit structure to one which relates benefits proportionately to earnings, computer programs and instructions for employees would have to be altered. Moreover, the inclusion of earnings sharing in the two-tier system would call for detailed records of each claimant's marital history in order to include earnings credits from marriage as part of his or her earnings record. This would require increased record keeping, since these data are not currently compiled by the Social Security Administration.

Because the proposed system would reduce protection for some groups, it would have to be phased in gradually, and thus numerous transitional provisions would be required. The new benefit levels would apply only to those individuals who become eligible for benefits—that is, reach age 62, become disabled or die—after enactment. In addition, the earnings-sharing option would not apply to couples divorced before enactment of the new system. Aside from these stipulations, the transition to a two-tier earnings-sharing plan could be designed in varying ways, depending upon the benefit levels to be guaranteed over the transition period and the length of the period itself.

Double Decker versus Two-Tier Option

Because both the double-decker and two-tier options include a second benefit tier which relates benefits proportionally to earnings in covered employment, the principal differences between the two stem from the design chosen for the first benefit tier; whether it provides means-tested benefits or a demogrant to all retired and disabled persons. Selection between the two proposals is therefore dependent upon whether means-tested benefits or a demogrant provision is preferred.

Opponents of a two-tier system argue that the stigma often associated with welfare programs also would be attached to means-tested tier I benefits. Moreover, it is held that because tier I benefits are unrelated to earnings they would be politically vulnerable to reduction during times of fiscal austerity. However, these concerns seem exaggerated for several reasons. First, studies examining perceptions of the current SSI program by both recipients and the general public indicate that the receipt of SSI benefits does not necessarily carry the stigma associated with other welfare programs, such as AFDC (see Tissue, 1978). Rather, because SSI benefits are intended exclusively for the aged, blind, and disabled, there is a tendency to view them as a necessary social good. Application procedures for SSI benefits are uncomplicated and, unlike AFDC, do not require that a social worker visit the applicant's home. Second, tier I benefits would be awarded to a much larger segment of the population than are current SSI benefits. As a greater percentage of the aged population comes to rely on these benefits for retirement income, any stigma associated with the present SSI program would be mitigated. Finally, as the proportion of the population receiving these benefits increases, it becomes increasingly unlikely that tier I benefits will be suddenly reduced as a result of changes in the political climate.

The weaknesses attributed to the two-tier approach must be weighed against the difficulties that could arise from the demogrant provision of the double-decker system. Had this demogrant been implemented in 1979, for example, it would have required that the Social Security Administration pay out approximately $50 billion (U.S. Department of Health, Education, and Welfare, 1979b, p. 81). In order for these funds to be targeted efficiently towards low-income groups, they would have to be taxed back from others. The taxation of these benefits through the personal income tax would require an increase in marginal tax rates, which would have adverse effects on labor force activity and savings behavior.

Impact on Women

While precise conclusions about the impact on women of a two-tier social security system with earnings sharing are not available without detailed simulations, some generalizations can be made about the major gainers and losers. The combined protection currently offered by SSI and social security is the relevant benchmark for evaluating issues of adequacy, equity, and efficiency.

ADEQUACY

The provision of means-tested tier I benefits under the two-tier earnings-sharing proposal would eliminate all of the benefit adequacy problems which face aged and disabled women under the present system.

First, the minimum income guarantee would be increased substantially above present SSI levels. Since a large percentage of elderly women currently subsist on incomes below the poverty level, this expansion of SSI should result in substantial gains for aged women. Second, an individual would become eligible for tier I benefits at age 62 as opposed to age 65 under the current SSI program. Finally, replacement rates for low-income workers would be higher than under the present social security system. Because the first benefit tier would insure adequate protection for all the aged and disabled poor, the following discussion will analyze the implications of a two-tier earnings-sharing system for nonpoor women.

Under the current system, women are eligible for social security benefits in their own right as workers and are also awarded retirement benefits as dependent spouses, as divorced wives if the marriage lasted more than 10 years, or as widows of insured workers. A two-tier approach with an earnings-sharing provision would change the level of benefits provided for each of these groups.

Women workers who spend most of their lives in the labor force would be relatively unaffected by the introduction of a two-tier system, although they would gain somewhat from the earnings-sharing provision which would establish an earnings record for them during any period they spend out of the labor force as homemakers. Depending on their earnings level, the composition of benefits which they receive would change in that, where all retirement benefits currently are provided through social security, under the two-tier system workers with below-average earnings would receive a portion of their benefits from the means-tested first benefit tier (SSI).

Aged homemakers would receive approximately the same level of benefits under the two-tier earnings-sharing system as under the current system. However, these benefits would no longer be based on dependency but rather on the homemaker's earnings record derived through earnings sharing in marriage. Disabled homemakers would also become eligible for disability benefits on the basis of this earnings record. It is important to note, however, that while the aged homemaker's benefit would be essentially unchanged under a two-tier system, the single-earner couple as a unit would receive substantially lower benefits owing to the elimination of benefits for dependents.

The earnings-sharing provision under the proposed two-tier system would attribute earnings to each spouse for the years of the marriage, thus providing divorced homemakers with continuous social security protection. Earnings credits acquired through marriage would be added to an individual's credits from work in covered employment, and the combined earnings record would provide a basis for both retirement and disability benefits. Thus, most divorced women would gain from the introduction of the proposed two-tier system in that they would qualify for both retirement and disability protection in their own right, regardless of the duration of the marriage. However, some homemakers divorced after 10 years might receive lower benefits under the proposed system. Whereas these women currently qualify for benefits based on their husbands' entire earnings record, under the two-tier system their benefits would be based on half the husbands' earnings for the years of the marriage.

Protection for widows would on average be reduced by the introduction of the two-tier earnings-sharing system. However, whether a widow gains or loses would depend on the distribution of earnings between the two spouses. Widowed homemakers would certainly end up with lower benefits, whereas the widow of a two-earner couple where the two spouses had equal earnings would acquire greater social security protection than she currently receives.

A widowed lifelong homemaker currently is entitled to benefits at age 60 equal to 100% of her husband's PIA. Under the proposed system, the homemaker would receive a benefit equal to 50% of the couple's PIA based on the earnings-sharing provision, and this 50% benefit would continue after the husband's death. Additional protection would be available through the joint–survivor option. However, since this option requires an actuarial reduction in the worker's benefit (approximately 12%) to compensate for the additional protection afforded his survivor, the ultimate benefit received by the aged widow would equal approximately (.88 × 50% + 50%) 94% of the survivor's benefit which is provided under current law.

In contrast, widows of two-earner couples where each spouse had a history of maximum earnings could in some cases receive considerably more than under the present system. Since the widow currently is entitled to 100% of the PIA of the spouse with the higher earnings, the survivor of a two-earner couple where each earned up to the maximum taxable earnings limit is not eligible for any additional survivor benefits based on her husband's earnings. Under the proposed system, the joint–survivor option would entitle her to a portion of her deceased husband's PIA, thereby increasing the total amount of protection available.

The introduction of a two-tier system with earnings sharing would create an additional problem for the nonaged widow in that she would not be eligible for benefits until age 62, as opposed to age 60 under the current social security system. Prior to this time the only protection she would receive would be a lump-sum benefit equal to the contributions made by her husband and his employer plus the accrued interest. Thus, the treatment of nonaged widows remains one of the most difficult problems under the proposed system. While the earnings-sharing provision would insure that a widow has an earnings record on which to base benefits at age 62 or upon disability, it would not alleviate the plight of the homemaker widowed after age 45 or 50 who has had little or no labor force experience.

The two-tier earnings-sharing system would effect one additional reduction in widows' benefits in that it would not provide for widows with young children. If no other programs were introduced, women in this category with no source of income would be forced to turn to the AFDC program.

In short, evaluation of the adequacy of benefits for women under the proposed as compared to the current system yields mixed results. Were a two-tier system with earnings sharing introduced, protection for low-income individuals would be increased through the expansion of the SSI program. No aged or disabled person would be forced to subsist below the poverty level. Among the nonpoor, however, some women would gain and some would lose.

EQUITY

Although the proposed two-tier system with earnings sharing yields mixed results with respect to the adequacy of benefits for women, it resolves all the equity problems which exist under today's social security program. The elimination of the spouse and survivor benefits eradicates the inequities between one-earner and two-earner couples and between married couples and single individuals. Moreover, the removal of the spouse benefit avoids the duplication in protection for married women who are employed. Since individual equity is not a relevant criterion on which to evaluate a public-assistance program such as SSI, the following discussion will focus on the equity aspects of the wage-related second benefit tier only.

Since spouse benefits under the current system are not paid to two-earner couples (unless one spouse has a low AIME), a two-earner couple generally receives lower total benefits than a one-earner couple with the same total AIME. As illustrated in Table 5.5, elimination of the spouse benefit and introduction of a proportional benefit formula will insure that the benefit which a couple receives is directly related to its earnings history, thus removing the advantage currently awarded one-earner couples.

An additional problem under the current system is that the benefits received by two two-earner couples with the same AIME can vary according to the proportion of the total AIME earned by each spouse. This inequity results from the progressive benefit formula and would be eliminated by the introduction of a proportional benefit structure.

Table 5.5
Monthly Benefits for Single Worker and One- and Two-Earner Couples under
Present Law and Two-Tier Earnings-Sharing Proposal, 1979

			Two-Tier Earnings Sharing		
	AIME	Present Benefits	Tier I	Tier II	Total
Single worker	$815	$365	0	$393	$393
One-earner couple					
Husband	815	365	$36	196	232
Wife	0	183	36	196	232
Total	815	548	72	392	464
Two-earner couple					
Husband	543	278	36	196	232
Wife	272	191	36	196	232
Total	815	469	72	392	464

Notes: This oversimplified, hypothetical example assumes that the couple were married throughout their working lifetimes and that both spouses retire at age 62 in 1979. Benefit amounts do not take into account actuarial reductions for early retirement.

AIME assumes earnings history at average wage (see Tables 5.2 and 5.3).

Tier I guarantees a minimum income of $366/married couple. Tier II benefit equals 48.2% of individual's AIME. Tier I benefits are reduced by 75¢ for every $1 of unearned income, which includes the tier II benefits.

An inequity also exists between the aged survivors of one-earner and two-earner couples under the current system. Because the widow benefit equals 100% of the PIA of the spouse with the higher earnings, the larger the proportion of the couple's earnings earned by one spouse, the higher the benefit awarded to the aged survivor. The proposed system would eliminate survivor benefits and, in their place, earnings splitting would insure the widow a benefit in her own right. The joint–survivor option would provide additional protection. Thus, benefits received by the survivors of two couples with equal AIMEs would no longer depend on the distribution of earnings between the spouses.

Although all workers contribute to the social security system at the same rate, the provision of a spouse benefit yields the one-earner couple a benefit 50% larger than that awarded a single individual with the same AIME. Moreover, widows of deceased workers are entitled to additional protection in the form of survivor benefits. Under the proposed system the elimination of survivor and dependent benefits would almost totally remove the greater protection now enjoyed by couples. Therefore, as shown in Table 5.5, the tier II wage-related benefits awarded to a married worker and a single worker with equal AIMEs would be equal. The joint–

survivor option, while affording additional protection for widows, would not introduce any new inequities between married and single individuals, since it would be paid for through a reduction in the worker's retirement benefit. However, the lump-sum benefit awarded to widows of deceased workers under the two-tier system would be the source of a new inequity between married couples and single individuals. Because single individuals would not benefit from this option, married couples would continue to be treated somewhat favorably.

The problem created by the duplication of protection for working women who contribute toward their own benefits and also are entitled to spouse benefits would be completely eliminated under the proposed scheme. Because of the elimination of dependent benefits and the introduction of earnings sharing, women would receive tier II benefits based on their own earnings while unmarried plus credits from earnings sharing while married. Any covered earnings by either spouse would increase the couple's benefits, and payroll tax contributions therefore would not be considered wasted.

EFFICIENCY

The inefficiencies which arise from the progressive benefit formula and the provision of dependent and survivor benefits under the current system would be eliminated by the introduction of a two-tier system. Because tier II would provide benefits directly proportional to workers' earnings and tier I would insure a socially desirable minimum income level, the need for a progressive benefit formula would be eliminated. Thus, workers with short earnings histories in covered employment would no longer be awarded those benefits intended for low-income individuals. Similarly, the creation of an earnings record for each spouse through earnings sharing would eliminate the need for dependent and survivor benefits. Instead, a worker's dependent or surviving spouse would qualify for a wage-related tier II benefit on the basis of his or her own earnings record and the means-tested first tier would efficiently target those benefits provided on social adequacy grounds to the poor aged and disabled.

Conclusion

Although the introduction of a two-tier system with earnings sharing would eliminate some of the adequacy problems and all of the inequities and inefficiencies found under the current system, it would not uniformly increase the benefits for women. This result should not be surprising, since the two-tier proposal is not motivated by a desire to increase benefits for women. Rather, it is intended to increase equity, to provide workers with a higher rate of return on their contributions, and to promote a rational distribution of the income maintenance burden between the payroll and income taxes. In addition, the expanded means-tested first benefit tier is intended to funnel funds to low-income individuals in a more efficient manner than the present progressive wage-related system. Indeed, the status of the very low-income aged and disabled would be improved through the expansion of the SSI program.

The choice between a two-tier system and a double-decker system requires the examination of such issues as the stigma of means-tested programs and the risk of cutbacks in income maintenance schemes that are subjected to annual congressional review. Were a two-tier or double-decker system introduced, the introduction of a wage-related benefit structure and the elimination of dependent and survivor benefits would highlight the need to provide for the unpaid homemaker. However, the dramatic change in the opportunities available to women implies that those who choose to have children and not to work should assume responsibility for this decision. Moreover, since both spouses participate in such decisions, the burden of support for the homemaker should rest with both members of the one-earner couple.

In essence, a two-tier earnings-sharing system involving expenditures equivalent to current social security and SSI outlays would reallocate some benefits currently provided for one-earner couples above the poverty level towards low-income individuals. Not only would one-earner couples as a group lose benefit protection, but within one-earner couples, benefit protection would be shifted from the husband to the homemaker.

Appendix

A comparison of the major provisions of the present law, the two-tier earnings-sharing option, and the double-decker option is given in Table 5.6, which follows on page 122.

Table 5.6
Comparison of Major Provisions under Present Law and Two-Tier Earnings-Sharing and Double-Decker Options

Provision	Present Law	Two-Tier Earnings Sharing	Double Decker
Eligibility for retirement benefits	Person must have worked in covered job long enough to be insured for benefits or be a dependent of such a person.	No insured status requirement for tier I or tier II.	No insured status requirement for deck I or deck II.
Earnings credits	Person gets earnings credits based only on his or her own work in covered employment.	For tier II, earnings record based on person's own earnings in covered employment while single plus one-half of couple's earnings credits while married.	For deck II, earnings based on person's own work in covered employment. Earnings credits of married couples (while married) divided equally at divorce. Surviving spouse credited with 80% of earnings credits of couple (or 100% of higher earner's credits).
Benefits			
A. Retired worker (married, separated, or divorced)	Gets weighted benefit based on own earnings credits.	Gets tier II benefit equal to flat percentage of earnings record as described above. Tier I benefit payable if person's income falls below the guaranteed minimum income level.	Gets deck I benefit of $122 plus deck II benefit equal to 30% of own average earnings and earnings credits acquired as a result of divorce or death of a spouse.
B. Aged homemaker (married, separated, or divorced)	Dependent spouse benefit equal to 50% of retired worker's benefit.	No dependent spouse benefit; gets tier II benefit based on any earnings credits acquired through work or marriage. May be eligible for means-tested tier I benefit.	No dependent spouse benefits; gets deck I. Gets deck II if has any earnings credits acquired through work or as a result of a prior marriage.

C. Aged widow(er)	Dependent benefit equal to 100% of deceased worker's benefit.	No dependent surviving spouse benefit; at age 60 gets tier II benefit based on earnings record as described above. Also joint–survivor annuity if deceased spouse had purchased this extra protection through an actuarial reduction in his own benefit. May also be eligible for means-tested tier I benefit.	No dependent surviving-spouse benefit; gets deck I. Also, deck II if has any earnings credits as described above (including credits inherited when spouse died).
D. Child	Benefit equal to 50% of worker's benefit paid to child of retired or disabled worker (75% for child of deceased worker) until child reaches age 18 (or 22, if a student). Where several children eligible family maximum applies.	No children's benefits; benefits for children of retired, disabled, and deceased workers provided through the AFDC program.	Deck I benefit payable to child of retired, disabled, or deceased worker subject to maximum of 250% of deck I benefit. In addition, in survivor cases, one deck II benefit equal to 100% of worker's benefit payable; benefit divided equally among children.
E. Young mother's or father's benefits	50% benefit (75% in death cases) payable to young parent caring for child under age 18 (or disabled).	No young mother's or father's benefits; these are provided through AFDC.	Deck I benefit payable if there is an entitled child under age 7 in his or her care.
F. Adjustment benefit for young widow	No comparable benefit. (Lump sum of $255 payable on death of worker.)	Lump-sum benefit equal to deceased spouse's payroll tax contributions plus accrued interest.	100% of deceased spouse's deck II benefit payable for 1 year.
G. Disabled person	Disabled worker who meets recency-of-work test gets benefit based on own earnings credits. Surviving spouse who meets stricter definition of disability can get a reduced dependent benefit if age 50 or older.	Gets tier II benefit based on earnings record as described above. May qualify for means-tested tier I benefit.	Deck I payable. Also gets deck II if has any earnings credits acquired as described above. Where recency-of-work requirement is not met, a more strict definition of disability must be met.

Source: Description of present law and double-decker proposal from U.S. Department of Health, Education, and Welfare (1979a, pp. 100–101); authors' description of two-tier earnings-sharing system.

Discussion

HENRY AARON

The Munnell–Stiglin paper is a clear brief on behalf of a major structural change in social security, the replacement of the current progressive ("kinked") benefit formula by a two-tier system. I confess to some chagrin at being unpersuaded either that the two-tier system is the best way to fix up the flaws in the way the present social security system treats the family or women or that, on balance, it is a desirable overall structural reform. My chagrin derives from the fact that I must admit publicly to having changed my mind. Twelve years ago, Joe Pechman, Mike Taussig, Alicia Munnell, and I labored through a Washington summer to produce a book that concluded—you guessed it—that a two-tier system was the way social security should go. To make matters worse, I cannot point to any analytical advance to explain my switch, just to a revision of political prejudice.

The two-tier plan would consist of one tier that pays a benefit proportional to average earnings, and one tier, an expanded version of SSI, that constitutes a negative income tax for the aged, blind, and disabled. In contrast to the present system, no dependent benefits would be paid.

Clearly, the strengths and weaknesses of this proposal go far beyond the changes in the treatment of women. It would have important effects on children and surviving adults for example. Such effects need to be weighed in any complete evaluation of the two-tier proposal.

The Munnell–Stiglin paper correctly stresses that the present system in all major respects is objectively nondiscriminatory toward women.

Rather, the widely remarked inequities occur because the present system is not well designed to take account of normal variation in behavior of both men and women: Some people stay single, some stay married, and some do a bit of both. Some married couples have one earner and some have two. And among two-earner couples, some spouses earn similar amounts, while in others one spouse accounts for most of the earnings.

The interaction between these pedestrian facts of late-twentieth-century American life and the social security system lead to the following problems, some of which result in unequal treatment of people or couples we now think should be treated equally and some of which result in inadequate benefits for people deemed to be needy. Thus

1. Family earnings (up to the earnings base) generate a larger potential retirement benefit, the greater the degree to which one spouse receives them. Two spouses with equal earnings do worst of all.
2. If one spouse in a couple initially is working, an increase in the worker's earnings raises potential family benefits, but the initiation of earnings by the other spouse does not increase potential retirement benefits.
3. Dependent retirement benefits for a divorced woman (or man) depend not only on earnings of the former husband (or wife) during marriage but also on his (or her) full lifetime earnings. Furthermore, the wife (or husband) is entitled to benefits only when the former husband (or wife) retires.

Each of these features of the present system appears by present standards of equity to be unfair. None would be very serious if nearly all people married 'til death did them part and if each couple supplied one worker to the labor force. Such patterns were never universally representative, but they characterized America far better in 1940 than they do in 1980.

In addition, the present system provides no benefits for work in the home or, for that matter, volunteer work outside the home. The present system expresses the principle that benefits should be paid only when money earnings or money support is lost, not when unpaid services are lost. Thus, the death of a homemaker precipitates no survivor benefits; the incapacity of a homemaker creates no entitlement to disability; the retirement or sixty-second birthday of a homemaker precipitates no entitlement to primary retirement benefits. Many people regard the failure to provide some or all of these benefits as a serious gap in coverage. Whether it is or not, it is an issue different from those described above—it is a disputed decision not to spend tax resources for certain purposes rather than the flawed calculation of benefits that we have decided should be paid.

THE TWO-TIER SYSTEM

Against this background, how effectively does the two-tier system deal with these problems? Before answering this question directly, I want to make two points. First, the two-tier proposal presented by Munnell and Stiglin is really an amalgam of components some of which are defining characteristics of the two-tier plan, and some of which are extrinsic to it and could be added to the present system or another alternative. Thus, Munnell and Stiglin are really describing a two-tier, earnings-sharing, joint–survivor, increased-SSI, no-dependent-benefits plan. Earnings sharing, for example, could be grafted onto the present system or to a double decker. In considering alternatives to the present system and to the particular two-tier plan described by the authors, one should not limit oneself to the two-way or even (when they include the double-decker plan) the three-way choice set forth in their paper.

Second, this paper is somewhat short on discussion of who gains and who loses from the proposed switch. Tables 5.2 and 5.3 show that the proposed new system reduces some benefits by large amounts for certain classes of recipients, but raises some benefits significantly. The authors point out in the text that some groups lose, notably widows, but the pluses and minuses receive scant attention.

They need extensive attention, for at least two reasons. The first is that some groups lose a great deal. That such losses must occur is revealed by the fact that the proposed system raises some existing benefits significantly, creates a new class of beneficiaries (disabled homemakers, married and divorced), and leaves overall costs unchanged. Table 5.5 in passing shows that one-earner couples with earnings of $815 per month would lose 15% of their present entitlement. The changes in benefits will be larger for some income histories, smaller for others.

The second reason why the distribution of losses needs more attention than it gets is that politicians and ordinary citizens regard benefits provided under current law as entitlements. They will regard the two-tier plan as a combination of increases and decreases in existing entitlements and will want to know, for example, why the benefits of one-earner couples should be reduced 15%. The point that I am trying to make is not that people don't like reductions in benefits; of course, they don't. Rather, it is that legislated reductions in a present entitlement are regarded as a breach of faith, an act verging on betrayal, the politically expressed disutility of which far exceeds the utility of increased benefits for others that such reductions would make possible. Economists who have long observed downward wage inflexibility and who now are studying the pervasive influence of implicit contracts should not dismiss this viewpoint with scorn.

While this popular sensitivity should not inhibit legislative reforms that would reduce the entitlements of some potential beneficiaries, it should alert us to the need to explain why certain cuts are justifiable and to make sure that we have a transition plan that works. I cannot explain, and I doubt that Munnell and Stiglin can explain, why a one-earner couple whose average earnings are $815 per month should have their benefits reduced 15%, cutting their replacement rate from 67% to 57%.

To many people, I suspect, a two-tier plan, adjusted to have the same costs as the present system, would be regarded not as a new structure that elegantly distinguishes earnings replacement and income redistribution and that achieves the goal of own-entitlements for women and improved protection for homemakers; but rather as a melange of benefit increases for some classes of beneficiaries—those with low-earnings histories, disabled nonworkers (most of whom are women), divorced women—and of benefit decreases for others—one-earner couples, divorced men, widows. I believe that it would be difficult to justify this reallocation; some parts are appealing, some are not, and it would be hard to make an intellectually coherent case for the mix.

Part of the problem is that any structural reform that does not boost costs must cut someone's benefit one dollar for every dollar by which someone else's is increased. This law of arithmetic may well step over the border between truism and banality, but it does carry the useful reminder that improving benefits for one group necessarily entails either lower benefits for another or higher program costs. It also suggests that major structural reforms are easier to enact when present law can be liberalized than when it cannot. The budgetary limits so very much with us today suggest that the best prospect for improving the equity with which social security treats the diversity of modern families is through incremental modifications in the present program structure that cause the minimum number of "irrelevant" redistributions. Such a "tinkering" approach minimizes the degree to which benefits are redistributed among demographic groups for reasons that have nothing to do with improving treatment of women and the family.

THE TREATMENT OF WOMEN

I believe there are three kinds of problems and that all of them can be modified within the present program structure, provided that social security coverage is extended to essentially all workers.

First, the problem of divorced people who have worked little or not at all and receive no credits toward retirement benefits if they were married fewer than ten years can be corrected if earnings received by the couple are divided equally on divorce. I would provide for such division only if the marriage lasted some minimum period to avoid administrative complexity that has little effect on entitlements.

Second, the problem of lesser earners who often do not add to the retirement benefits of the couple by their work and may receive larger benefits as dependents than as workers can be reduced by stipulating that when both spouses claim retirement benefits, the earnings of the two spouses must be averaged, so that each spouse receives a benefit based on half of the sum of their total joint earnings. Alternatively (and *not* equivalently), one could share earnings received during a marriage not only at divorce, but also at retirement. Generally speaking, both procedures reduce the benefits of one-earner couples to the level paid two-earner families. Both create equal entitlements for each spouse based on half of the couple's combined earnings. They differ in the treatment of earnings received before marriage. Both would provide widows who worked little or not at all with much smaller benefits than they receive under current law. Because widows have lower benefits than do any other group among the aged, permitting surviving spouses (usually women) to inherit earnings credits of deceased spouses (usually men) would be necessary in my opinion.

Third, it is possible to extend disability benefits to married homemakers, by allowing earnings sharing when a disability claim is made, or for divorced homemakers, by permitting credits shared at divorce to be used for disability as well as retirement benefits.

Each of these steps raises benefits for some workers and lowers them for others. All are subject to the stricture that redistribution that does not raise total benefits must reduce benefits of some beneficiaries as much as it increases those of others. But the tinkering approach entails less shuffling of benefits for purposes other than improving the equity with which social security affects women and families than does the two-tier system. It improves the treatment of women without restructuring the whole system.

I personally would favor the first two steps and oppose the third. Although disability of a married homemaker increases family expenses, I think that full earnings sharing for disability benefits creates costly benefit entitlements where, in many cases, no earnings loss has been suffered. And the most pressing needs can be met through means-tested programs and direct provision of services. Other claims on the fisc, in my opinion, deserve higher priority than this one. Providing speedier disability coverage for divorced homemakers has great appeal if an administratively feasible way can be found to do so specifically for this group.

THE CONDITIONS FOR STRUCTURAL REFORM

If total expenditures under social security are not to rise as a fraction of earnings, the way the present social security law is written maximizes the difficulty of structural reform. By indexing wage histories and the benefit formula by the full increase in average wages, the present law assures that structural reform can be purchased only by raising the total cost of the system as a percentage of earnings or by lowering the benefits of some workers. The achievement of desired reforms in the treatment of women and the family illustrates this dilemma.

The prospects for improving the treatment of women and for other reforms would be far better if the benefits of some groups could be increased without legislating a decrease in others. The original drafters of social security did not anticipate that the next generation would want to change the treatment of the family, and we cannot anticipate what changes the next generation will want to make. The arrangements for indexing the benefit formula constitute a straitjacket hampering structural reform.

For this reason, as well as others, I think that Congress should reconsider the policy of indexing the benefit formula by wage growth and should index it instead by price growth. In the past few years price indexing would have pushed initial entitlements up faster than wage indexing has done, but that will not be true over the long run (we hope!). The prospects of achieving reform in the way social security treats women and the family and of achieving other reforms would be far better if Congress could achieve them without having either to raise taxes or to cut someone's benefits. Under a price-indexed system, structural reforms could be achieved gradually by holding constant real (price-indexed) benefits for some groups while benefits for other groups were increased faster than prices.

THE DOUBLE-DECKER SYSTEM

If a major restructuring of social security were to be sought, I believe that a double-decker system (a demogrant plus an earnings-related benefit) would have advantages over the two-tier system (a negative income tax plus an earnings-related benefit).

The first advantage is one that Munnell and Stiglin consider and reject—the absence or diminished importance of a means test under the double decker and its heightened importance under the two-tier system. Munnell and Stiglin assert that by extending means-tested benefits to half or more than half of all social security recipients, we will convert means tests from something soiled by association with the poor into something made bland by association with the middle class. They may be right. But, they may be wrong. And there is no way we can be sure. Because conclusive evidence is lacking and probably unobtainable, and because the social and political consequences if they are wrong would be serious, I would lean toward a double-decker system that decreases reliance on means tests and away from a change that embraces increased reliance on them. (Advocates of the present system argue that in the United States a double decker would inevitably "degrade" into a two-tier system because, sooner or later, a demogrant would be means tested. I think such a fear is exaggerated. But honesty requires me to acknowledge that the reasons of those who oppose a double decker are similar to my reasons for opposing the two-tier system. The lesson, I suppose, is that one person's prudent caution is another's hysterical fear.)

The second advantage of the double-decker over the two-tier system is that means tests use more real resources for administration than do programs without them (SSI spends roughly 10% of program costs on administration, compared with less than 2% by social security). This saving in resources of a double decker should be weighed against the cost of less accurate aiming of transfer payments. I do not know how different the distribution of benefits between a two-tier system and a double decker would be, but that is an easy issue to settle empirically. In any event the cost of poorly aimed benefits under the double-decker system should be weighed against the savings in administrative costs. I suspect that the advantages of the two-tier system in accuracy would be substantially undercut by higher administrative costs.

6

The Double-Decker Alternative for Eliminating Dependency under Social Security

JENNIFER L. WARLICK
DAVID E. BERRY
IRWIN GARFINKEL

The dependency provisions of Old Age and Survivors Insurance (OASI), commonly known as social security, pursue their goal of income adequacy at the cost of creating inequities between working and nonworking women and men. Several strategies have been suggested to correct these inequities while simultaneously assuring an adequate, guaranteed minimum income. Among these is the plan commonly referred to as the double decker, which combines a universal, flat-rate benefit (often called a "demogrant") with a proportional earnings-related benefit.

The double decker is a familiar proposal to followers of the debate over the priorities which should be assigned to the dual objectives of social security: earnings replacement and basic income support (Burns, 1965; Pechman, Aaron, and Taussig, 1968; Munnell, 1977; Schorr, 1977). It has also been studied as a possible remedy for the problems of stigma and nonparticipation associated with means testing under public assistance programs (Berry, Garfinkel, and Munts, forthcoming). Thus, unlike most of the other proposals examined in this volume, the double decker has not been devised recently to address the problem of inequitable treatment of working women under social security. Its goals spread far beyond this immediate concern. Consequently, it is not surprising that the double-decker proposals which we examine not only eliminate the inequities arising from dependency provisions, but also transfer more income to the aged poor than does the current system.

This paper analyzes the distributional effects of instituting a double-decker system for the aged—those 65 years and older. It makes use of a microsimulation model and of data from the 1973 Exact Match Study to compute three sets of annual benefits: those that would have been payable in 1972 under the social security and SSI programs as amended in 1977, and potential benefits under two versions of a double-decker program. The first is the plan discussed in U.S. Department of Health, Education, and Welfare (1979a), which we call the "HEW proposal." This program combines a demogrant of $122 per month (1979 dollars) with a benefit equal to 30% of average indexed monthly earnings (AIME). There are no dependent benefits for spouses, surviving spouses, or divorced spouses; however, a widow or widower inherits 100% of the couple's combined earnings credits,[1] and a divorced person receives 50% of the total. The second version is distinguished from the first in that (a) the demogrant for an individual is raised to the level of the SSI basic benefit under current law; (b) a couple's demogrant is only 50% greater than that for an individual (rather than 100% greater, as in the HEW proposal); and (c) earnings-related benefits are reduced so that total benefits are roughly the same as in the HEW proposal. In the first version, SSI benefits are available, but in the second the SSI program is eliminated because of the higher demogrant.

We start by describing the dependency issue as it has evolved within the context of the current social security program, setting forth the basic features of a double-decker system, and outlining the anticipated distributional impact of the HEW double-decker proposal. A brief description of the microsimulation model is then provided. The amounts and incidence of simulated benefits by entitlement and marital status, along with the distribution of total income by income class, are presented for each system, with the economic welfare of aged widows, who constitute a disproportionately large share of the aged poor, highlighted. Finally we discuss some fundamental questions about the overall benefit structure that are raised by the simulation results.

---

[1]This provision, advocated by the Advisory Council on Social Security (U.S. Department of Health, Education, and Welfare, 1979b) departs from the HEW proposal as described below.

The Double-Decker Alternative for Eliminating Dependency under Social Security

DEPENDENCY UNDER SOCIAL SECURITY

The present social security system seeks to achieve three goals of social policy toward the aged: earnings replacement, equity, and adequacy.

Provisions designed to promote adequacy include a progressive benefit structure, in which the earnings-replacement rate (ratio of benefit to preretirement earnings) is higher for low-income workers than for high-income workers; a minimum benefit for all insured workers; and a special minimum benefit available only to individuals who have worked for many years in covered employment.[2]

In addition, a series of provisions promotes the economic welfare of dependents of insured workers in a variety of situations: a living spouse of a retired or disabled worker; a widow or widower; a divorced spouse whose marriage lasted at least 10 years; and a disabled spouse of a current worker who will be entitled in the future. A recent study by the Social Security Administration (U.S. Department of Health, Education, and Welfare, 1979a) considers the implications of each of these provisions in light of the changing roles of men and women. Our investigation, however, is limited to those dependency provisions making benefits available to the aged spouses of retired and deceased workers. (We devote only minor attention to divorced persons because of insufficient data.)[3] These provisions compromise the equity goal in several ways:

1. Working wives often find that their benefits are no greater than—or only slightly larger than—those of their nonworking counterparts, so that they have little or nothing to show for their contributions.

[2] In 1979, the OASI basic monthly benefit formula was 90% of the first $180 of AIME, 32% of the next $905, and 15% of the remainder. (The bracket widths are adjusted annually by the rate of wage growth.) The minimum monthly benefit available to all insured workers was frozen by the 1977 social security amendments at $121 per month. The special monthly minimum benefit in 1979 was $11.50 times the number of years of covered employment above 10 and up to 30. The amount is adjusted annually for inflation. (See Snee and Ross, 1978.)

[3] An aged spouse of a retired worker is entitled to a benefit of 50% of the worker's basic benefit, the primary insurance amount (PIA). A divorced spouse may collect a benefit of the same amount if the marriage lasted at least 10 years. A widow or widower is entitled to a benefit equal to 100% of the deceased spouse's PIA. In all cases, the benefit is reduced if claimed before age 65. An individual who is entitled to benefits both as a worker and as a dependent receives the worker's benefit plus the amount by which the dependent benefit exceeds the worker's benefit.

2. One-earner couples receive greater combined benefits than do two-earner couples with the same total past earnings and contributions.
3. Survivors of one-earner couples receive greater benefits than do those of two-earner couples with equal total earnings and contributions.
4. Married workers on the whole realize greater rates of return than single workers, although all workers pay the same tax rate irrespective of marital status.[4]

These inequities, in combination with other perceived failings of social security, have prompted serious consideration of alternative systems of social insurance for the aged, among them the double decker.

BASIC FEATURES OF A DOUBLE-DECKER SYSTEM

The basic features of a double-decker system are shaped by three underlying principles regarding social insurance for the aged: (a) each aged individual should receive a benefit regardless of that individual's experience in covered employment; (b) retirement benefits should be directly related to the covered earnings of the individual worker; and (c) the adequacy and earnings-replacement elements of social insurance should be separated (U.S. Department of Health, Education, and Welfare, 1979a, pp. 36, 71).

These principles are implemented by combining a demogrant or flat-rate pension (first deck) with a proportional earnings-related benefit (second deck). The demogrant is intended to place a floor under the incomes of the aged, while the earnings-related benefit is designed to replace earnings that cease upon retirement. The system relies upon the sum of the demogrant and earnings-related benefit to achieve the desired replacement rate. All persons become entitled to the demogrant upon reaching a specified age.

Because the first deck of the double-decker system explicitly addresses the issue of income adequacy, the earnings-related benefit program is freed from pursuing this goal. Unlike the current system, which employs a single benefit structure to treat simultaneously the concerns of adequacy and earnings replacement, there are no spouse benefits or minimum benefits in the second deck of the double decker. However, in two recently discussed double-decker proposals (U.S. Department of Health, Educa-

---

[4]These inequities are discussed in U.S. Department of Health, Education, and Welfare (1979a), and in Chapters 1 and 2 of this volume.

tion, and Welfare, 1979a, 1979b), couples split evenly their total earnings credits in the event of divorce, and widows and widowers inherit some or all of the former couples' combined earnings credits. These features of the two proposals are their only departures from the double decker's principle of purging the earnings-related benefit program of all adequacy elements.[5]

Since the second-deck benefit in the double decker is strictly proportional to the beneficiary's earnings index (which may include earnings credits of a former spouse), there is no requirement of insured status based on quarters of coverage. Finally, it should be noted that the double-decker system is progressive in that the combined earnings-replacement rate, based on the sum of the demogrant plus the earnings-related benefit, declines as the earnings index increases.

Related to the double-decker system are two important issues: (*a*) the size of the demogrant for an individual; and (*b*) whether a couple's demogrant should be twice as large as that for an individual or a smaller amount. A demogrant large enough to replace SSI would result in administrative savings; it would also eliminate the problems of stigma and nonparticipation, which would bring about a greater transfer of income to the aged poor. Indeed, the main body of argument in favor of the double decker, at least until recently, has been on these grounds rather than on the ground of eliminating the inequities of dependency provisions. Those opposed to such a large demogrant argue that it would treat aged persons with significant other income too generously and would carry the risk of ruining the carefully nurtured "insurance image" of social security by relying too heavily on general revenues and by reducing rates of return on total "contributions"—payroll taxes plus those income taxes directed toward the demogrant—below acceptable levels for the upper-middle-income and high-income aged.

Because the demogrant is intended to promote adequacy, some argue that it should take account of economies of scale derived from shared living arrangements. For example, the demogrant for a couple could be set at 1.5 times that for an individual, following the model established by the SSI guarantee levels. Those opposed to this arrangement argue that it amounts to a marriage tax; they feel that the demogrant should be neutral with respect to marital status so that each individual, whether married or not, receives a demogrant of the same amount. It should be recognized,

---

[5]Under the HEW proposal, there are two exceptions: First, a surviving spouse under age 62 would receive a 12-month adjustment benefit based on the deceased worker's earnings and subject to an earnings test. Second, the surviving children of a deceased worker would receive, as a group, a benefit based on the worker's earnings (U.S. Department of Health, Education, and Welfare, 1979a, p. 197).

though, that neutrality with respect to marital status must come at the expense of either (*a*) a lower demogrant for individuals; (*b*) lower earnings-related benefits; or (*c*) higher total benefit costs.

ANTICIPATED EFFECTS OF THE DOUBLE DECKER ON
THE DISTRIBUTION OF BENEFITS

In this section, we compare the changes in benefit levels for different groups of the aged that would arise under a transition from the current system to the double-decker plan in the HEW proposal. The main features of the two systems are summarized in Table 6.1. The only provision that we have not yet discussed is earnings inheritance for widows and widowers under the HEW proposal (No. 6).

Figure 6.1 plots the benefit structures for single individuals and married couples reaching age 62 in 1980 under both the status quo and the HEW double-decker proposal. In two-earner couples, both spouses are assumed to have the same AIME. Surviving spouses are assumed to have no past earnings; the horizontal axis for these people measures the AIME of the deceased spouse. The horizontal lines, which show SSI benefits, are drawn under the assumptions that (1) an individual or couple has no other income and (2) the person or couple decides to participate in the program if eligible.

Figure 6.1 shows that under these assumptions, benefits for those who are unaffected by the dependency provisions of OASI—never-married individuals and two-earner couples—are roughly the same under the two systems at all AIME levels below the maximum.[6] This, of course, depends upon the specifications of the HEW plan: in particular, the level of the demogrant ($132 per month[7] for all aged individuals regardless of marital status) and the level of earnings-related benefits (30% of AIME).

Under the assumptions made for surviving spouses, their benefits at any given AIME level are the same as those of never-married individuals under both systems, so that they, too, would experience little change in benefits under a transition to the double decker. However, those widows

---

[6]In the future, the maximum possible AIME will move further beyond the second bend point in the OASI benefit structure as greater proportions of the working lives of retiring workers are affected by the increase in the annual covered-earnings limit legislated in 1977 (Snee and Ross, 1978). As a result, high-wage earners in the future would have larger benefits under the HEW proposal than under the current system.

[7]The demogrant under the HEW proposal is indexed by average wage growth. The $132 amount for 1980 is arrived at by raising $122—the 1979 amount—by the same percentage wage increase used by the Social Security Administration to adjust the bracket widths in the 1979 OASI benefit formula to 1980.

Table 6.1
Main Features of the Current System and the HEW Double-Decker Proposal

Current System (OASI and SSI)	HEW Double-Decker Proposal
1. Persons with low OASI benefits and those not entitled may be eligible for a means-tested income supplement from SSI.	1. All aged persons, regardless of work experience or marital status, are entitled to a demogrant (deck I) equal to $122 per month (1979 amount). Low-income persons may be eligible for a means-tested income supplement from SSI.
2. Earnings-related (OASI) benefits are determined with a progressive benefit formula which yields higher replacement rates for low-wage than for high-wage earners.	2. Earnings-related benefits (deck II) are determined with a proportional benefit formula (30% of AIME).
3. A minimum benefit is available to all insured workers. Low-wage earners with many years of covered employment are also eligible for a special minimum benefit.	3. There is no minimum or special minimum benefit.
4. Entitlement to benefits based on one's own earnings is contingent on the satisfaction of an insured-status requirement.	4. There is no insured-status requirement.
5. Spouses are entitled to a benefit equal to the larger of 50% of their husband's or wife's benefit or the amount based on their own past earnings.	5. There is no spouse benefit.
6. Surviving spouses are entitled to a benefit equal to the larger of 100% of their deceased spouse's benefit or the amount based on their own past earnings.	6. There is no surviving-spouse benefit. A surviving spouse inherits the greater of 80% of the couple's total earnings credits (up to the taxable-earnings limit) or 100% of the earnings credits of the higher-earning spouse, for each year of the marriage. These earnings credits are combined with those for years outside of the marriage in order to compute the surviving spouse's AIME.

and widowers with significant past earnings of their own stand to gain from the inheritance provision in the HEW proposal. This part of the plan is considered in more detail below.

The replacement of the spouse benefit with a demogrant in the HEW proposal gives rise to a reduction in total benefits for one-earner couples at middle and high AIME levels. Note that the gap increases with AIME; since the spouse benefit in the current system is tied to the worker's

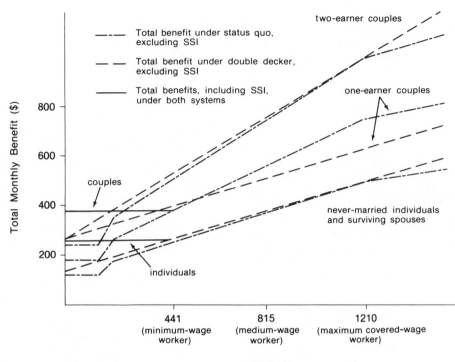

Figure 6.1. Benefit structures in 1980 for never-married individuals, surviving spouses, and married couples age 62 under status quo and the HEW double-decker proposal. Benefits have not been actuarially reduced to reflect early retirement. AIME is interpreted as follows: for one-earner couples, AIME of working spouse; for two-earner couples, AIME of each spouse; for surviving spouses, AIME of deceased spouse, assuming that the couple were married by the time the survivor reached age 22, that the deceased spouse lived until the survivor reached age 62, and that the survivor had no earnings. (Figure by University of Wisconsin Cartographic Laboratory.)

benefit, it also depends on the AIME level. Whereas one-earner couples in which the working spouse received the minimum wage throughout the work life would experience little change in a transition to the double decker, those with average or better wages would experience significant reductions: 9% for those with a medium-wage history and 15% for those with the working spouse earning the maximum taxable wage. Consequently, the position of one-earner couples with medium and high AIME levels would fall relative to both single individuals and two-earner couples.

Figure 6.1 also indicates that those who are not entitled to benefits under OASI or who have low AIMEs would be unaffected by a transition to the double decker because of the availability of SSI benefits. However, some of these people do not receive SSI benefits, either because they decide not to participate in the program in order to avoid stigma or other costs associated with participation, or because they have enough other income to make them ineligible. Among the people not receiving SSI benefits, those who are not entitled to benefits under OASI would gain under a transition to the double decker by collecting the demogrant; those who are insured but have low AIMEs (because of small amounts of time spent working in covered occupations) would experience smaller gains.

Although we have used the case of a one-earner couple to analyze the distributional effect of eliminating the spouse benefit under a transition to the double decker, this case is the extreme; most wives who currently collect dependent benefits have some covered earnings of their own. Under the double decker, such women would collect earnings-related benefits as well as demogrants, while nonworking wives would receive only the latter. This would be true not only for those dually entitled under the current system (entitled to benefits in their own right as well as to [larger] spouse benefits), but also for those without sufficient quarters of coverage for insured status (entitled only as dependents), since there is no insured-status requirement under the double decker. Although those women with past earnings but currently receiving spouse benefits would receive reduced benefits under a transition to the HEW plan relative to those now receiving benefits based on their own earnings, the decline would be smaller than for nonworking wives.

The potential effects of the HEW double-decker plan on the benefits of surviving spouses of two-earner couples are illustrated in Figure 6.2 and Table 6.2. For these survivors, the inheritance provision in the HEW plan (No. 6 in Table 6.1) is more generous than the status quo, under which benefits of widows and widowers are unaffected by the earnings credits of the lower-earning spouse. Note that because inherited earnings credits under the HEW proposal may not exceed the taxable maximum, survivor benefits are limited to the corresponding amount—$495. Excepting cases where one or both spouses earned the maximum taxable wage, survivors of two-earner couples are better off under the proposed inheritance provision (abstracting from other program changes) whenever the AIME of the lower-earning spouse exceeds 25% of that of the higher-earning spouse.[8] (It is assumed here that the couple were married by the time the survivor reached age 22 and that the deceased spouse lived until the survivor reached 62.) Moreover, the gains are greater the more nearly

[8]For example, if the deceased spouse's AIME is $100 and that of the survivor is at least $25, then 80% of the total is at least as great as the deceased spouse's AIME.

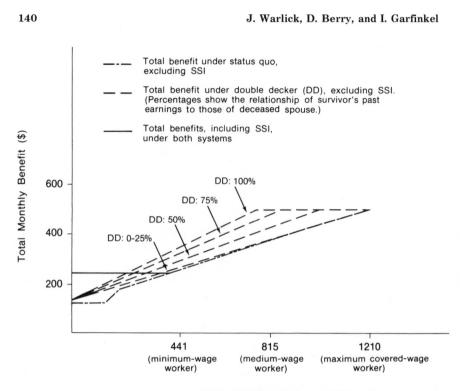

Figure 6.2. Benefit structures in 1980 for surviving spouses age 62 with different work histories under status quo and the HEW double-decker proposal. Benefits have not been actuarially reduced to reflect early retirement. It is assumed that the couple were married by the time the survivor reached age 22 and that the deceased spouse lived until the survivor reached age 62. Benefits can be no greater than the amount shown by the dashed horizontal line because the survivor's earnings credits inherited from the marriage may not exceed the taxable-earnings limit. (Figure by University of Wisconsin Cartographic Laboratory.)

equal are the AIMEs of the two spouses; in cases where the deceased earned low to medium wages, surviving spouses with the same AIMEs as those of the deceased experience benefit increases of almost one-third (last col., Table 6.2). Note that because of the SSI tax rate of 100% on nonemployment income, increases in total benefits accrue only to those who are not SSI beneficiaries—primarily middle- and upper-income survivors. The overall effect is to increase substantially the overall benefits of survivors, most of whom are widows.

It should be emphasized, however, that there are some survivors who stand to lose from the replacement of the current survivor provision with earnings inheritance. The survivor benefit under OASI is equal to the benefit of the deceased and is thus based on his or her AIME. Under

Table 6.2
Benefits in 1980 for Surviving Spouses Age 62 with Different Work Histories under
Status Quo (SQ) and the HEW Double-Decker Proposal (DD)

Work History and AIME of Deceased	Total Monthly Benefit When AIME of Surviving Spouse, as a Percentage of AIME of Deceased, Is			
	0–25%	50%	75%	100%
Minimum wage (AIME = $441)				
Status quo (SQ)	$258[a]	$258[a]	$258[a]	$258[a]
Double decker (DD)	264	291	317	344
DD as % of SQ	102%	113%	123%	133%
Medium wage (AIME = $815)				
Status quo	$373	$373	$373	$373
Double decker	377	425	474	495
DD as % of SQ	101%	114%	127%	133%
Taxable maximum (AIME = $1,210)				
Status quo	$493	$493	$493	$493
Double decker	495	495	495	495
DD as % of SQ	100%	100%	100%	100%

Notes: Benefits have not been actuarially reduced to reflect early retirement. Computations
are based on the assumptions that the couple were married by the time the survivor reached
age 22 and that the deceased spouse lived until the survivor reached age 62.
[a]Includes SSI.

earnings inheritance, however, a survivor's AIME, which is the basis for
his or her benefit, can be lower than that of the deceased: It is an average
of earnings credits inherited from the marriage and covered earnings for
years outside of the marriage over the period between ages 22 and 62. The
problem would affect those whose earnings were substantially lower than
those of their deceased spouses—primarily women—and who married
late or were widowed at an early age.

Although we are unable to include divorced persons in the simulation
analysis (below) because of insufficient data, we can draw some conclusions about how they would fare under a transition to the HEW double-
decker proposal. In general, though the earnings-sharing provision in the
HEW proposal would work to the advantage of most divorced women (and
to the disadvantage of most divorced men), some divorced women would
have lower benefits under this proposal than under the current system.

Under the HEW proposal, a couple's combined earnings are split at
divorce. A divorced person's benefit is based on his or her own AIME,
which is an average of half of the couple's total earnings during the

marriage and the divorced person's own earnings for years outside of the marriage. This contrasts with the present system, in which a divorced person may collect a benefit based on his or her own earnings or those of the former spouse, but not both. As a result of this difference, the HEW proposal would work to the advantage of most divorced women, who could add some of their former husbands' earnings to their own earnings records. Correspondingly, most divorced men would suffer.

If a divorced woman had very low earnings throughout her life relative to those of her former husband, she might have a lower benefit under the HEW proposal than under the current system. Although she would receive half of the couple's total earnings credits for the years of the marriage, her overall AIME would be pulled down by the inclusion of her low earnings for years outside of the marriage into the average. Under the current system, by contrast, her benefit would be equal to half of her former husband's benefit, which is based on his earnings credits for his entire career (specifically, the period between ages 22 and 62).

We have calculated the benefit changes that would occur under a transition to the HEW proposal for divorced women under varying circumstances: (a) different relative earnings (compared to those of the former husband) for the years of marriage; (b) different relative earnings for the years outside of marriage; (c) different durations of marriage; and (d) different earnings levels of the former husband. The calculations are limited to those cases in which there is no remarriage. The results show that instituting the HEW proposal would reduce benefits for divorced wives of middle- and high-wage earners whose own earnings were very low, in cases where the marriage had lasted 10–20 years.[9] For divorced wives of low-wage earners, however, the demogrant would be almost as large as, or larger than, the dependent benefit under present law. (In 1980, the dependent benefit for the divorced wife of a worker who earned the minimum wage throughout his career would be $127 per month; the demogrant under the HEW proposal would be $132.) In addition, all divorced women whose earnings throughout their careers were at least one-third of (but no larger than) those of their former husbands, or whose marriages lasted at least 30 years (regardless of relative earnings), would gain under a transition to the HEW proposal. Finally, it should be noted that instituting the HEW proposal would work to the advantage of all divorced women whose marriages lasted less than 10 years (and whose earnings were less than those of their husbands), because they are ineligible for divorced spouse benefits under the current system.[10]

[9]The detailed results of our calculations are available upon request.

[10]The median duration of marriages ending in divorce is slightly less than 7 years (U.S. Department of Commerce, 1979b, p. 82).

While earnings-related benefits in both the current system and the HEW proposal are indexed by inflation, the demogrant in the latter is indexed by average wage growth, *for those in retirement as well as those reaching retirement age.* If wages grow faster than prices, therefore, total benefits in the double decker will grow faster throughout the retirement years than do those in the present system. We will refer to this phenomenon as the *"aging effect."* Because of the aging effect, people who have roughly equal benefits under the two systems at age 62 (as depicted in Figure 6.1) will have higher benefits under the double decker than under the status quo in later years. In addition, the reduction in benefits experienced by one-earner couples under the double decker will be counteracted and possibly reversed as these couples advance beyond age 62. However, the *relative* benefits of one-earner couples (as compared with those of other types of beneficiaries) will still be lower under the HEW proposal than under the current system.

Since the bracket widths in the current OASI benefit formula as well as the demogrant in the HEW proposal are indexed by wage growth, the benefit structures under the two systems (as they apply to the year a person reaches age 62) bear the same relationship to each other for all cohorts as they do for the cohort depicted in Figure 6.1. (This, of course, ignores SSI benefits, which are indexed by inflation.) Consequently, it is also true for other cohorts that survivors, never-married individuals, and two-earner couples who are older than 62 will have greater benefits under the double decker than the current system as a result of the aging effect. However, it cannot be predicted in advance whether one-earner couples beyond age 62 will experience an increase or decrease in benefits.

The Simulation

THE THREE SYSTEM MODELS

In addition to the status quo and the HEW proposal, we simulate a double-decker plan with demogrants for individuals and couples that are higher than in the HEW plan. Specifically, they are equal to the SSI guarantee levels, so that the need for SSI no longer exists. Our interest in this version of the double decker arises from the fact that the demogrant has often been viewed as a means for meeting the adequacy goal without the assistance of means-tested supplements, such as SSI.

The major features of the status quo and the two double-decker plans are summarized in Table 6.3 and will not be repeated here. A few additional details should be noted, however.

Table 6.3
Characteristics of Simulated System Models

Earnings-Related Benefits

Model	Basic Structure	Additional Benefits Spouse	Additional Benefits Surviving Spouse	Retirement Test[a]
Status quo	OASI as under 1977 amendments	50% of insured's PIA	100% of insured's PIA	$3,100 disregard, 50% tax rate
HEW double-decker proposal	30% of AIME	none	} inherits 100% of couple's total earnings credits up to the taxable-earnings limit	$3,100 disregard, 50% tax rate
Double decker with higher demogrant	22% of AIME	none	}	$3,100 disregard, 50% tax rate

Non-Earnings-Related Benefits

Model	Demogrants Individual	Demogrants Couple	SSI Guarantees Individual	SSI Guarantees Couple	SSI Tax Rates Current Earnings	SSI Tax Rates Other Income
Status quo	none	none	$1,500	$2,250	$780 disregard, 50% tax rate	$240 disregard, 100% tax rate
HEW double-decker proposal	$ 966	$1,932	1,500	2,250	$780 disregard, 50% tax rate	$240 disregard, 100% tax rate
Double decker with higher demogrant	1,500	2,250	none	none	none	none

[a]Applies only to people under age 70.

The status quo incorporates the benefit structure as set forth in the 1977 social security amendments. The model includes the minimum benefit, but not the special minimum, for the data set does not provide sufficient information for us to calculate it. Nor have the assets test and state supplements payable under SSI been modeled, for the same reason. The provision that reduces SSI benefits by one-third for persons living in the homes of others has also been excluded. Since SSI did not exist in 1972—the year of our data—we have determined the guarantee levels by adjusting the current amounts by the Consumer Price Index (CPI). We have modified the HEW plan in the computation of benefits for widows and widowers by allowing the surviving spouse to inherit 100% of the couple's total earnings credits for each year of the marriage (not to exceed the taxable-earnings limit).[11] A widow's or widower's benefit is then computed from an index based on these earnings credits plus his or her own earnings for years outside of the marriage. The demogrant levels in the HEW plan have been computed by indexing the amounts specified for 1979 to 1972 by the ratio of average wages for the two years. We do not include divorced persons in the simulations because of insufficient data.

COMPARABILITY OF THE SYSTEM MODELS

The three models have the same minimum income guarantees—$1500 for an individual and $2250 for a couple. Benefit levels for high-wage earners are also roughly equal, based on calculations for insured primary earners (assumed to be men), age 66 in 1972, in the top fifth of the income distribution of the aged. The earnings-replacement rate for this group is .43 in the status quo model, .44 in the HEW plan, and .43 in the double

[11]This is the earnings inheritance proposal of the Advisory Council (U.S. Department of Health, Education, and Welfare, 1979b). The council rejected the approach of the HEW plan (described above) "because it would not eliminate the differential in benefits that exists under present law between couples with the same total earnings but earned in different proportions by the two spouses [p. 99]."

Because of insufficient data, we compute the survivor's earnings index under the inheritance provision directly from the individual earnings indices of the two spouses, rather than by combining the spouses' earnings for each year of the marriage. In our data, annual covered earnings are available for the period after 1950; for earlier years (1937–1950) only total earnings are given. Individual earnings indices for persons in the sample are based on data for both periods. Since earnings data are not available for deceased spouses, we estimate their earnings indices using data for their surviving spouses.

In computing a survivor's earnings index under the inheritance provision, we follow the advisory council proposal as closely as possible by making assumptions, based on demographic data, about the ages of the survivor at marriage and at the death of his or her former spouse. The latter is an increasing function of the survivor's current age.

decker with higher demogrant.[12] We set the level of earnings-related benefits in the latter model lower than in the HEW proposal in order to make the "high-income replacement rate" the same as in the status quo.

The three models also share other features. All include a retirement test with a disregarded amount (Table 6.3).[13] It is assumed that all persons first receive both earnings-related and non-earnings-related benefits at age 65, eliminating the necessity of modeling delayed retirement credits and actuarial reductions. Earnings-related benefits are financed with payroll taxes and non-earnings-related benefits with income taxes. In all of the models, benefits are taxed, and the special aged exemption is eliminated. We believe these changes from present law are desirable in the double-decker models, which distribute a flat-rate pension to all aged persons regardless of income class. The tax provisions of the status quo model are similarly modified to maintain comparability with the double-decker models.

DATA

The data used in the simulations are from the 1973 CPS/IRS/SSA Exact Match Data Set, which links data from the Internal Revenue Service and the Social Security Administration to the March 1973 Current Population Survey. The social security data include annual covered earnings from 1951 to 1972 and total covered earnings for the period 1937–1950. Other data refer to 1972. The sample consists of family units with at least one single person 65 years or older in 1972 or one couple with both spouses at least 65, and unrelated individuals meeting the same age criterion. Nonaged members of family units are included because their incomes affect the well-being of old people with whom they live. There are 9420 aged persons in the sample.

---

[12]In the status quo model, the replacement rate is based only upon earnings-related benefits; that is, SSI benefits are excluded in the computation. In the double decker, the replacement rate is based on the combined benefit.

[13]The actual disregarded amount was $2100 in 1972. Under the 1977 amendments, the disregard is raised in yearly increments to $6000 in 1982. Thereafter, it will be adjusted automatically in the same proportion as the growth of average wages. The $3100 amount for 1972 is obtained by applying such an adjustment to the 1982 amount, using actual covered-wage growth from 1972 to 1977 and the wage growth projected for 1977 to 1982 by the Social Security Administration at the time of the amendments. (See Snee and Ross, 1978, pp. 13–14.)

SIMULATION PROCEDURE

The simulation routine computes benefits, income and payroll tax rates, tax payments, and net income for the aged under the three system models. Tax payments are based on actual 1972 provisions, except that the income tax base is expanded (as described above) and the rates are altered in order to finance the simulated benefit levels, taking account of the income tax base expansion. We do not take account of labor supply responses to program provisions. We do, however, include two other behavioral effects: intrafamily transfers (see footnote 15) and participation in the SSI program. Roughly 50% of all aged persons eligible for SSI benefits do not apply for them. We account for this by predicting the probability of participation for each eligible individual and couple, based on socioeconomic characteristics and the potential benefit level (Warlick, 1979, pp. 283–330).

The Immediate Impact of Adopting a Double-Decker System

BUDGET COSTS AND TAX RATES

The budget costs and tax rate changes in the three models are given in Table 6.4. When compared to the status quo budget cost of $35.6 billion, the total cost of income maintenance for the aged rises by 20% under the HEW plan and by a slightly larger amount under the double decker with higher demogrant (DDHD). In addition, the share of total budget cost accounted for by earnings-related benefits declines dramatically under both double-decker models: from 96% in the status quo to 54% and 38% in the double-decker models. This implies substantial decreases in payroll taxes and comparable increases in income taxes as indicated in the table.

Because the nonaged bear a smaller proportion of total income taxes than of total payroll taxes, the shift toward general revenue financing under the double-decker models vis-à-vis the status quo implies that the increases in cost to the nonaged[14] are less than the increases in total budget cost: although budget costs rise by roughly 20%, the increases in

[14]Cost to the nonaged is the tax burden on those under 65 arising from the benefit levels under the model at hand, computed under actual 1972 tax provisions as modified by (1) the expansion of the income tax base for the aged (see text above) and (2) the tax rate changes implied by the simulated benefit levels and the income tax base expansion.

Table 6.4
Budget Costs, Tax Rate Changes, and Costs to the Nonaged in the Three System
Models, 1972

	Status Quo	HEW Double-Decker Proposal	Double Decker with Higher Demogrant
Total budget cost (billions)	$35.6	$42.6	$43.2
Earnings-related benefits	34.0	22.8	16.2
Non-earnings-related benefits	1.6	$(0.5)^a$ 19.8	27.0
Changes in tax rates[b]			
Payroll tax rates	0	−20%	−31%
Income tax rates	0	18%	25%
Cost to the nonaged (billions)	$29.8	$33.2	$32.9

[a]Portion of non-earnings-related benefits accounted for by SSI benefits.

[b]Tax rate changes are expressed relative to those in the simulation of the status quo model rather than to actual rates in 1972.

cost to the nonaged are only about 10%. Since DDHD relies even more heavily on general revenues than does the HEW plan, it registers a slightly lower cost to the nonaged while at the same time a higher total budget cost.

EFFECTS OF THE HEW DOUBLE-DECKER PROPOSAL ON
THE DISTRIBUTION OF BENEFITS

Widows, Widowers, and Never-Married Persons

We first consider the effects of a transition to the HEW double-decker proposal on the benefits of widows, widowers, and never-married persons (Table 6.5). The most noticeable result is that these people experience a large overall gain in moving to the double decker. A large portion of this increase is attributable to the aging effect described above. Widows and widowers also benefit substantially from the replacement of the dependent survivor provision with earnings inheritance; under the dependency provision, the earnings credits of the lower-earning spouse do not affect the benefit, while under the inheritance provision, both spouses' earnings are taken into account. As a result, widows and widowers show larger gains than do never-married persons. Notice also that among widows, the increases are greatest for those entitled as workers, followed by those dually entitled, and finally dependents; the increases for workers reflect their former husbands' earnings, while those for widows in the other categories reflect their own earnings.

The exception to the pattern of large overall gains is that dependent widows in the youngest cohort show an increase of only $90. Since the husbands of most widows in this cohort died before their wives reached age 62, these widows' earnings indices under the inheritance provision are often lower than their husbands' had been (as explained above); as a result, the replacement of the dependent survivor provision with earnings inheritance reduces benefits for many of these widows. This problem is not as widespread for older (dependent) widows, because a higher proportion of their husbands lived until their wives turned 62. This difference among cohorts is reflected in our results because the simulation program takes account of the expected age of the survivor at the time of his or her spouse's death, as a function of the survivor's current age, in computing the earnings index under the inheritance provision.

Finally, note that as a result of the aging effect, the benefit increases under the double decker tend to be larger for older cohorts. This tendency, however, is counteracted for widows and widowers by the fact that the gains from earnings inheritance are relatively small for the oldest cohort. (This statement is based on simulation results not presented in the table.)

Married Persons

Table 6.6 shows benefit changes for married persons and couples under the HEW double-decker proposal. Since married men (with some exceptions) and those married women who are entitled as workers under the status quo are not affected by the elimination of the dependency provision, they experience large benefit increases on account of the aging effect. As before, the gains are more pronounced in older cohorts. For dependent and dually entitled wives, though, the effect of eliminating the spouse benefit is felt along with the aging effect. Since dually entitled wives have greater past earnings than do dependents, they feel a relatively mild impact from the elimination of the dependency provision. (Remember that those dependent wives who have earnings credits receive earnings-related benefits under the double decker because there is no insured-status requirement.)

Because of the presence of the aging effect, one must consider *relative* benefit changes to see the effects of eliminating the spouse benefit. Dependent wives' benefits fall by $410 relative to those of wives entitled

Table 6.5

Mean Benefits for Widowed and Never-Married Persons Aged 65 and Over under Status Quo (SQ) Compared to HEW Double-Decker Proposal (DD), 1972

Age	Widows					Widowers				Never Married			
	SQ	DD	DD – SQ	Percentage of Total	Percentage of All Widows	SQ	DD	DD – SQ	Percentage of Total	SQ	DD	DD – SQ	Percentage of Total
Dependent: Entitled Only on Basis of Spouse's Earnings Credits													
65–71	$2,290	$2,380	$ 90	33%					NA				NA
72–78	2,080	2,560	480	36									
79+	1,820	2,400	580	30									
All dependents 65+	2,070	2,450	380	100	36								
Dual: Entitled on Basis of Own Past Earnings but Eligible for Larger Benefit as Dependent													
65–71	2,260	2,660	400	23					NA				NA
72–78	1,800	2,540	740	25									
79+	1,850	2,560	710	52									
All dually entitled 65+	1,930	2,580	650	100	16								

Worker: Receiving Benefit Based on Own Past Earnings

Age													
65–71	1,850	2,450	600	46		$2,360	$2,690	$330	29%				
72–78	1,870	2,680	810	46		2,300	2,700	400	33				
79+	1,750	2,580	830	9		1,960	2,460	500	38				
All workers 65+	1,850	2,570	720	100	32	2,190	2,610	420	100				
All Aged Persons[a]													
65–71	1,890	2,310	420	35		2,170	2,540	370	29	$1,750	$2,050	$300	51%
72–78	1,750	2,420	670	37		2,040	2,490	450	33	1,700	2,060	360	30
79+	1,570	2,240	670	28		1,810	2,330	520	38	1,570	2,000	430	19
All persons 65+	1,750	2,330	580	100		1,990	2,440	450	100	1,700	2,040	340	100

Notes: No data are given for dependent and dually entitled widowers because they represent less than .05% of all widowers.
NA = not applicable.
[a] Includes those not entitled to benefits under OASI.

Table 6.6
Mean Benefits for Married Couples and Persons Age 65 and Over under Status Quo (SQ) and HEW Double-Decker Proposal (DD), 1972

Age	Married Couples			Married Men			Married Women			Percentage of Total	Percentage of All Married
	SQ	DD	DD – SQ	SQ	DD	DD – SQ	SQ	DD	DD – SQ		
	Dependent: Entitled Only on Basis of Spouse's Earnings Credits										
65–71	$3,610	$3,540	$–70	$2,280	$2,530	$250	$1,330	$1,010	$–320	31%	
72–78	3,680	3,700	20	2,440	2,690	250	1,240	1,010	–230	43	
79+	3,190	3,530	340	2,110	2,530	420	1,080	1,000	–80	26	
All dependents, 65+	3,540	3,610	70	2,310	2,600	290	1,230	1,010	–220	100	54%
	Dual: Entitled on Basis of Own Past Earnings but Eligible for Larger Benefit as Dependent										
65–71	4,220	4,270	50	2,710	2,920	210	1,510	1,350	–160	45	
72–78	4,260	4,470	210	2,840	3,120	280	1,420	1,350	–70	36	
79+	3,870	4,410	540	2,580	3,080	500	1,290	1,330	40	19	
All dually entitled, 65+	4,160	4,370	210	2,730	3,020	290	1,430	1,350	–80	100	11

Worker: Receiving Benefit Based on Own Past Earnings

65–71	4,010	4,400	390	2,090	2,320	230	1,920	2,080	160	36	
72–78	4,250	4,680	430	2,320	2,550	230	1,930	2,130	200	43	
79+	3,670	4,270	600	1,930	2,310	380	1,740	1,960	220	20	30
All workers, 65+	4,050	4,500	450	2,160	2,420	260	1,890	2,080	190	100	

All Aged Couples[a]

65–71	3,700	3,850	150	2,200	2,450	250	1,500	1,400	−100	34	
72–78	3,780	4,000	220	2,350	2,610	260	1,430	1,390	−40	42	
79+	3,270	3,740	470	2,030	2,460	430	1,240	1,280	40	24	
All persons, 65+	3,630	3,890	260	2,220	2,520	300	1,410	1,370	−40	100	100

Notes: Only those couples with both spouses at least 65 and those persons whose spouses are at least 65 are included. Married couples and married men are classified according to the entitlement status of the wife.

[a]Includes those not entitled to benefits under OASI.

as workers; for dually entitled wives the relative decline is $270 (compare DD − SQ amounts). Corresponding changes take place for married couples in the three categories. Finally, the overall benefits of married women fall by $340 relative to those of married men.

EFFECTS OF THE HEW PROPOSAL AND THE DOUBLE DECKER
WITH HIGHER DEMOGRANT ON THE DISTRIBUTION OF INCOME

In this section we compare the distributional effects of the two double-decker models. Since the double decker with the higher demogrant was introduced on account of the concern of its proponents with the welfare of the aged poor, we begin with distributional effects by income class.

Income Class

Table 6.7 presents the mean adjusted after-tax income of aged individuals by quintile, with the first and fifth quintiles broken down by decile, for the status quo (SQ), the HEW proposal (DD), and the double-decker with higher demogrant (DDHD).[15] The average incomes of persons of every marital status in the lowest two deciles are higher by substantial amounts under both double-decker models than under the status quo. This is a reflection of higher benefits (other than SSI) under the double-decker models for two groups of people: (*a*) those who choose not to participate in SSI in order to avoid stigma or for other reasons and are therefore not subject to the 100% tax rate on nonemployment income, and (*b*) those who collect SSI benefits under the status quo but whose incomes (other than SSI) are raised under the double-decker models beyond the point where they lose eligibility. The first group is a large proportion of the aged poor; the participation rates arising in our simulations are roughly 60%. With regard to the second group, note that all of the aged become ineligible for SSI under DDHD; hence the elimination of SSI in that model.

---

[15]Total family income is adjusted for family size by a formula which lowers the incomes of large families relative to those of small families, so that adjusted incomes represent levels of economic welfare controlled for family size. Specifically, family income is multiplied by the ratio of the poverty line for a two-person family to the poverty line for the family's own size. A family's adjusted income is attributed to each of its aged members for the purpose of computing income distribution.

This procedure implicitly assumes that family income is shared evenly among all members—a reasonable assumption for families with aged heads, including aged individuals and couples. Where elderly people live in the homes of younger relatives, we think it is more reasonable to assume that there is only partial sharing of income between the two groups. We determine the magnitudes of these intrafamily transfers by applying the procedure set forth by Marilyn Moon (1977).

Table 6.7
Mean Adjusted Income of Aged Individuals under Three Plans: The Status Quo (SQ), the HEW Double-Decker Proposal (DD), and the Double Decker with Higher Demogrant (DDHD), 1972

Programs	1st Decile	2nd Decile	2nd Quintile	3rd Quintile	4th Quintile	9th Decile	10th Decile
All Aged Individuals							
SQ	$1,790	$2,490	$3,600	$5,250	$7,520	$10,670	$20,760
DD	2,190	2,940	3,970	5,480	7,660	10,680	20,170
DDHD	2,390	3,050	3,960	5,360	7,480	10,440	19,670
Married Persons							
SQ	1,710	2,550	3,720	5,270	7,450	10,580	21,130
DD	2,330	2,870	3,970	5,400	7,470	10,490	20,450
DDHD	2,400	2,890	3,880	5,170	7,180	10,140	19,870
Widows							
SQ	1,800	2,460	3,490	5,250	7,650	10,930	19,340
DD	2,220	3,040	3,970	5,630	7,980	11,120	19,040
DDHD	2,420	3,170	4,010	5,630	7,920	11,050	18,710
Widowers							
SQ	1,750	2,500	3,570	5,210	7,550	10,790	21,560
DD	2,050	2,800	3,970	5,500	7,840	11,000	21,000
DDHD	2,240	2,980	4,030	5,500	7,840	10,930	20,600
Never Married							
SQ	1,740	2,420	3,590	5,130	7,540	10,650	20,330
DD	2,050	2,690	3,910	5,350	7,750	10,830	19,780
DDHD	2,260	2,910	4,060	5,450	7,840	10,850	19,500

Because of the higher demogrant in DDHD, the gains for single individuals in the lowest income classes are substantially larger under that model than under the DD. However, poor married persons are not significantly better off under DDHD than under DD, since the demogrant for a couple in DDHD is only 50% greater than for an individual.

While the overall income increases under the double-decker models are felt by the middle-income classes as well as the poor (married persons excepted), the direction of the impact is reversed for persons of every marital status in the top decile. Average incomes in this group drop by amounts from $300 to $680 under the DD, and from $630 to $1260 under DDHD, in the wake of increased income tax liability. For married persons, the average income decline dips down into the ninth decile under the DD, reflecting the elimination of the spouse benefit. In DDHD, the fall in income for these people extends into the third quintile, since the couple's demogrant is only 50% higher than for an individual.

Marital and Entitlement Status

Table 6.8 compares mean benefits under DDHD to those under the other two models by marital and entitlement status. The figures for married men and women under DDHD are computed by attributing half of the couple's demogrant to each spouse. Since the demogrant is conditioned upon marital status in DDHD, replacement of the DD with the DDHD brings a decline in benefits for couples relative to those of unmarried individuals by amounts ranging from $340 to $440 (compare differences in last col.). Married men experience absolute decreases

Table 6.8
Mean Benefits for Couples and Persons Age 65 and Over under the Double Decker with Higher Demogrant (DDHD) Compared to the Status Quo (SQ) and the HEW Plan (DD), 1972

Marital and Entitle- ment Status	DDHD	DDHD − SQ	DDHD − DD
Married couples	$3,640	$ 10	$−250
Dependent	3,440	−100	−170
Dual	3,990	−170	−380
Worker	4,080	30	−420
Married men	2,230	10	−290
Dependent	2,290	−20	−310
Dual	2,590	−140	−430
Worker	2,160	0	−260
Married women	1,410	0	40
Dependent	1,150	−80	140
Dual	1,400	−30	50
Worker	1,920	30	−160
Widowers	2,530	540	90
Widows	2,440	690	110
Dependent	2,550	480	100
Dual	2,640	710	60
Worker	2,620	770	50
Never married	2,230	530	190

Note: For each marital status, the overall benefit level for DDHD as well as the differences between DDHD and the other models include those who are not entitled to benefits under OASI. A dependent is entitled to benefits only on the basis of his or her spouse's earnings credits. Those dually entitled are eligible on the basis of their own past earnings but are eligible for a larger dependent benefit. Workers are entitled to and receive benefits based on their own past earnings.

because the decline in earnings-related benefits for them (from 30% of AIME to 22%) outweighs the increase in their share of the couple's demogrant.[16] Note that the reduction in earnings-related benefits also causes the overall benefits of married women entitled as workers under the status quo to fall by $300 relative to those of dependents.

The Overall Social Security Benefit Structure and the Objectives of Old-Age Income Maintenance Policy

The comparison of the results for the two double-decker models raises some fundamental questions about the overall social security benefit structure and more broadly about the objectives of old-age income maintenance policy. In both models, the inequity between working and nonworking wives arising from the dependency provision in the status quo is eliminated. However, while the average annual benefit of working wives would increase by $410 relative to that of dependent wives under the HEW proposal, the corresponding figure for the double decker with the higher demogrant is only $110 (Tables 6.6 and 6.8). This is because second-deck benefits under the DDHD rise *less* steeply with past earnings than under DD. A two-tier system with income-tested bottom-tier bene- fits, such as that proposed by Munnel (1977),[17] would result in a greater differentiation between working and nonworking wives than would either of the double-decker models we have considered.

These comparisons give rise to two interrelated questions: (*a*) How large a role should be played by income-tested benefits, as opposed to a demogrant or a progressive earnings-related benefit structure, in the provision of minimum income support? (*b*) What relative emphases should be placed on the income-adequacy and earnings-replacement goals of social security? The connection between these questions is that with cost to the nonaged constant, a relatively heavy reliance on non-income-tested benefits to achieve the adequacy goal requires smaller benefits for middle- and high-wage earners because it increases the outlay necessary for minimum income support.

With regard to the first question, the principal argument against using income-tested benefits is that it stigmatizes and isolates beneficiaries.[18]

---

[16]This seems surprising in light of the fact that earnings-related benefits in DDHD were set at a level to give roughly equal replacement rates for high-wage earners under the two double-decker models (see above); the reason is that the high-income replacement rate under DDHD was based on the individual's demogrant ($1500) rather than on one spouse's share of the couple's demogrant ($1125).

[17]See also Chapter 5 in this volume (Eds.).

[18]For other arguments and a detailed discussion, see Garfinkel (forthcoming).

To many beneficiaries and potential beneficiaries, one of the costs of participating in a welfare program is loss of pride. To receive benefits, they must declare themselves poor. In our country, where so much stress is put on economic success, where independence is so valued, and where the dominant ideology is that "with hard work, anyone can make it," to declare oneself poor is almost synonymous with declaring oneself to be a failure.

On the other hand, it has been alleged that transfer programs that employ an income test are more efficient than those that do not. This claim is based on the concept and measure of target efficiency. Target efficiency is the ratio of benefits to the poor to total benefits. While target efficiency may have some appeal, it has nothing to do with economic efficiency. Economic efficiency is defined by most people as maximizing the total output of goods and services in the economy.[19] As of now, we do not have sufficient information to say with confidence whether relying on income-tested benefits to provide minimum income support for the aged would result in more or less total production.

Furthermore, one cannot say in general whether using income-tested benefits will bring about higher or lower incomes for the poor. As demonstrated in another study (Berry, Garfinkel, and Munts, forthcoming), the outcome depends on which parameters—the high-income replacement rate, the guarantee, or cost to the nonaged—are held constant in the programs being compared.

Another important criterion for evaluating alternatives for pursuing the adequacy goal is administrative efficiency. Administrative efficiency, of course, is one aspect of economic efficiency because running transfer programs consumes productive resources. If providing a minimum income were the only goal of old-age income maintenance policy, it would be uncertain whether income testing would increase administrative efficiency: On one hand, paying benefits to only a minority of the aged, as opposed to all of the aged, would reduce administrative costs; on the other, investigating people's incomes would increase these costs. If the earnings-replacement goal is also accepted, however, the administrative efficiency consideration weighs against using income-tested benefits to pursue the adequacy goal, because a majority of the aged will be processed administratively anyway as they receive earnings-related benefits.

The relative emphases that should be placed on the income-adequacy

---

[19]Economists have a more precise definition: efficiency is a condition in which it is impossible to improve the economic well-being of one individual without diminishing that of another.

and earnings-replacement goals depend, of course, on a value judgment. Our own values are such that we would welcome a double-decker system because it would make explicit the tilt of the present benefit structure toward the lower-income aged. We would also prefer a program without an income test, in order to avoid the stigma engendered by the current SSI program and to ensure that all of the aged poor receive the benefits to which they are entitled. We recognize, however, that if a double-decker program were enacted today with a demogrant equal to the SSI guarantee, earnings-related benefits would have to be so low as to run counter to the values of many Americans, in the absence of a large increase in the burden on the nonaged. As for attitudes in the future, we are not prepared to make a judgment.

It is important to emphasize, however, that many possibilities exist for pursuing the twin goals of old-age income maintenance policy. As an example, we have devised an alternative that forms a compromise between relying on income-tested benefits and depending solely on a demogrant for providing a minimum income. It consists of a demogrant and a proportional earnings-related benefit at roughly the same levels as those set forth in the HEW proposal, and a supplement for those with low benefits (regardless of other income) to raise the total to the SSI guarantee level. (Remember that the demogrant and earnings-related benefit levels in the HEW proposal give rise to a combined benefit structure that closely approximates the current OASI benefits structure.) The supplement, of course, would require covering the entire population under the earnings-related benefit program. It would be financed, along with the demogrant, from general revenues.

Although the supplement may seem to be a great departure from current provisions, it is actually very close to the present special minimum benefit. For those who have worked 30 years in occupations covered by OASI, this benefit is roughly equal to the SSI standard. Under universal coverage, only a trivially small number of people other than homemakers and the disabled would fail to qualify for the special minimum. We see no reason why these two groups should not also be entitled to a supplementary benefit.

Under the arrangement we have outlined, the demogrant would be freed from pursuing the adequacy goal, so that the desired relationship between the combined benefit and the AIME, for those with benefits above the poverty level, could be brought about through appropriate adjustment of the demogrant and earnings-related benefits. Moreover, adequacy would be achieved without the stigmatizing means test.

The program we have suggested stands among many alternatives for eliminating the inequities of the dependency provisions in OASI. These alternatives encompass a wide range of emphases on the objectives of minimum income provision and earnings replacement, with or without an income test; the choice among them requires judgments about these larger issues.

Discussion

COLIN D. CAMPBELL

What I want to do is first to look at the double-decker plan and the findings in this study from the point of view of the various criticisms of the way the social security system treats women, and then to review some of the calculations in the Warlick–Berry–Garfinkel study and the issues raised by the double-decker plan.

The 1977 amendments to the Social Security Act required the Department of Health, Education, and Welfare to prepare a study of proposals to eliminate dependency as a factor in determining entitlement to spouse benefits and to bring about equal treatment of men and women taking into account such factors as the increased labor force participation of women, the increasing divorce rate, and the economic value of women's work in the home (U.S. Department of Health, Education, and Welfare, 1979a). Somewhat surprisingly, at least to me, in the HEW report, one of the two major proposals to eliminate dependency and discrimination was the double-decker plan. As stated by the authors of this paper, the usual objective of double-decker plans has been to provide minimum incomes to all aged persons without a means test, not to change the way in which women are treated.

The study by Warlick, Berry, and Garfinkel is primarily concerned with the effect of the double-decker plan on the distribution of income, and the

161

major conclusion of the paper is that such a plan would substantially improve the adequacy of the social security system by providing a guaranteed minimum income for all elderly persons. Despite this, I want to start by considering the effect of a double-decker system on problems related to the coverage of women—dependency, married women workers, and divorced homemakers.[1]

DEPENDENCY

The principal way in which a double-decker system is alleged to eliminate dependency is by giving the homemaker a flat-rate pension instead of one-half her spouse's primary insurance amount (PIA). If this were done, the homemaker's pension would no longer be dependent on the earnings of her spouse. However, the flat-rate pension is still similar to the present supplemental spouse benefit—both are welfare payments that have not been paid for by the persons receiving them. Dependency cannot be eliminated by changing the name of the benefit from "spouse benefit" to "first-deck benefit." In the double-decker system, the dependency aspect of the flat-rate benefit for spouses is to some extent alleviated by also giving the husband a flat-rate benefit. Nevertheless, to eliminate dependency completely, the homemaker needs protection that has been paid for in her own name, such as through earnings sharing.

Another aspect of dependency in the existing social security system is the way survivors' benefits are determined—a survivor is entitled to 100% of the pension of a deceased spouse. The double-decker system does not attempt to eliminate this type of dependency. If a survivor had to rely on her flat-rate pension and whatever earned pension she was entitled to in her own right, her pension could drop sharply when her spouse died. To avoid this, double-decker plans have retained the relationship of survivors' benefits to deceased spouses' earned benefits found in the existing social security system. This is significant because approximately 23% of the total number of OASI beneficiaries are survivors.

In the second of the two double-decker systems analyzed by Warlick, Berry, and Garfinkel, a person's flat-rate benefit depends on his marital status—the flat-rate benefit for a married couple is set only 50% higher than the benefit for a single person. This is different from the double-decker plan in the report prepared by the Department of Health, Education, and Welfare, in which every individual, whether married or not, receives the same flat-rate pension. Having the flat-rate pension depend

[1] For a discussion of the treatment of women in the social security system, see Gordon (1979, pp. 223–255).

on one's marital status is not far different from treating the wife as a dependent—it assumes that if a woman gets married, her flat-rate pension should be reduced because she can now depend for part of her support on her husband. (In addition, such a policy would have the disadvantage of again inducing individuals to live together without marrying, a problem which the 1977 amendments attempted to solve by permitting a widow who remarries after age 60 to receive benefits based on her deceased husband's coverage.)

MARRIED WOMEN WORKERS

The inequitable treatment of married women workers in the social security system is a topic that has been discussed for many years. Because of the growing number of married women workers, one would expect increasing political pressure in their favor (see Flowers, 1977).

According to Table 6.6, the double-decker system would, on the average, give some—but not all—married women workers a significantly better deal. Table 6.6 shows, for example, that for the age group 65–71, the shift to the double-decker system would increase significantly the benefits of two-earner couples in which the benefit received by the wife is based on her own past earnings. On the other hand, the increase in benefits is very small for two-earner couples in which the wife receives a larger benefit as a dependent than that based on her own earnings.

The effect of the double-decker system on married women workers relative to homemakers depends on two opposing forces. In the types of double-decker systems analyzed in this study, the earnings-related pension on the average amounts to only 40% to 50% of a person's total pension. Giving a low weight to the earnings-related pension tends to lower the pensions of two-earner couples relative to the pensions of one-earner couples. On the other hand, the elimination of an earnings-related spouse benefit raises the pensions of two-earner couples relative to the pensions of one-earner couples.

The double-decker system tends to improve the relative position of low-income groups regardless of whether they are one-earner or two-earner couples (*Social Security Bulletin*, May 1979, p. 30). The reason why the double-decker system benefits persons with low incomes is that for many persons with low incomes, a flat-rate pension together with an earnings-related pension would be larger than the pension that they would have received based solely on earnings. For persons with high earnings, if the portion of a person's pension based on earnings is reduced sufficiently, there would be a relative decline in the size of the pensions received by them.

Despite the uncertain effect of the double-decker plan on the level of benefits of married women workers, the double-decker plan would reduce the disincentives to labor force participation of married women workers. Under the existing system, a married woman worker often does not receive any increase in her social security benefit as a result of employment and the payment of payroll taxes. This occurs when the benefit she is entitled to as a spouse is larger than the benefit she has earned. Under such conditions, the tax she pays is a real tax rather than a type of forced saving, and such taxes would be expected to reduce the supply of labor consisting of married women workers (Feldstein, 1977, pp. 86–88; Kotlikoff, 1978, pp. 122–124). In the double-decker system, because a married woman worker earns in her own right a second-deck benefit, the size of which depends on her earnings, there should be less effect on the supply of labor of married women workers than under the existing system. This advantage of the double-decker system is still not very significant because the bulk of a person's total pension in a double-decker system is expected to consist of the flat-rate pension, which is unrelated to earnings.

DIVORCED HOMEMAKERS

The way in which social security treats divorced homemakers has become a matter of concern in recent years. The difficulty here is that the dependent benefit received by a divorced homemaker who has been married at least 10 years is only 50% of the husband's PIA. The double-decker system without earnings sharing is unsuited to solving this problem. In a double-decker plan without earnings sharing, a divorced homemaker who had no earnings credits would receive only the flat-rate benefit—set at $1500 a year in this study. In the existing social security system, one-half the average retired worker's PIA currently amounts to about $1750 a year—a better deal than under the double-decker plan.

Because of this problem, double-decker plans usually include earnings sharing for divorced homemakers—that is, earnings credits received by married couples during their marriage are divided equally at the time they are divorced. However, in such a plan, it is the earnings sharing rather than the double-decker system that improves the position of the divorced homemaker relative to the position of the covered spouse.

SURVIVORS

The first comment that I have about the calculations in this study concerns Table 6.8. This table shows that a change to the second type of double-decker plan analyzed in this paper would have little effect on the average benefits of married couples, but would increase sharply the benefits of widows and persons who had never married. As I have already mentioned, in the second type of double-decker plan analyzed, the flat-rate benefit for a couple is set only 50% higher than the benefit for a single person. In the double-decker system proposed by HEW, the flat-rate benefit of a couple is 100% higher than that for a single person. The relative improvement in the benefits of widows and single persons shown in this example in Table 6.8 is partly the result of this special assumption rather than the shift to a double-decker system.

ADEQUACY

My second comment about the calculations in the paper concerns the conclusion that shifting to a double-decker plan would substantially improve the adequacy of the system. Although the simulation in the study supports this conclusion, the way in which these results were obtained is not very convincing.

In the current social security system, the goal of adequacy has been largely taken over by the Supplemental Security Income (SSI) program. Because of SSI, some economists have advocated that adequacy (defined as a guaranteed minimum income) no longer need be a major objective of the old-age and survivors insurance (OASI) program. Partly as a result of this change in attitude, the 1977 amendments to the Social Security Act froze the minimum OASI benefit at $121 a month so as to gradually phase it out.

In the calculations made in this study, certain assumptions about the SSI program play an important role. The authors assume in their simulations that 50% of the persons who qualify for old-age SSI benefits do not apply for them. If this were true, there would be several million eligible persons who are not covered. The 50% figure is similar to an estimate made by the Social Security Administration in 1973, before the SSI program was started. At that time, the Social Security Administration overestimated by 50% the expected number of SSI recipients (see Grimaldi, 1980, pp. 24–27). Since then there have been substantial efforts to publicize the availability of SSI benefits, and one would expect that a larger percentage of those who qualify for SSI benefits would be receiving them.

The means test for SSI benefits is the usual explanation of the large number of eligible persons who have not applied. I would not expect a means test to have the significant effects attributed to it in this study.

While persons with low incomes may find the means test objectionable, such persons are apt to become dependent on relatives or charitable organizations. This causes the relatives or charitable organizations to see to it that the persons with low incomes get all the public assistance they are entitled to, despite the opposition of the recipients to the means test.

If 50% of the persons eligible for SSI benefits are in fact not receiving such benefits, but would receive the flat-rate pension in the double-decker system, one would expect a substantial increase in the number of persons receiving the amount of income considered to be minimally adequate. The estimated total budget cost of the double-decker system shown in Table 6.4 reflects the large increase in the number of persons expected to receive the minimum pension under the double-decker system. The total budget costs of the two double-decker systems examined are estimated to be about 20% higher than the existing OASI and SSI systems combined—an increase of approximately $7 billion. A principal reason for this additional cost is the increase in the number of beneficiaries receiving the minimum benefit. The estimated increase in budget cost is not the result of higher benefits. The calculations are based on the assumption that double-decker benefits are no higher than OASI and SSI benefits.

The assumption about the participation rate of SSI beneficiaries significantly affects the conclusions drawn from the figures in Table 6.7. In that table, a shift to a double-decker system greatly benefits low-income groups, and especially the first decile. According to this table, a shift to the double-decker system would raise the mean income of aged persons in the first decile by as much as 22% to 33%, depending on the type of double-decker system.

INCOME REDISTRIBUTION

I have two general comments about basic issues raised by the double-decker system. The first of these has to do with the expected effect of the double-decker system on income redistribution from the rich to the poor. In the double-decker plan, there is greater reliance on progressive income taxes and less on payroll taxes, and egalitarian flat-rate benefits would be substituted for part of the earnings-related benefits. Whether the social security system should be altered in these ways so as to redistribute income from rich to poor or should be treated as a program of forced saving is a subject that has been debated for a long time. The most important argument against using the program for income redistribution from rich to poor is that this would risk eroding its strong public support. The social security system, which up to now has been viewed by the public as an insurance system and which probably does little to redistribute income within a given generation from persons with high incomes to those with low incomes, has had considerable appeal.[2]

GENERAL REVENUES

A second major issue raised by the double-decker proposal is that the first deck would be financed by general revenues rather than by payroll taxes. In the double-decker plan proposed by the Department of Health, Education, and Welfare, 46% of the total revenues required would be financed by general revenues, payroll tax rates would be reduced 20%, and the average income tax rate would be increased 18%. In the second double-decker plan discussed, 62% of the revenues would be financed by general revenues, payroll tax rates would be cut by 31%, and income tax rates raised 25%. Of the arguments concerning payroll taxes versus general revenues, probably the most important is that earmarked payroll taxes with benefits related to earnings are viewed by the individual taxpayer as forced savings rather than taxes. The significance of viewing payroll taxes as forced saving is that under such conditions payroll taxes for social security need not reduce work effort. At the present time, this argument is especially important because of the social security system's long-run financing problem—the rising payroll tax rates expected in about 30 years because of the sharp decline in the birth rate that started in 1957. If an increase of either 18% or 25% in the average income tax rate—one of the results of the double-decker plans described in this paper—reduced the supply of labor in covered employment, the long-run financing problem would become even more serious than it is. Although the long-run financing problem of the social security system could be substantially solved by raising the eligibility age for full old-age benefits from 65 to 68, in addition it will be necessary for other government policies to attempt to reverse the current trend toward earlier retirement.

---

[2]See Rosen (1977, pp. 103–106). The social security system has redistributed income from the young to the old, and within a given generation from single persons to married couples, from two-earner couples to one-earner couples, from males to females, from blacks to whites, from employees to the self-employed, from nongovernment workers to government workers, and from those who continue working after age 65 to those who retire at age 65.

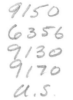
7

Disability Insurance under Proposed Reforms

WILLIAM G. JOHNSON
WILLIAM B. BURFIELD

Introduction

The proposed changes in the social security program are designed to eliminate inequities in the distribution of benefits between men and women who are or have been marriage partners. The effects of the major proposals on retirement benefits are analyzed in the other papers in this volume. This paper considers the effect of the various options on disability insurance (DI) benefits.

The proposed changes are based on the objectives of the retirement component of social security and fail to recognize the fundamental difference between retirement and the risk of disability.

Retirement is, from the individual's viewpoint, a predictable event, subject to the risk of prior death or disability. Subject to well-known institutional constraints on the retirement age, the time of retirement is a matter of individual choice. An individual could, therefore, act as his or her own "pension fund" by saving during the labor force years and consuming the savings plus accrued interest when retired (Schulz, 1980). Since, for any individual, the risk of death or disability prior to retirement and economic need during retirement are difficult to estimate at any reasonable level of certainty, there is a demand for voluntary, risk-pooling arrangements (Boulding, 1958). Voluntary organizations of this type are quite feasible and form an important part of the retirement system (Munnell, 1977).

Why then, have we created a compulsory "savings" (tax and transfer) retirement program? The prevailing answer to this question is that the objective of social security old-age insurance is to guarantee that persons who would not voluntarily save for retirement would not require, when old, support from the more prudent members of society (Brown, 1972; Munnell, 1977). The rationale for the public provision of insurance against economic losses caused by disabling illness and injury is quite different. The definitions and concepts presented in the next section are important to an understanding of the differences between retirement and disability.

Definitions and Concepts

THE GENERIC DEFINITION OF DISABILITY

"Disability" is a form of health-related inability or limitation in performing one or more of the tasks (such as attending school, performing market work, or managing a household) that a society defines as valuable. The causal chain between illness or injury and disability is, except at extreme levels of severity, neither simple nor short. One cannot, therefore, define disability solely by reference to clinically measurable symptoms. "Disability" is the final outcome of the following process (Nagi, 1979, pp. 2, 3):

1. Pathology—the active stage of a disease process or trauma characterized by the interruption of normal bodily processes and the simultaneous efforts of the organism to restore a normal state of existence.
2. Impairment—a physiological, anatomical, or mental loss or other abnormality. The most important category of impairments are residual losses that remain after the active pathology has ended.
3. Functional limitations—limitations in an individual's ability or capacity to perform functions (e.g., walking, lifting) due to the existence of an impairment.
4. Disability—a form of inability or limitation in performing roles and tasks (e.g., education, recreation, employment, household production) expected of an individual within a social environment.

At any stage in this process, medical or vocational interventions may return the individual to his or her primary, prepathology activity, thereby averting "disability." The rather well-developed technology for replacement of amputated limbs with prostheses, for example, permits many persons to perform practically all of the relevant functions (walking, lifting, etc.) even though they are permanently and severely impaired. In these cases, therefore, neither the pathology (traumatic injury) nor the resulting impairment can be assumed to be disabling.

In situations in which the functional limitations created by an impairment cannot be significantly reduced, it is often possible to redesign the environment in which the person's primary activity takes place (i.e., job redesign, "mainstreaming" impaired children by adapting classrooms to their requirements, special controls on autos, etc.). There are other technologies and adaptive techniques that are used to compensate for the loss of physical or mental function. These examples are cited to clarify the distinctions among impairment, functional limitation, and disability.

As these examples indicate, the definition of "disability" is meaningful only in the context of the requirements of a specific activity. In general, a person is "disabled" when he or she, in consequence of functional limitations, is limited in or unable to perform the activity that society considers primary or usual for that person.

Children in our society are disabled, for example, if they suffer a functional limitation that limits or precludes their ability to function as students. In an earlier time, their disability would have been judged according to their ability to work in the labor force or on a family farm.

Although a substantial proportion of men aged 65 or over have significant functional limitations, they are not generally considered to be disabled, because of the convention that the primary activity of older males is retirement. If age 70 becomes the generally accepted retirement age, many men who would have been considered "retired" will be defined as "disabled."

It follows that persons whose primary activity is homemaking are disabled *if* their uncompensated functional limitations affect their capacity for household production. (Do homemakers retire?)

These examples should make it clear that the state of being "disabled" is defined by reference to both the presence of a health-related limitation of function *and* a social expectation as to what is the individual's most important form of activity. In recognition of this fact, some scholars adopt the term "work-disability" to more accurately represent the risk against which programs such as DI provide protection.

The situation is further complicated by the fact that, except at the extremes of severity of functional limitation, the ability or inability to perform an activity differs among individuals whose clinically measurable limitations are equally severe. In other words, whether or not a limitation is disabling depends in part on individual preferences (e.g., preferences between work and leisure); and perceptions (e.g., individual responses to pain or anxiety related to a limitation) (Johnson, Mudrick, and Wai, 1980).

As we shall see in our subsequent discussion, these distinctions are extremely important for an understanding of the implications of options that extend DI coverage to homemakers.

THE SOCIAL SECURITY DEFINITION OF DISABILITY

The DI program definition of "disability" for disabled-worker benefits is "the existence of a medically determinable physical or mental impairment or impairments expected to result in death or which have lasted or can be expected to last for a continuous period of not less than 12 months and of a level of severity deemed sufficient to preclude an individual from engaging in substantial gainful activity [U.S. Department of Health, Education, and Welfare, 1978, p. 96]."

Benefits are provided to *disabled widowers* (see Glossary—who were married to an insured worker), who are 50 or more years of age. The definition of disability is the same as above except that the criterion is the inability to perform *any* gainful activity.

Both definitions use the health-related inability to perform market work as the criterion for determining whether or not someone is disabled.

With these concepts and definitions in mind, we can now compare the objectives of the current program with those of the proposed extensions and subsequently evaluate the administrative feasibility of the proposals.

The Objectives of Disability Insurance (DI)

OBJECTIVES OF THE CURRENT SYSTEM

The DI program provides protection to insured workers and their dependents against the economic costs (foregone wages, medical-care costs) of permanently and totally disabling illnesses and injuries. Permanent and total disability occurs very rarely in the population and, unlike retirement, is universal only in a probabilistic sense. The risk to any individual is quite low, although the costs of each event of disability are extremely high. From an individual point of view, it is extremely difficult (and expensive) to obtain and evaluate the information required to estimate the probability of a disabling event, and even if such information is obtained, individual assessments of the likelihood of a disabling event are surrounded by very high levels of uncertainty.

The advantages of market insurance relative to individual planning for low probability, high cost, uncertain risks are well known. One would expect, therefore, that risk-averse individuals would purchase insurance against disabling illness or injury. There is substantial evidence, however, that in the 20 years prior to the creation of the DI program, private insurance against earnings losses due to disability was not generally available (Berkowitz, 1979). Workers' Compensation insurance is provided in most workplaces for illness and injuries that are presumed to be or can be proved to be work-related. With few exceptions persons who were disabled by chronic illnesses were unlikely to be eligible for Workers' Compensation benefits (Barth and Hunt, 1979). The reluctance of private insurers to cover the risk of the disability of wage earners was based on the losses that they incurred on disability policies during the 1929 depression (Dixon, 1973). One important cause of these losses was the inability of the insurers to distinguish between unemployed persons whose health prevented them from working and unemployed persons who, although physically impaired, would have been employed had the demand for labor not been so low. The creation of the DI program is, therefore, a classic example of public intervention in response to the failure of the market to supply risk-aversion services (Johnson, 1979). The social insurance approach does not, however, eliminate the uncertainty that plagued the private insurers. That is, that except at the extremes of severity, one cannot determine whether a person is able to work solely by reference to clinically measurable symptoms.

Some persons who meet the medical criteria for disability will, in fact, be able to work. The introduction of the element of choice in the decision to work means that disability is subject to moral hazard (that is, the risk is changed by the provision of insurance). Insurers traditionally defend against moral hazard by requiring persons at risk to coinsure for part of the expected costs. In the case of social security disability insurance, the waiting-period requirement, the recency-of-employment test, the limit on beneficiaries' wage income, and the limits on replacement of earnings require that medically eligible persons who *can* work sacrifice wage income in order to receive DI benefits, and thereby become coinsurers.

The limitation of DI coverage to persons who work in the labor force reflects not only the objective of insuring against wage loss, therefore, but also a coinsurance requirement to guard against the inherent uncertainty surrounding purely medical determinations of an individual's ability to work.[1]

The extension of DI coverage to spouses who do not and who may never have worked for wages is not, therefore, a simple redistribution of benefits between marriage partners. It would, instead, redefine the risk that the program is designed to insure and effectively eliminate coinsurance against moral hazard. We will consider these issues in terms of the following proposals for the extension of coverage: (a) earnings sharing; (b) the double decker; (c) the two-tier system; and (d) homemaker credits.

In general, the options change eligibility for DI benefits in one or more ways: They extend insured status to persons who have either never performed market work or who have worked in the market but who have not worked in covered employment in 20 of the 40 calendar quarters preceding the onset of disability. This extension of coverage is either based on a spouse's earnings records (as in earnings sharing), imputing market wages to homemaking activities (homemaker credit), or by eliminating covered employment as a condition of eligibility (double-decker and two-tier systems). The proposals also change eligibility through the adoption, as the definition of disability, of both the disabled worker SGA standard (the standard of gainful activity used by the Social Security Administration) for persons who meet the recency-of-work test on the basis of their own earnings history, and the disabled widow (widower) standard, modified to exclude the age condition, for all others. Although the proposal is not clear on this point, the homemaker-credit approach would presumably also adopt the disabled-widow (widower) standard.

The proposed changes affect benefits, but we concentrate our discussion on the question of coverage which, we think, is a more important issue. We consider whether the proposed extensions of coverage are (a) consistent with the objectives of the current program, and (b) administratively feasible.

OBJECTIVES OF EXTENDING DI COVERAGE

Although the objectives of the options for change are well defined for retirement benefits under social security, their extension to DI creates several anomalies. In general, these anomalies reflect a failure to recog-

---

[1]The congressional debates on DI legislation contain many examples of concerns with moral hazard being met by the defense that the DI program will insure only those who have demonstrated a continuing attachment to the labor force (see U.S. Congress, 1974, pp. 85–88).

nize that the objective of DI is to insure against the risk of income losses due to a permanently disabling illness or injury.

The proposed extensions of coverage for DI to homemakers, for example, do *not* insure homemakers against the inability to do household work. With the possible exception of the homemaker-credit option, all the options define disability by reference to the ability to do market work. The standard currently applied to those who apply for disabled-widow benefits is the one adopted. As was mentioned earlier, it uses the phrase "gainful activity."

DI coverage of disabled widows (who are 50 years of age or over) does not insure against the inability to perform nonmarket work. Subject to a limit of 7 years after spouse's death, the benefits are a transitional insurance scheme that provides a widow or widower, who is not insured in his or her own right at the time of the spouse's death, "with enough time to gain protection on his or her own record," by working in the labor force (U.S. Congress, 1974, p. 117). The object of these benefits is to protect persons who are moving from household work to market work from the consequences of an illness or injury that prevents them from doing *market* work.

Unless one assumes (we would not do so) that all persons who meet the medical criteria for the proposed disability standard necessarily cannot do household work, the proposals in effect restrict DI coverage to the inability to work in the labor force.

Since the risk is defined to be "work-disability," it would be appropriate to calculate benefits on the basis of foregone wages. The options are structured to reflect the earnings of persons with some labor force experience. For those who have not worked, benefits are either fixed at a flat amount (as in the two-tier and double-decker systems) or paid as a fraction of the benefits to which an insured spouse would be entitled (earnings sharing). Benefits under the homemaker credit would presumably reflect homemakers' valuations of offer wages in the market (assuming that the option defines disability as it has been defined in the past).

The attempt to treat DI benefits as if they were a shared income (earnings-sharing option) creates an anomaly in that if both partners to a marriage become disabled, the high earner's benefits are reduced when the low earner is disabled. If the married couple obtain a divorce, earnings are shared at the time of the divorce and the high earner retains full benefits and the low earner receives benefits based on the couple's shared earnings (U.S. Department of Health, Education and Welfare, 1979b, p. 366).[2]

[2]This proposal creates some obvious incentives for divorce (with or without the physical separation of the marriage partners).

The effective benefit structure is, therefore, no longer solely related to the losses that a disabled individual incurs because of his or her inability to work. Although the goal of economic security for disabled persons with insufficient quarters of covered employment is desirable, it is one that is more appropriately achieved through the SSI program. This fact is explicitly recognized, we think, in the double-decker proposal.

As these examples indicate, it is difficult to identify the objectives of the proposals that extend DI coverage. The inconsistencies, such as the retention of the market-work test of disability when a stated objective is "recognition of the contribution of homemakers," or the payment of larger DI benefits to persons if divorced than if married, on the basis of their participation in an economic partnership, are the apparent result of a failure to adequately consider the differences between old-age retirement and disability.

One fact that is clear, however, is that most of the proposed options effectively create a new disability insurance program. The size of that program is the subject of the next section.

The Effects of Extending DI Coverage

The extension of coverage should produce three effects. One is to add to the DI program disabled persons who are not eligible under the current program. This effect should occur rather quickly. The number of new beneficiaries is limited to some subset of those who are now disabled. The estimates that we present are limited to this component of the increase in beneficiaries under the new plan.

The elimination (double-decker and two-tier systems and the home-maker credit) or modification (earnings sharing) of a covered market-earnings record as a requirement for eligibility means that applicants who can prove the existence of a severe, permanent impairment *and* that they do not work in the market will face a rather high probability of being granted benefits. If the proposed changes are instituted, therefore, married, divorced, or widowed homemakers who have never worked in the market and who are permanently impaired but not institutionalized would represent a major group of new beneficiaries.

Another large group of new beneficiaries can be found among all married, divorced, or widowed persons who now receive long-term care in mental, medical, or "rehabilitative" facilities. All those who are patients in chronic-care hospitals or private and public mental hospitals, it seems to us, will be eligible. In addition, one would also expect that persons receiving continuing care for disorders such as drug addiction and alcoholism would, depending upon the frequency of treatment and some professional clinical or psychological certification as to work capacity, also be eligible for benefits. The *immediate* impact of the proposed changes on the number of beneficiaries can, therefore, be estimated from data on the number of persons in the categories described above.

The second effect, which we cannot predict, is the growth in the beneficiary population that can result from the fact that some proposals provide incentives for functionally limited persons who work (in the market *or* in the home) to define themselves as "disabled" (that is, functionally limited *and* not working). It seems to us, for example, that persons who have never worked in the market and who are severely limited but who can perform household work, would under most of the proposals be able to obtain DI benefits at no cost (except for the application process) to themselves or to the household. The differences between this polar case and persons with some work history are differences in degree rather than in kind.

A third effect can be predicted from the attempt (common to most of the proposals) to rely on clinical definitions of the inability to perform gainful activity. As we have indicated, the link between impairment, functional limitation, and disability cannot be adequately explained by medical criteria alone, except in cases of extreme severity. Persons who are limited to a significant degree but who receive medical care on an outpatient basis pose a difficult problem for those who must determine whether or not they are "able to perform any gainful activity." If, however, these same people are institutionalized, it would be impossible to rebut the presumption that they meet the program definition of disability.

The adoption of the proposed changes would, therefore, create incentives to institutionalize some persons who might otherwise remain in their community. The most important incentives for institutionalization are likely to occur where the person's limitation is the result of a behavioral disorder. Persons who are "mentally ill" are the classic example of the uncertainties surrounding purely clinical definitions of disability since, in most cases, the limitations that exist are *defined* by individual behavior.

It is ironic that one potential effect of proposals designed to simply distribute benefits more equitably is to create economic incentives to institutionalize mentally ill persons. The irony is reinforced by the fact that one of the goals of the federal government has been to promote de-institutionalization of the mentally ill.

THE DATA

Our information on the nonaged, noninstitutionalized women who could become beneficiaries under the proposed changes is obtained from the

Social Security Survey of Health and Work Characteristics for 1972 (Allan, 1976). Each woman's history of covered employment is available from the data set but, unfortunately, the earnings histories of their spouses (past or present) are not.

Three estimates of the number of "new" beneficiaries are presented. The first and simplest measure is obtained by counting the number of married, divorced, separated, and widowed women who, by their own evaluation, are "unable" to work and excluding those who already receive DI benefits.

The second estimate is based on the number of married, divorced, separated, and widowed women who consider themselves to be "occupationally" disabled, that is, either limited in the amount or kind of work they can perform or limited in their ability to perform housework, *and* report being unable to perform the same kind of work as they performed prior to the onset of illness or injury. The total number of women in this category is reduced by the exclusion of those for whom (in our best judgment) the observed evidence on severity of impairment and labor force behavior support the presumption that it is extremely unlikely that they would be determined to be eligible. Those who received DI benefits in their own right are also excluded.

The final estimates from those "unable" to work are added to those from the "occupationally disabled" category to estimate the increase in the number of DI beneficiaries likely to result from the extension of coverage to noninstitutionalized married, divorced, separated, and widowed women.

The probability that these women would apply for DI benefits, if coverage were extended to them, is predicted by using an applications equation whose parameters were estimated from data from the same survey on insured women. We recognize that to be strictly correct this approach requires the characteristics of the women in the two groups be essentially identical except for coverage by the DI program. We know, *a priori*, that this is not likely to be true but feel the extent of the bias will not seriously affect our estimates.

We now present our estimates of the increase in beneficiaries that is likely to be produced by the proposed changes.

THE UNABLE-TO-WORK ESTIMATE

In 1972 approximately 3.1 million women living outside institutions reported that they were unable to perform any work. The 1972 survey included separate questions concerning the ability to perform market or household work. The household-work question was only asked of women.

Those who indicated that they were "unable to work" were *presumed* to be unable to perform household work and the household-work question was not asked. Approximately 13% of the women who reported being unable to work also reported that they had never worked in the labor force.

Only a small number (352,000) of the women had never married. In other words, approximately 89% of all women who are unable to work would be covered by the earnings-sharing options, and all would be covered by the extensions of coverage proposed under the double-decker plans. The effect of the homemaker-credit proposal is somewhat less obvious, as we shall discuss in a subsequent section.

In general we exclude all disabled women who receive DI benefits (1971) or who were nonbeneficiaries but insured for benefits by their *own* work histories. Women age 65 and over are excluded because, as under the current system, disability benefits at this age convert to retirement benefits, whose size and distribution are discussed in other papers in this book. The estimates for the remaining women who are unable to work assume that each would satisfy the definitions of disability under the new programs.

As stated above, approximately 3.1 million women reported being unable to work in 1972. Approximately 1.2 million (39%) of these women are excluded from our estimates since they either receive or are eligible nonrecipients of some form of DI benefit (disabled widow or wage earner; 628,300); or receive social security retirement benefits or are over 64 (583,500). These exclusions result in an estimated total of 1.9 million additional DI eligibles (see Table 7.1), should DI eligibility be extended.

The extent to which these individuals are likely to be beneficiaries of the new program under earnings sharing depends upon the extent to which their own earnings histories, combined with those of past or present spouses, would be sufficient to satisfy the program criteria for insured status. The data do not include marital histories, but one can make some gross estimates by reference to the women's ages.

If average labor force participation rates for the spouses of married women (average age = 52) apply, one would project that approximately 94% of the currently ineligible married women who have a spouse present ($N = 1,074,000$), or 1,009,600, would receive credits from their husbands' and their own earnings history, which would be sufficient to provide them with DI coverage.

It is more difficult to evaluate the situation of widows and separated and divorced women under the earnings-sharing option. (Never-married women are, of course, excluded.) The only estimate known with any degree of certainty is that no more than 590,600 of these women would be potentially eligible. (That is the total number of women in these categories

minus those who can be identified as beneficiaries or as insured nonbeneficiaries under the current system.)

In total, then, had the earnings-sharing proposals been applied to the
noninstitutionalized women who are unable to work but had some labor
force experience, as many as 1,600,200 new beneficiaries could have been
added to the DI rolls. Of this total, 1,009,600 would be married; an
additional 291,200 would be divorced or separated; and 299,400 would be
widows (see Table 7.1).

The following inferences can be made concerning increases in program
expenditures under the earnings-sharing option. If one assumes that no
current or former husbands were receiving DI benefits, all the benefits
and Medicare payments made on behalf of these women would represent
a net addition to program expenditures. If some of the living spouses were
DI beneficiaries, then both partners in previous or existing marriages

Table 7.1
Estimated Increases in DI Eligibles and Applicants under New Proposals (in Thousands)

| Marriage Status | Eligibles | | | Applicants | | |
	Unable to Work	Occupationally Disabled	Estimated Application Rate	Unable to Work	Occupationally Disabled	Total
Earnings Sharing						
Married	1,009.6	239.8	.495	499.8	118.7	618.5
Separated	130.0	5.9	.617	80.2	3.6	83.8
Divorced	161.2	1.7	.617	99.5	1.0	100.5
Widowed	299.4	30.6	.617	184.7	18.9	203.6
Never married	0	0				
Total	1,600.2	278.0		864.2	142.2	1,006.4
Double Decker (Deck I) or Homemaker Credit						
Married	1,074.0	255.1	.495	531.6	126.3	657.9
Separated	130.0	5.9	.617	80.2	3.6	83.8
Divorced	161.2	1.7	.617	99.5	1.0	100.5
Widowed	299.4	30.6	.617	184.7	18.9	203.6
Never married	198.9	24.4	.617	122.7	15.1	137.8
Total	1,863.5	317.7		1,018.7	164.9	1,183.6

Note: For explanations of the unable-to-work and occupationally disabled categories
and the estimated application rate, see text.

would share benefits and some of the transfers to the "new" beneficiaries would be offset by reductions in benefits to their spouses. Presumably both partners, given a 2-year period as a DI beneficiary, would receive full Medicare benefits. Total DI expenditures on behalf of the widows would represent a net increase in DI payments.

If the double-decker proposal is adopted, all women, regardless of marital status or earnings record, would be eligible, given our assumptions, for the deck I disability benefit of $122 per month.[3] Under the two-tier approach, those women who satisfy the means-test requirement would be eligible for tier I. Tier II or deck II disability benefits would be based on earnings credits acquired in prior marriages. Lacking the data on earnings histories of spouses, we cannot estimate tier II or deck II benefits.

Given sufficient time for credits to be accumulated, one would expect the same women to be eligible if the homemaker-credit option is approved. The only uncertainty in this regard is whether never-married women would be permitted to participate. Since never-married women account for almost 200,000 women in the unable-to-work category, their participation is an important policy question (see Table 7.1).

It is not clear to us whether the homemaker-credit proposals would allow the accumulation of credits and payment of taxes by never-married women. This raises an interesting question concerning what would be defined as "homemaking" by the regulations of the new DI program. If the effective definition is nonparticipation in the labor force, then the exclusion of never-married women would seem to be inconsistent with the equity objectives of the homemaker credit proposed. A related question is whether all persons, regardless of sex, who usually work for wages would be eligible for homemaker credits during periods in which they are unemployed or have temporarily withdrawn from the labor force.

Although the intent of the modifications is to provide credits for homemaking for women, it seems likely, if the provisions are not to be discriminatory, that men who are not employed should also be eligible. Consider, for example, situations in which a wife is employed but her husband is not. Unless the regulations are written to exclude the possibility that men perform household work, it is possible that the courts might require that such benefits be provided. This situation is one example of the problems surrounding the disparity between the traditional roles of the sexes and the reality of contemporary society.

We would predict, therefore, that the number of new eligibles immediately created by the extension of coverage under the homemaker or double-decker options would be 1,863,500. Let us now consider the

---

[3] Benefit amount from U.S. Department of Health, Education, and Welfare (1979b, p. 79).

potential number of new eligibles that would be drawn from the population of occupationally disabled women.

THE OCCUPATIONALLY DISABLED ESTIMATE

We assumed that women who considered themselves unable to work
satisfy the programmatic definition of disability. Although imperfect, that
assumption is likely to be a reasonable approximation of reality. That is
not true of those who indicate that ill health limits their ability to work.
There were 2.3 million women in this category in 1971, 5.7% of whom had
never worked in the labor force.

Many persons suffer functional limitations that will, in concert with low
skill levels, lack of labor force experience, and age, effectively preclude
them from working. It is well known, for example, that for given levels of
functional limitation, the probability of work disability increases sharply
with age (Haber, 1968). One also finds that a substantial proportion of
workers classified as having permanent–partial (not total) disabilities by
Workers' Compensation programs meet the DI criteria for permanent and
total disability (Johnson, Cullinan, and Curington, 1979).

The clearest evidence that occupationally disabled persons may satisfy
the criteria for DI is the fact that 0.7% of these women received DI
benefits in 1971. These women received disabled-widow benefits. Besides
these DI recipients, 719, 850 women were insured for, but did not receive,
DI benefits in 1972. An additional 367,000 women over age 64 received
social security benefits other than DI. Subtracting these three groups
from the 2.3 million figure yields an estimate of 1.5 million currently
(1971) noninsured potential eligibles who are occupationally disabled.

To address the problem of discriminating among the occupationally
disabled in terms of medical criteria, we consider the severity of functional
limitation using a measure developed by applying the AMA guidelines for
the evaluation of permanent–partial impairment to the survey responses
concerning functional limitation on the 1972 SSA survey (Burfield, 1978).

In prior research on Workers' Compensation and on the DI program, we
used a threshold value of the *functional limitation scale*, FLS $\geq$ 10%, to
represent the minimum level of severity at which a person might be
considered unable to work when weight is given to other characteristics.
To be conservative and to more closely reflect the program definitions of
disability as applied to persons with little or no work history, we adopt
FLS $>$ 25%[4] as the threshold value for this estimate.

[4]The FLS values are constructed by adding limitation percentages for separate body
functions. Someone is classified as being 25% functionally limited, for example, if he or she is
able to perform one or two of the following functions *but with difficulty*: walking, using stairs,
or lifting less than 10 pounds (Burfield, 1978).

The FLS > 25% threshold eliminates an additional 1.2 million women. Our estimate of potential new eligibles from the occupationally disabled population is, therefore, limited to 317,700 women (see Table 7.1).

Following the procedures described in the previous section, we estimate that all these women would be eligible for some benefits under the double-decker or the homemaker-credit option; and that 239,800 married women and no more than 38,200 divorced, separated, or widowed women would be eligible under the earnings-sharing option.

The decision of the OD women to apply for DI is likely to be more sensitive to DI benefit levels than that of the women in the "unable to work" group, because of the higher probability that work for wages is a feasible alternative.

APPLICATIONS EQUATION ESTIMATES

Prior research on DI applications (Johnson, Mudrick, and Wai, 1980) from *insured* women (SSA 1972 data) indicates that age, expected wage income, and severity of impairment are the major determinants of DI application. Using the elasticities of application (evaluated at means) from the estimated parameters for these variables, we can estimate the change in the number of DI applicants under the new program options. To find the percentage change in application rates, we sum the products of each determinant's elasticity and the percentage change in the determinant's mean between the insured and noninsured samples.[5]

The expected application rates for the insured samples of married and not-married women obtained from our prior research are .39 and .49 respectively. The effects of age, severity, and expected wage incomes increase the probability of application for married females in the current study by 27% and for nonmarried females by 26%. Thus the estimated expected application rates obtained are .495 and .617 for the married and not-married women and are reported for these groups in Table 7.1.

[5]The percentage change in the application rate is computed as follows:

$$\dot{p}_i = \sum_{j=1}^{3} \hat{\gamma}_{ij} \cdot (\dot{p}_{ij}/\hat{x}_{ij})$$

where $\dot{p}_j$ = percentage change in application rate;
  j = married, not-married;
  $\hat{\gamma}_{ij}$ = percentage change in mean of determinant (noninsured–insured)/insured;
  j = age, expected wage income, severity of impairment;
  $\hat{x}_{ij}$ = percentage change in mean of determinant; insured sample.

Table 7.2
Mean Values of Important Labor Supply Characteristics of Insured and Uninsured Women

	Married		Not Married	
Variable	Insured	Not Insured	Insured	Not Insured
Age (years)	49.0	53.1	49.8	48.3
Severity of impairment	0.26	0.36	0.29	0.36
Expected wage	$4,243	$3,686	$4,349	$3,411

It is not strictly correct to make even approximate estimates in this way unless the two groups (insured, not-insured) differ only in their insured status. The data indicate that, at least in terms of the most important influence on applications, the two groups are quite similar.

As indicated in Table 7.2, the not-insured women tend to be slightly older[6] and more severely impaired than their insured sisters, and their average expected wage is somewhat lower. In each instance, the difference is one that leads to higher expected application rates. Given their lack of labor force experience, our use of an instrumental wage substantially overstates their real labor force prospects. We expect, therefore, that our estimates of application rates for DI for these women are conservative.

ESTIMATE OF INSTITUTIONALIZED PERSONS

There are some data from the 1967 Social Security Survey of Institutionalized Adults that permit some extremely uncertain and limited estimates of the potential for increases in beneficiaries from among persons in long-term-care institutions other than nursing homes. Of the 648,000 persons represented by the sample, 37% were known to be DI beneficiaries, 18% were known to be nonbeneficiaries, and the beneficiary status of the remaining 45% was not determined (Frohlich, 1972). In our opinion, the only reasonable approach in using such fragmented data is to simply estimate that the number of new beneficiaries ranges from 116,000 (the known nonbeneficiaries) to 408,000 (known nonbeneficiaries plus not-determined cases), recognizing that the data are quite old.

[6]The married not-insured women are older, whereas the unmarried are slightly younger.

SUMMARY ESTIMATE OF EXTENDING COVERAGE

As indicated in Table 7.1, we estimate that the number of new Disability Insurance beneficiaries range from 1.0 million to 1.2 million if we assume that all new beneficiaries are drawn from the preexisting population of noneligible, disabled, and noninstitutionalized persons. For 1971, the total number of DI beneficiaries (including institutionalized persons) was approximately 1.3 million. The potential increase is, therefore, at minimum, equivalent to approximately an 85% expansion in DI beneficiaries.

These estimates assume that there is no increase in the prevalence of "disability" in response to the changes in economic incentives that are created by most of the proposals.

We think that these estimates are conservative in that they are based only on persons who perceive themselves to be severely disabled. There is evidence (of a fragmentary nature) from a feasibility study of a sample of the data from the Framingham Heart Study that indicates that the number of persons who meet or equal the existing criteria for DI benefits is much larger than the number who identify themselves as "disabled" or who apply for DI benefits (Boston University, 1981).

Our estimates are approximations, but we suggest that they are sufficient to conclude that the extension of DI coverage under most options can produce effects that have not been adequately considered by the policymakers. One aspect of these problems is the impact of the proposals on the disability determination process.

Administrative Feasibility of Extending Coverage

Under current rules, the determination of whether an individual is eligible for DI benefits is the primary duty of state "disability determination services." These agencies, under contract to the Social Security Administration, collect and evaluate the medical and vocational information on each person who applies for Disability Insurance benefits. The agencies are staffed by examiners ("disability specialists") and by consulting physicians.

The process of determination of disability is a highly individualized evaluation in which clinical judgments must often be made. Unlike the eligibility determination for retirement, it is a complex, time-consuming process. In 1978, approximately 6000 persons (medical consultants excluded) were employed to evaluate DI claims in these state agencies (Mashaw, 1979).

The regulations also provide for an appeal by denied applicants. The first step in the appeal process is a "reconsideration hearing" in which the DI application is reevaluated by another examiner within the same state agency (Treitel, 1979). If the original denial is affirmed, the unhappy applicant can request a hearing before an administrative law judge (ALJ). Such appeals are considered as original applications, and the ALJ may consider and collect any new evidence that he or she considers relevant to the case. Denials affirmed by ALJs can be appealed to a U.S. District Court. The inherent uncertainties surrounding current eligibility rules and determination procedures are reflected by the staggering increase in the number of appeals.

In 1977, there were approximately 1.3 million applications for DI, of which nearly 846,000 were initially denied. Of these denials. 234,000 were "reconsidered." Slightly more than 140,000 of the reconsiderations went, on appeal, to ALJs and nearly 7000 of the ALJ's decisions were appealed to district courts (Mashaw, 1979; Treitel, 1979).[7] As a result of the appeal process, approximately 50% of the cases that were appealed were reversed (that is, the applicant was found to be eligible for benefits).

If one considers each step in the appeal process as the administrative equivalent of a new claim, then the effective number of DI claims in 1977 was approximately 1.7 million.

These data are important as evidence of the complexity of evaluating eligibility for DI benefits, even when the applicants are persons with substantial work histories that permit comparisons between their functional limitations and the requirements of jobs that are usual for persons of equal education and experience.

If the 1977 ratio of appeals to applications is applied to our estimates of new beneficiaries, then the administrative equivalent of potential new claims (appeals included) ranges from 1.3 million to 1.6 million depending upon which option is adopted. This is not, of course, an annual estimate but one that reflects a one-time adjustment. Consider, however, the magnitude of the adjustment and its probable effect on the administration of the disability determination process. If the staffs of the disability determination agencies could, given some economies of scale, effectively administer 25% more cases than they now process, the "one-time" adjustment could require from 2451 to 3300 additional staff members and a substantial increase in the number of ALJs (now approximately 650 in number) and in program expenditures for medical consultants and legal

---

[7]It is also worth noting that the number of appeals has increased dramatically in recent years. Between 1960 and 1977, appeals increased from 14,000 a year to more than 190,000 (Treitel, 1979, p. 1 and Table 1).

fees. Given the highly individualized nature of the data collection and evaluation process it seems unlikely to us that the economies of scale are very significant. Our assumption of a 25% increase in caseloads is, therefore, conservative.

The adjustment problems are likely to be difficult and expensive to solve, although the phasing-in process could distribute the increase over time. In our opinion, however, the problems of adjustments are minor compared to some more basic administrative problems created by the proposed extensions of coverage.

The most fundamental problem is created by the need to define disability, using market work as the relevant activity, for persons with little or no work experience prior to becoming limited as a result of injury or illness. The importance of the work test under the current system is in its function as a coinsurance provision. That is, that a previously employed person must, in addition to providing clinical evidence of permanent impairment/limitation, be out of the labor market for a period of five consecutive months and cannot (trial work periods aside) remain eligible if he or she earns more than a fairly trivial monthly wage income (that is, the SGA requirement).

Through these provisions, clinical uncertainties concerning the extent to which an impairment is limiting or work-disabling can be effectively minimized by requiring applicants to incur wage losses *if* they are capable of earning wages. It is extremely important to recognize that, for many of the major disabling illnesses, clinical evaluations are inherently uncertain, no matter how skilled the physician.

The importance of the work criterion is stated quite simply in the handbook that Social Security provides to physicians who are evaluating DI applications: "If an applicant has an impairment or combination of impairments that meets or equals those described in the evaluation criteria—and he isn't working—he would generally be considered disabled. Of course, if he is doing substantial gainful work, he would not ordinarily be considered disabled [U.S. Department of Health, Education, and Welfare, 1973, p. 68]."

In other words, no matter how severely impaired an individual, the fact of working precludes granting DI benefits.

Most of the persons that we estimate to be beneficiaries under the new system have, by behavior and self-perception, concluded that they are severely disabled. Our minimum estimates assume that less than one-half of these women would apply for benefits if they are "insured." We have not, however, considered the question of how many persons, who do not now identify themselves as disabled, might apply under the new system.

Consider, for example, the fact that 1,166,000 women with little or no labor force experience who do *not* consider themselves to be either "unable" to work or occupationally disabled, report (1971) impairments which, by our measure of severity, are equal to more than 25% of their total bodily capacity. We do not know what proportion of these women could be eligible under the extended coverages that are proposed. It is obvious, however, that most of the proposals create significant incentives for these women to apply.

The impact of these *induced* applications on the administrative system is not restricted to the population of currently disabled persons. Although we cannot estimate it, the data described above raise the possibility that it could be substantial.

Lacking the coinsurance effects of the current system, the new DI program would be faced with evaluating large numbers of applications from persons who are likely to meet the clinical criteria with potentially large expected benefits and no wage losses from application, and, therefore, an incentive to invest in appeals.

Conclusion

Our first recommendation, therefore, is that the question of inequities in the DI program be reevaluated as an issue separate from the set of proposed changes in retirement and survivor benefits. We suggest that the reevaluation consider the following issues and strategies:

1. Consider the provision of earnings credits at an accelerated rate to persons making the transition from household to market work.

The objective of this type of approach is, within the structure of the existing DI program, to recognize that a divorced or widowed person with little or no prior covered employment faces a transition period during which (even though employed) he or she is not insured against the risk of work disability.

The accelerated credit scheme reduces the period of noncoverage without sacrificing DI coinsurance requirements or redefining the risk. This approach, which is based on the logic of the disabled-widow benefit amendment, could be used with any of the proposed options, if they were restricted to retirement and survivor benefits.

2. Recognize that, with the exception of welfare-type programs, proposals to extend coverage for disabled homemakers must answer the following questions: Is coverage to be restricted to persons who were or are married? Such a restriction is inconsistent with the rationale that coverage is to be extended in recognition of the economic contribution of homemakers. Is it to be restricted to women? If the answer to both of these

questions is no, then the proposal would effectively include all persons at any point in time at which they are not employed for wages. What is the criterion to be used to define a person as a disabled homemaker? This is the most serious problem. We suggest that the only *reasonably* accurate criteria require considerably more investigation on a case-by-case basis than do current DI criteria.

We hope that the information that we have provided stimulates a more detailed evaluation of the problems of disabled homemakers and of widowed and divorced persons. Although we have been critical of the proposed options, it is their structure with which we argue and not their intent.

Discussion

PAUL N. VAN DE WATER

William Johnson and Brad Burfield make two particularly important points in their fine paper. I would like to comment briefly on these two points and then discuss at greater length an area which they did not cover.

ELIGIBILITY CRITERIA

Johnson and Burfield explain the important difference between disability and impairment, and this distinction is vital to understanding how the Social Security Administration's disability programs are administered. In principle, social security disability insurance (DI) and SSI-disability benefits are paid on the basis of disability—that is, inability to perform paid work. In practice, however, benefit awards depend on the presence of an impairment and the actual absence of earnings. The causal link between the impairment and the lack of earnings is *presumed*, even though this presumption is far from exact. In recent years, about three-quarters of new social security benefits have been awarded on the basis of the applicant having one of a specified list of impairments, or another impairment of equal severity.

Discussions of the various plans to provide improved disability protec-

190

tion for homemakers have heretofore assumed that the impairment-based determination process now used in DI would continue to apply. Johnson and Burfield correctly point out that this process, already an approximate method of identifying persons with a work disability, is a particularly inadequate means of assessing disability for people with only a marginal attachment to the paid labor force.

The issue of eligibility criteria should not be thought of as simply or even primarily an administrative problem. Rather, determining the appropriate criteria requires a clearer definition than has yet emerged of the reasons for providing increased disability protections for homemakers. Johnson and Burfield are to be commended for pointing this out, and it is a matter to which I will return below.

COST OF EXPANDING DISABILITY PROTECTION
FOR HOMEMAKERS

The second major point made by Johnson and Burfield is that increased disability protection for homemakers will be very expensive. Based on the Social Security Administration's 1972 Survey of the Disabled and on a model of the DI application process, the authors conclude that an earnings-sharing, double-decker, or homemaker credit plan would increase the number of DI beneficiaries by about 85%.

While the authors' point is generally correct, I think that their specific estimate is considerably high. It also appears to be inconsistent with the cost estimates produced by the SSA actuaries. The discrepancy, I think, lies in the definition of benefit eligibility used by Johnson and Burfield. They categorize as newly eligible anyone who, in the 1972 survey, reported being unable to work, and who did not have social security insured status but would meet the insured-status test (if any) under the proposal. The Johnson–Mudrick–Wai model is then used to estimate the number of insured persons who would apply for benefits. Johnson and Burfield fail, however, to take account of the fact that not everyone who applies for benefits is awarded them. While the acceptance rate in the DI program has varied from year to year, it has generally been less than 50%. For severely disabled applicants in the 1972 survey, the acceptance rate was only 43%.[1] Using the 50% figure, however, the increase in beneficiaries would be only 42% instead of the cited 85%.

[1] The 43% average conceals a 65% acceptance rate for men and a 25% rate for women. Whether or not the individual applied for DI benefits is based on his or her response to a survey question, not on program records. Also, the data do not allow a distinction between denials for lack of insured status and denials for not meeting the disability criteria.

In addition, it is reasonable to assume that women newly eligible for disability benefits would have benefit amounts considerably lower than those of today's average beneficiary. For example, the $122 deck I benefit under the double-decker plan discussed by Johnson and Burfield is about 40% of the average disabled-worker benefit then projected for 1980. Roughly speaking, therefore, a 42% increase in the number of beneficiaries would translate into an approximately 17% increase in program costs. Coincidentally, this is almost identical to the cost estimate given in the HEW report (U.S. Department of Health, Education, and Welfare, 1979a, p. 99).[2]

Even this lower estimate, however, underscores a very important point—the major new cost of either the earnings-sharing or double-decker plan is accounted for by the additional disability protection for home-makers. In the full-scale earnings-sharing plan developed for the 1979 HEW report, a couple's earnings during marriage were to be shared at the time of divorce, retirement, or death, but not in the event of disability. As a result, disability protection for widowed and divorced spouses would improve, but full-career homemakers in intact marriages would remain without disability protection.[3] By the same token, however, the cost of additional benefits for new disability beneficiaries was held to 0.10% of payroll in this option (U.S. Department of Health, Education, and Welfare, 1979a, pp. 99, 185–186).

The full-scale earnings-sharing plan developed for the 1979 Advisory Council on Social Security *did* provide for earnings sharing in the event of disability, but only if it resulted in a higher benefit. If the higher earner became disabled before his or her spouse retired or became disabled, the higher earner would receive a benefit based on his or her own earnings, just as under present law. If the lower earner became disabled first, his or her benefits would be based on shared earnings, because for this spouse, sharing would produce the higher benefit. In this plan, the cost of providing for new disability beneficiaries amounted to 0.26% of payroll (U.S. Department of Health, Education, and Welfare, 1979b, pp. 373–375, 385).

The double-decker plan developed for the 1979 HEW report would have provided a benefit for all disabled persons, married or single, without regard to any test of insured status. It therefore provides the greatest

---

[2]The cost for new disability beneficiaries was estimated to be 0.40% of payroll. Since the cost of disability benefits under present law was estimated to be 2.22% of the payroll, this figure represents an 18% increase in the overall cost of the program.

[3]Paying benefits to a divorced person in circumstances where a married person would not be eligible is considered inequitable by some observers. While this situation does not arise under present law, it is a characteristic of many limited earnings-sharing plans.

increase in disability benefits of the three plans, at a cost for new beneficiaries of 0.40% of payroll (U.S. Department of Health, Education, and Welfare, 1979a, p. 99).

In addition to these comprehensive approaches, it is also possible to provide improved disability protection for women through incremental changes in present law. One frequently mentioned possibility is to eliminate the requirement that, in addition to being fully insured, a worker also have earned 20 quarters of coverage during the most recent 10 years.[4] Complete elimination of the recency test would cost 0.51% of payroll, but a lower cost could be incurred by merely making the test less stringent. Another possibility is to provide full benefits (100% of the primary insurance amount) to disabled widows at any age; this would cost about 0.04% of payroll. For another 0.04% of payroll it would also be possible to provide a benefit of 50% of PIA to disabled spouses of retired and disabled workers.

ALTERNATIVE SOCIAL NEEDS

Because of the large costs involved, and in the present atmosphere of cost cutting and budget balancing, the need for additional disability protection for homemakers must be carefully weighed against alternative social needs. On the one hand, the desire for better disability protection for part-career or full-career homemakers must be weighed against the need to increase the adequacy of benefits for aged widows, to help divorced women, and to deal more equitably with two-earner couples, issues that have been discussed extensively at this conference. In addition, it must take into account the major gaps that remain to be filled in our country's disability income system. It is to these alternatives that I will now turn.

Other Proposals to Improve Benefits for Women

In Table 7.3, I have displayed the costs of the proposals discussed above and compared them with the cost of some other proposals to assist women and/or disabled workers. For example, the Advisory Council's interim recommendation for earnings sharing at divorce and inheritance of earnings credits by the surviving spouse, a proposal which was intended to improve old-age benefits for widows and divorced wives, is estimated to

---

[4]The recency test is somewhat less strict for persons under age 31.

Table 7.3
Comparison of Costs of Various Proposals to Benefit Women or Improve Disability Coverage

Proposal	Cost as Percentage of Payroll
Proposals to expand disability protection for women	
Earnings sharing in HEW report	0.10[a][b]
Advisory Council full-scale earnings-sharing plan	0.26[a]
Double decker in HEW report	0.40[a][b]
Eliminate recency-of-work test	0.51
Full benefit for disabled widow(er)s at any age	0.04
Benefits for disabled spouses of retired and disabled workers	0.04
Other proposals to improve benefits for women	
Advisory Council's interim recommendations for earnings sharing at divorce and inheritance of earnings credits	0.06
Inheritance of earnings credits, with a guarantee that survivors receive no less than the benefit under present law	0.23
Working spouse's benefit for aged survivors	0.35
Up to 10 child-care credit years in computing special minimum benefit	0.14[c]
Other disability proposals	
Occupational definition of disability	
True occupational definition	0.28
Advisory Council recommendation	0.07
Coverage of occupational diseases	
Eliminate 5-month waiting period	0.30
Eliminate recency-of-work test	0.51
Furnish supplemental benefits to victims of occupational diseases	d
Changes in Supplemental Security Income	
Liberalize definition of disability	e
Raise guarantee to the poverty line	f

Note: Unless otherwise indicated, cost estimates are based on the assumptions underlying the 1979 social security trustees' reports. Where sources are not indicated in the text, the figures are unpublished Social Security Administration estimates.

[a] Cost for new disability beneficiaries only.

[b] Based on 1978 trustees' report assumptions.

[c] Based on 1980 trustees' report assumptions.

[d] No estimate available.

[e] Roughly estimated to cost about $1 billion per year. While SSI costs are not generally expressed as a percentage of taxable payroll, for comparison purposes this is roughly equal to 0.1% of payroll.

[f] About $4.3 billion, which is roughly equivalent to 0.33% of payroll.

194

cost only 0.06% of payroll (U.S. Department of Health, Education, and welfare, 1979b, pp. 114–117).

Under the Advisory Council's plan, benefits based on inherited earnings credits would replace the present law benefit for widows and widowers—that is, present benefits for aged or disabled survivors would be phased out. If inheritance were adopted with a provision that survivors would receive no less than the benefits under present law, the cost would be 0.23% of payroll.[5]

Another proposal for improving retirement benefits for working women is that the special minimum benefit for long-term low-wage workers be changed to allow credit for up to 10 child-care years. As recommended by the National Commission on Social Security, a child-care credit year would be one in which the worker had a child under age 7 and did not earn enough to gain a year of coverage. In addition, the number of years countable toward the special minimum benefit would be increased from 30 to 35. The long-run average cost of this change is estimated to be 0.14% of taxable payroll (U.S. National Commission on Social Security, 1981, pp. 235–236).

Still another option—the working spouse's benefit—has been advocated by Robert Myers (Chapter 10 in this volume). Under this approach an individual eligible for benefits both as a worker and as a surviving spouse of a worker would be paid the larger of the two benefits plus 25% of the smaller benefit. The long-range cost of this proposal is estimated to be 0.35% of taxable payroll.

While many other proposals have been made to deal with the issues discussed in this volume, the foregoing provides a general indication of the costs involved. Viewing the issue of disability protection for homemakers as a disability issue as well as a women's issue, however, it is also important to compare the costs of these proposals with the costs of the major disability-related proposals now under discussion.

Other Disability Proposals

At present, the definition of disability used for DI and SSI is the inability to engage in *any* substantial gainful activity. This is admittedly a very stringent definition. One study has found that, even of those who apply for benefits and are turned down, four-fifths never return to sustained competitive employment.

---

[5]This cost estimate is for inheritance of earnings credits only and does not include earnings sharing at divorce. The estimate is an unpublished Social Security Administration figure.

Because of the stringency of this definition there have been repeated calls, particularly from organized labor, to adopt a so-called occupational definition of disability in the DI program, at least for workers age 55 and over. The definition used in the Federal Civil Service Retirement System is an example of what might be called an "easy" or "true" occupational definition of disability. Federal civil servants are eligible for a disability annuity if they are unable to perform even one significant function of their current job; they cannot be required to accept a modified or less demanding assignment.

Adopting such a definition in social security for workers age 55 and over would increase DI costs over the next 75 years by 0.28% of payroll. Since taxable payroll is now over $1 trillion per year, this represents a long-run average cost of over $3 billion in today's terms. This figure represents an increase of 23% in cash benefit payments to workers age 55 and over.

The 1979 Advisory Council on Social Security endorsed a much more limited occupational definition of disability for older workers. In particular, the council recommended that skilled or semi-skilled people age 55 through 59 who are able to perform no more than light work should be considered disabled if they do not have skills that are transferable to closely related occupations. The long-run cost of disability payments under this recommendation is estimated to be 0.07% of payroll (U.S. Department of Health, Education, and Welfare, 1979b, pp. 148–149).

While the payment of social security disability benefits is not conditional on the source or nature of a person's disability, social security does supplement the Workers' Compensation program in paying benefits to people with a job-caused disability. The Workers' Compensation system, however, was designed to deal with on-the-job accidents, such as falling off of a scaffold or losing a hand in a machine, and generally does not provide benefits for job-caused occupational diseases with long latency periods.

A recent study by the Department of Labor, for example, finds that only 5% of persons suffering from occupational disease are receiving Workers' Compensation benefits. Social security disability insurance, on the other hand, is the major source of income support for those severely disabled from an occupational disease and is estimated by the Labor Department to pay benefits to 53% of those so disabled (U.S. Department of Labor, 1980, p. 61).

Since social security already pays considerable benefits to the occupationally disabled, and since the costs of administration and litigation of Workers' Compensation claims are high, it is often suggested that social security provides the best vehicle for dealing with occupational disease.

The Department of Labor report (1980) gives several examples of ways in which DI might be modified to provide improved protection for victims of occupational disease. One possibility is that DI beneficiaries who are occupational-disease victims be paid a supplemental benefit to bring their total benefit up to a specified fraction of prior earnings. Although the cost of this option has not been determined, it is likely to be quite expensive. Among other possible modifications to DI suggested in the report are eliminating the 5-month waiting period for cash benefits, estimated to cost 0.30% of payroll, and eliminating the recency-of-work test, which would cost 0.51% of payroll. As noted earlier, relaxing the recency test is often advanced to help women workers rather than workers with occupational diseases.

Because of the stringency of the current definition of disability in SSI and DI, many disabled people do not qualify for benefits, and among this group the incidence of poverty is extremely high. According to the 1972 Survey of the Disabled, of noninstitutionalized persons who were severely disabled 18 months or more and were not social security beneficiaries, 44% were living in poverty. Of those severely disabled nonbeneficiaries who were unmarried, the poverty rate was 77%. Table 7.4 gives a detailed breakdown by sex and marital status, as well as more detail on disabled persons with incomes below specified fractions of the poverty threshold.

Figures like these led the 1979 Advisory Council on Social Security to recommend a more liberal definition of disability in the SSI, but not the DI, program. "Since disability insurance benefits are paid without regard to need," the Advisory Council argued, "it is appropriate to restrict eligibility to those whose medical impairments are quite severe. However, in the SSI program, where benefits are generally lower and paid only to those with little or no other income and only limited assets, such strict standards for eligibility are neither necessary nor desirable. The SSI program should . . . protect those in need whose impairments are not quite severe enough to qualify them for disability insurance, but are severe enough to prevent them from working when the impairments are combined with other personal and economic factors [U.S. Department of Health, Education, and Welfare, 1979b, pp. 150–151]." Since a specific alternative definition of disability for SSI has not been developed, no precise cost figure is available. The current cost of federal SSI disability benefits, however, is about $4 billion per year, and I would guess that the additional cost of such a change would be in the $1 billion range.

Another perennial proposal is to raise the guaranteed income level in the SSI program to the poverty level. This would, by definition, eliminate poverty among the aged and among those disabled who would qualify for benefits. The cost of this change is estimated to be $4.3 billion per year.

Table 7.4
Adequacy of Income for Disabled Persons (Percentage of Persons below Specified Percentage of Poverty Line)

Percentage of Poverty Line	Married	Widowed	Divorced or Separated	Never Married
Disabled Worker Beneficiaries, Male				
51%	4%	16%	13%	12%
76	13	39	27	23
91	20	43	35	32
101	24	43	42	36
126	32	62	62	56
151	42	80	71	70
Disabled Worker Beneficiaries, Female				
51	5	1	15	15
76	6	19	32	40
91	7	22	45	51
101	10	28	55	57
126	12	49	64	66
151	14	73	74	76
Severely Disabled Nonbeneficiaries, Male				
51	11	18	33	53
76	22	46	56	73
91	29	48	62	78
101	36	51	68	83
126	46	80	80	85
151	52	83	82	87
Severely Disabled Nonbeneficiaries, Female				
51	6	26	39	46
76	16	43	62	78
91	19	63	78	82
101	22	71	80	83
126	28	79	88	97
151	32	84	93	98

Note: Data derived from the Social Security Administration's 1972 Survey of the Disabled for noninstitutionalized individuals disabled 18 months or more as of the survey date. Poverty status is based on household income. The author appreciates the assistance of Bernie Trieber and Mary Ellen Burdette in preparing this table.

CONCLUSION

Johnson and Burfield have correctly emphasized the costs and complexities involved in providing improved disability protection for homemakers. In light of these considerations, I think that their implicit suggestion to focus first on the needs of widowed and divorced persons is a reasonable one. As Table 7.4 shows, the poverty rates among severely disabled widows and divorcees who are not receiving DI benefits are extremely high—71% and 80%, respectively. But the poverty rate is even higher (83%) for severely disabled nonbeneficiaries—both women and men—who have never married. Conversely, the lowest poverty rate (22%) among severely disabled nonbeneficiaries is for married women. Designing a proposal to target benefits on those most in need, alleviate existing inequities, and avoid creating new problems will be a difficult task but is one well worth doing.

ACKNOWLEDGMENTS

The views expressed in this paper are personal and not necessarily those of the Department of Health and Human Services or the Congressional Budget Office. The author wishes to thank Virginia Reno and Melinda Upp for valuable comments.

8

Occupational Pension Plans and Spouse Benefits

FRANCIS P. KING

This paper traces the development and describes the current status of provisions for spouses of active and retired employees under public and private pension plans in the United States, reviews the current treatment of pension assets and benefits by state family and divorce statutes, and raises some policy issues related to possible new directions that might be taken in spouse protection under occupational pension plans.

Historical Background

Although the major growth in occupational pension plans in the United States did not occur until after World War II, the roots of current pension practice are sunk deeply into the social and economic grounds of the late nineteenth and early twentieth centuries. In these decades, pension plans were developed in response to new social and industrial situations. They established basic philosophies and objectives that are still clearly visible as distinguishing features. This includes their emphasis on benefits related to employee service, on individual equity (as opposed to criteria of social adequacy or presumed need, as under social insurance plans), and their ultimate identification of the need for a sound financial base, leading to the use of reserve funding (as opposed to the pay-as-you-go inter-generational transfer method used for social insurance programs).

The employee—not the family—was the entity on which the early pension plans focused. There was little attention to benefit provisions for wives, widows, or children. What is generally regarded as the earliest private pension plan (established by the American Express Company in 1875), provided its benefits only for long-service employees who had both reached a stated age and were unable physically to continue work.[1] Other plans took this approach, but it later appeared that defining eligibility for pension benefits in terms of physical ability was less practicable from an administrative standpoint than an age test. Retirement for age thus became a surrogate for disability retirement.[2]

An important early question concerned the nature of the pension benefit. Once offered, was it an entitlement or a gift? In the plan documents, private employers took great care to make it clear that benefits were considered gratuitous payments, that is, gifts. One company's plan, for example, stated: "The allowances are voluntary gifts from the company and constitute no contract and confer no legal rights upon any employee. The continuance of the retirement allowance depends upon the earnings of the company and the allowances may at any time be reduced, suspended, or discontinued on that, or any other account, at the option of the Board of Directors [Conant, 1922, pp. 50–51]."

Even while qualifying the pension reward as a gift, however, many of the early industrial pension plans asserted that the benefits were paid as a reward for long and faithful service. For example, an oil company plan stated: "This plan was adopted by the Company to reward long and faithful service. It is a purely voluntary provision made by the Company for the benefit of its employees, and constitutes no contract, and confers no right of action [Conant, 1922, p. 51]."

---

[1]The early history of industrial pension plans in the United States is documented in Conant (1922); National Industrial Conference Board (1925); National Industrial Conference Board (1931); Latimer (1932); and Dearing (1954).

[2]Conant, writing in 1922, viewed the common practice of fixing an arbitrary age of retirement as "objectionable." He stated that "a more desirable arrangement is to make the retirement age subject to the discretion of a pension committee, provided there is adequate guarantee that the worker's rights will be protected [p. 214]." This author's further views might have been as appropriate as arguments in support of amendments in 1978 to the Age Discrimination in Employment Act as they were in 1922 when he wrote them: "If a worker is fully able to perform his task there is no real reason for retiring him simply because he has reached, say, age sixty or sixty-five. Ordinarily his wages, even at that age, will be considerably larger than his pension, while, moreover, it is desirable, both from his standpoint and from the standpoint of society, that he should continue to be a producer as long as he is able to do so [pp. 214–215]."

There were seeds for conflict here, for if pension benefits were considered rewards for long service, it could be argued that they were earned
and were not simply the benefice of charity. As if to confirm the view that
benefit amounts were earned, benefit formulas normally related pension
amounts to years of service and wages (Conant, 1922, pp. 231–250). A
1925 Conference Board report on industrial pensions appeared to acknowledge a degree of employer obligation when it noted that while the
granting of a pension was the voluntary act of an employer "who admits no
contractual obligation nor any legal right on the part of the employee," the
same employer "does acknowledge a moral obligation and a corresponding moral claim to the payment of a pension actually 'earned'
[National Industrial Conference Board, 1925, p. 25]."

The idea that an employee earns pension benefits as a reward for long
service emerged early in pension history, but it took many decades for
pension philosophy and practice to proceed from a concept of "moral"
obligation to one of "legal" obligation, with many social, economic, and
legal conflicts along the way. Whether or not a pension was "earned" or
was truly a gift, social welfare or redistributive concepts were absent;
pensions and wages generally shared the same philosophical ground (i.e.,
both were measured by employee service), despite the ambiguous nature
of the pension benefit.

Few of the early plans, public or private, established pension reserves
for the financing of future benefits. Most plans paid all benefits out of
current earnings (private), or revenue (public) (National Industrial Conference Board, 1925, p. 21). This meant a lack of financial stability and
considerable uncertainty about the ability to assure pension payments in
bad times. It explains, in part, the unwillingness of employers to offer
pensions as binding obligations, as well as the early limitations on benefits
and the lack of interest on the part of employers in establishing benefits
for widows of retired employees under their pension plans.

Benefits for widows were rare in the early pension plans. Out of 94
industrial pension plans analyzed in 1922, only 3 reported pension
benefits for widows (Conant, 1922, p. 250). The study noted that "under
some plans, only one monthly payment is made to the estates of such
annuitants [Conant, 1922, p. 202]." The study's author concluded the
following: "Specific provision for widows and dependent children cannot
reasonably be expected of an ordinary pension plan. Industry cannot
provide against all the hazards of life. Moreover, the private employer may
with justice take the ground that his criterion should be the service
rendered and not the number of an employee's dependents." He added
that "it is ... reasonable to provide that a retirement benefit shall
continue to go to the estate of a pensioner who dies shortly after going on

the pension roll, until the net value of the pension earned or accumulated up to the time of his retirement had been paid out. . . . Beyond this, provision for dependence may properly be regarded as the concern of society as a whole, rather than that of a private retirement scheme [Conant, 1922, pp. 209–210]."

On the question of preretirement death benefits, the same study concluded it advisable to provide them under separate arrangements, such as group insurance (Conant, 1922, pp. 203–204).

A few years later, a National Industrial Conference Board study (1925) of 245 industrial pension plans found that 52 provided for some pension coverage for widows of retired employees, but that none of the 52 provided a lifetime annuity benefit for the widow. In 14 plans, the widow's pension continued for one year following the retiree's death; in 8 plans the pension continued for less than one year (p. 100). For death benefits prior to retirement, the Conference Board study found that 85 plans reported modest group life insurance or other programs providing lump-sum death benefits, usually graduated according to years of service. Some of these provided from $75 to $250 for funeral benefits. Death benefits prior to retirement were normally provided for outside of the scope of the regular retirement plan (pp. 95–100).

The lack of widows' benefits in the early plans was consistent with explicitly stated company views that pension benefits, although in the nature of a reward for long service, implied no contractual obligation on the part of the employer to pay such benefits, to continue them once started, or to pay them to persons other than the retired employee. There was little pressure on employers to extend benefits to widows of retired employees, since labor did not view the developing private pension plans with much warmth, and consequently did not attempt to influence their provisions. (See Latimer, 1932, pp. 8–9; Webb and Webb, 1894, 1, 158; Peterson, 1945, pp. 128–146.)

By the end of the 1930s private and public employee pensions had reached a low point in their development. It was only with the advent of World War II that occupational pensions began to expand to their present size and strength. The economic prosperity of the war years was a powerful stimulant, but there were a number of other important influences: the provisions of the 1942 Internal Revenue Code, the operation of excess-profits taxes, and the wartime wage stabilization policies of the National War Labor Board, which aimed at maintaining wage stability at the price of "greater flexibility on secondary lines," specifically, fringe benefits. The wartime focus on fringe benefits popularized them and helped create in the minds of labor leaders and workers the view that they were entitled to such benefits as a matter of right (U.S. Department of Labor, 1950, p. 166).

The Internal Revenue Act of 1942 placed the tax treatment of pension plans in a clearer light and delineated criteria regarding nondiscrimination of employee classes within plans. Combined with the sharp increases in corporate and excess-profits tax rates of the 1940s, the tax treatment that was accorded pension contributions and reserves under the 1942 act enhanced employer receptiveness to union pension and other fringe-benefit demands. And once labor groups began to see pensions as a right, they took an active interest in influencing the structure, operation, and benefits of the plans. In the meantime, public employees were also expressing greater interest in improved retirement provisions.

By 1950, private and public employee pension plans were poised for their post–World War II growth. In the private sector, the Labor Management Relations Act of 1947 (the Taft–Hartley Act) had extensively amended and supplemented the original basic Labor Relations Law of 1935, the Wagner Act. When a question arose between the Inland Steel company and the Steelworkers' Union as to whether the law imposed a duty on employers to bargain with representatives of their employees on the subject of pensions, the National Labor Relations Board ruled (April 1948) that companies were required to bargain on pension plans.[3] The Federal Court of Appeals (7th circuit) affirmed the view that retirement plans were included under the act as a proper subject for collective bargaining. The court skirted the "pensions as wages" issue and concluded that a pension plan was a condition of employment.[4]

The Inland Steel case effectively closed the era of union noninvolvement with employer-sponsored pension plans. Thereafter, many private plans ceased to be a matter of voluntary, unilateral employer action. It thus became possible to perceive pension plan provisions—including spouse benefits—as an expression of the fringe-benefit priorities of organized workers.

Table 8.1 shows the distribution of occupational pension plans in the United States in 1978 by major type, number of participants, and plan assets.

[3] *Inland Steel Company*, 77 NLRB (April 1948), p. 1.

[4] *Inland Steel Company* v. *NLRB*, affirmed 170 F. 2d 247 (CCA 7, 1948) Cert. Den. as to the welfare fund issue, April 25, 1949, 336 U.S. 960, pp. 251, 253.

Table 8.1
Pension Plans in the United States, 1979

Pension Plans	Persons Covered[a]	Percentage of Covered Persons	Assets (millions)	Percentage of All Pension Assets
Private plans				
With life insurance companies	21,615,000	31%	$119,110	23%
Other private plans	31,000,000[b]	44	202,237	39
Public employee plans				
State and local	13,540,000	19	57,677	11
Federal civilian employees[c]	4,380,000	6	142,573	27
Total	70,535,000	100	521,597	100

Source: American Council of Life Insurance (1978–1979, pp. 8–10).

[a]Includes workers and retirees.

[b]Estimated.

[c]Includes U.S. Civil Service Retirement System, Tennessee Valley Retirement System, and Retirement Systems of the Federal Reserve Banks.

Current Pension Plan Benefits for Spouses

Current provisions for surviving spouses under public and private occupational pension plans can be divided into two survivor-benefit classifications: (1) postretirement benefits, and (2) preretirement benefits, also sometimes designated as death benefits. Data on the extent and characteristics of survivor-benefit provisions are somewhat limited.

PRIVATE PENSION PLANS

A study by the Bureau of Labor Statistics in 1971 (reported in Hodgens, 1973) concluded that survivors' annuities—defined as monthly payments to which the spouse or dependents of deceased active or retired workers are automatically entitled if the worker has satisfied specified age or service requirements—emerged as "an important employee benefit" in private pension plans during the late 1960s. The study reported that "by 1971 . . . 3.8 million workers, or almost one of five plan participants, were in plans with these annuities [Hodgens, 1973, p. 31]," and noted that collective bargaining by large unions was largely responsible for the growth in survivor provisions. About half the workers with such coverage participated in plans negotiated by the Automobile Workers, Communications Workers, Steelworkers, or Teamsters.

Employees covered by multi-employer plans generally were less likely to have survivors' pensions than employees covered under single-employer pension plans; only about one in ten workers in multi-employer plans had survivors' pensions compared with one in four workers in single-employer plans. Some of the largest differences were related to the number of participants. While survivors' pensions were seldom provided by plans covering less than 1000 workers, about half of all workers in large plans (100,000 participants or more) were covered by such benefits (Hodgens, 1973, p. 31).

The 1971 BLS study reported that while survivor benefits are generally designed to aid the surviving spouse, provisions for minor children were included in such plans covering more than one-fourth of the workers. Plans covering 17% of the workers provided the regular survivor's pension to minor children in the absence of a surviving spouse.

Most of the plans covered in the 1971 study aimed at protecting survivors of long-term employees. Four out of five workers had to satisfy a minimum age and service requirement before their survivors would be eligible for a benefit. The most common requirement was age 55 and 10 to 15 years of service (Hodgens, 1973, p. 33). The amount of the basic survivor's benefit depended on the worker's accrued pension, but the age or other characteristics of the survivor usually entered into the actual determination of the benefit. Reductions for one or more of these factors were present in plans covering about 7 of 10 workers. Standard actuarial reductions for the difference in the worker's and surviving spouse's age or an approximation of such reductions covered 48% of the workers. More liberal age reductions (for example, benefits reduced 0.5% for each year that the survivor's age was under 50) applied to the survivors of 20% of the workers. Reductions applicable when survivors attained age 62 covered the survivors of 25% of the workers. The pensions were generally paid out for the survivor's lifetime but in plans covering 12% of the workers they ended at age 62. Plans for one-fourth of the workers discontinued payments if the spouse remarried (Hodgens, 1973, p. 33).

A few years later the BLS reported significant changes between 1970 and 1974 in 144 of the 149 pension plans regularly monitored (Hodgens, 1975, pp. 22–27). The report stated: "Concern for survivors of longtime workers and retirees led to a significant expansion in the prevalence of survivors' pensions. By 1974, nearly half of the plans had such a provision [p. 22]." The study also indicated that four-fifths of the 149 major pension plans provided some type of death benefit, usually for survivors of both working members and retirees. The report observed that pension plan death benefits vary considerably and may include the return of employee contributions with interest (less any benefits received), lump-sum payments, guarantees of a certain number of benefit payments to beneficiaries (less payments already made to the retiree) and lifetime or long-term monthly pensions to surviving spouses or children or both (p. 27). It noted that death benefits may also be provided by insurance plans not covered by the study.

Studies of corporate pension plans by the Bankers Trust Company have also helped to document the development of private pension plans. The most recent full study covered 190 companies and 271 single-employer retirement plans, representing approximately 8,400,000 employees, or about one-quarter of all employees covered in 1975 by pension plans of employers in private industry (Bankers Trust Company, 1975, pp. 5–23). This study reported that a majority of the surveyed pension plans provide for payments to a beneficiary upon the death of a retired employee, either (a) through the operation of a joint-and-survivor option; or (b) through a refund of employee contributions. Under the first method, the employee elects an actuarially reduced pension payable for a lifetime upon retirement, with some or all of the reduced pension continuing to the surviving spouse. Under the second method, a contributory plan would refund any excess of the decedent's contributions with interest over the aggregate pension payment that had been received.

The study concluded that a growing number of pension plans were providing postretirement death benefits requiring additional company contributions. Out of 87 pattern plans (plans following an industry pattern and usually originating as flat benefit plans) and conventional plans (plans relating benefits to salary and service) with postretirement death benefits, 25 provided a greater than actuarially equivalent joint-and-survivor benefit. Standard joint-and-survivor and refund methods require no additional employer contributions.

The Bankers Trust study also reported that 63% of the plans studied provided a spouse's benefit as a *preretirement* death benefit. A trend towards providing preretirement death benefits and survivors' pensions was first noted ten years earlier, when 28% of plans provided such benefits. In the 1965 to 1970 period this figure increased to 56%, with the 1975 study reporting 63%. The preretirement death benefits in the pension programs usually supplemented a group life insurance coverage, provided by most companies.

ERISA

In 1974 the Employee Retirement Income Security Act (ERISA) became law, effective January 1975. ERISA (Sec. 205) requires that if a retirement plan provides for the payment of benefits in the form of an annuity, a "qualified joint-and-survivor annuity" be made available if the participant has been married throughout the 12-month period preceding the date on which the annuity payments are to begin.[5]

The specific ERISA provisions are summarized as follows (Sec. 205):

1. A retirement plan may set a minimum age which the surviving spouse must attain in order to receive annuity payments.

2. If a retirement plan provides for early retirement, a survivor's annuity must be payable if the participant reached early retirement age before dying and had been married for at least 12 months preceding death.

3. The participant may elect not to receive a joint-and-survivor annuity prior to reaching regular retirement age at any time after the later of (a) attaining early retirement age or (b) a date which is 10 years before the date on which he will reach regular retirement age.

4. A plan may provide that the election not to take a joint-and-survivor annuity (or the revocation of such an election) is not effective if the participant dies within a specified period not in excess of two years after making a revocation of the election.

5. An employee's rights to benefits attributable to employee contributions may not be forfeited, even upon death. However, a plan may provide for the forfeiture of an employee's vested benefit derived from employer contributions in the event of the employee's death before retirement. This forfeiture rule does not apply if the employee continued to work after becoming eligible to retire and a joint or survivor annuity was to be provided.

As a matter of public policy, the significance of this ERISA legislation is in its recognition of the importance of survivor-benefit provisions, the encouragement of married workers to take a joint–life annuity, and its implicit support of equity among pension plan participants through provision for the survivor benefit as an actuarial equivalency.

[5]ERISA defines a qualified joint-and-survivor annuity as an annuity for the life of the participant with a survivor annuity for the life of the spouse which is not less than one-half of, or greater than, the amount of the annuity payable during the joint lives of the participant and the spouse and which is the actuarial equivalent of a single annuity for the life of the participant [ERISA, Sec. 205(g)].

PUBLIC EMPLOYEE PENSION PLANS

A recent study of public employee retirement systems was carried out by the U.S. Congress, House of Representatives, Committee on Education and Labor, Pension Task Force (1978). The report included brief summaries of the pre- and postretirement death-benefit provisions currently incorporated in these plans. It concluded that postretirement survivor benefits in public plans normally take the form of an annuity income option selected by the employee to provide a continuing benefit for life to the spouse in the event of the employee's death after retirement. Practically all plans provided a joint-and-survivor annuity option; most did not provide an automatic survivor annuity; normally, the single-life annuity is provided unless the employee selects a survivor annuity.

For preretirement death benefits, the Pension Task Force reported that a return of member contributions is usually the minimum death benefit for nonvested employees in public plans. Where survivor annuities are payable, eligibility requirements (employee service and/or age) are stated. Survivor annuities for spouses (and, sometimes, minor children) are usually provided for vested employees meeting specified age and service requirements. Benefits tend to be more generous than under private plans, including survivor benefits that are greater than the actuarial value of benefits accrued by the employee. The task force study did not cover eligibility requirements for preretirement death benefits.

Generally, public retirement systems provide for preretirement survivor benefits more frequently than private plans, and for more liberal eligibility conditions, as well as for an often extensive array of annuity income options designed to provide a continuing life income for a retiree's surviving spouse. Since statistical summaries of survivor-benefit provisions cannot fully reflect the sometimes rather complex whole of such provisions, the following two descriptions are offered as more detailed examples of survivor provisions in public pension plans.

California Public Employees' Retirement System

Preretirement death benefit: Return of employee contributions with interest (6%) plus lump-sum death benefit equal to 6 months' salary plus $5000.

If the employee was at least age 50 with 5 years of service, a lump sum of $5000 plus, for surviving spouse if married at least one year before death, or, if there are unmarried children under age 18, an allowance equal to 50% of the benefit formula based on service to date of death. The benefit for the surviving spouse is payable until death or remarriage. Or, spouse may elect to receive the amount that would have been payable had the employee retired at the date of death based on a joint and full survivor option (Cook, 1979, pp. 21–22).

Postretirement survivor benefits: The following annuity income option elections are available to the employee: Joint and full continuance, joint and one-half continuance or continuation of any amount, within certain limits, specified in advance by the retired employee; or a reduced annuity to the retired employee with the balance of employee contributions payable to a survivor at death (California Public Employees' Retirement System, 1977, pp. 21–24).

Florida Retirement System

The preretirement death-benefit provisions of the Florida Retirement System are somewhat closer to the provisions typical of private plans (and less generous and less costly than the California plan), except for the age credit for benefit deferral, the eligibility of other dependents in absence of the spouse, and the liberal service-connected death benefit, as indicated below:

Preretirement death benefit: For non-service-connected death: If the employee has completed 10 years of service, spouse or other dependent may elect to receive a benefit calculated as if the employee had retired at the date of death, based on a joint-and-full-survivor option. Payment of the benefit may be deferred to a later time when it will be calculated on the age the employee would have attained at the time the benefit commences. For service-connected death, no service requirement and spouse receives 50% of final monthly salary per month until death or remarriage. If spouse dies, unmarried children continue receiving the benefit to age 18. Cost-of-living provisions in the pension benefit formula are applied after the date the employee would have reached age 65 (Cook, 1979, p. 27).

Postretirement survivor benefits: Employee may elect among the following income options: At retired employee's death, refund of remaining employee contributions, if any; annuity with 10-year guarantee; joint and full continuance to a coannuitant; joint annuity with two-thirds continuance upon the death of either the retired employee or the survivor (Florida Retirement System, 1975).

COMPARISON OF BENEFITS FOR SPOUSES IN
PUBLIC AND PRIVATE PENSION PLANS

Provisions for pre- and postretirement survivor benefits for spouses vary widely between public and private pension plans, and also within the public–private categories. Some data are available to provide statistical information on the distribution of survivor-benefit provisions by type of provision, but their usefulness is limited, largely owing to the difficulty of collecting and classifying complex benefit provisions. Generally, it appears that public employee retirement systems are more likely to offer preretirement death benefits, and have more liberal eligibility provisions, than private pension plans. This is consistent with the generally more liberal benefits of public employee retirement systems. Public and private pension plans are more similar to each other in their structural provisions for postretirement benefits (though not in benefit levels) than for preretirement benefits. For postretirement benefits, retiring public and private employees may choose a basic single life-annuity benefit, or elect among a variety of income-payment methods that provide for continuation of a lifetime income to a surviving spouse. ERISA requires private pension plans to provide for the automatic payment of a joint–life option (at least half to survivor) unless the employee specifically elects otherwise.

As individual equity, reserve-funded pension plans, both public and private pension plans are distinguishable in type from social insurance plans (social security, social welfare) by the absence of redistribution features and presumed or actual needs criteria, and by their use of reserve financing methods (at least their intention to do so) instead of a pay-as-you-go system.

Public and private pension plans generally share the philosophy that the postretirement benefit to a surviving spouse is to be paid as an actuarial equivalency of the employee benefit stated as a single life annuity. There are exceptions, however, particularly among public employee pension plans, usually in the direction of a more costly benefit.

Rights of a Spouse to Employee Pension Entitlements on Dissolution of Marriage

Due to growth in pension plan coverage and improvements in vesting provisions and benefits, pension accruals for many workers can represent substantial asset values. With increasing divorce rates, such accruals have become subject to greater attention from attorneys and courts regarding the question of spousal interests on the dissolution of marriage. A considerable body of law has developed in this area. In at least one state, it has been held to be malpractice of law if an attorney fails to secure a client's community-property interest in a pension plan.[6]

---

[6]*Smith* v. *Lewis*, 13 Cal. 3d 349, 530 P. 2d 589 (1975).

How spousal rights to pensions are treated depends on whether a particular state (*a*) embraces community-property rules for husband and wife; (*b*) subscribes to common-law rules modified by the adoption of the Universal Dissolution of Marriage Act; or (*c*) subscribes to the pure common-law concept of the property of husband and wife. The different treatment of spousal rights on the dissolution of marriage is briefly reviewed for each of these jurisdictional categories.

COMMUNITY-PROPERTY JURISDICTIONS

Community-property rules generally prevail in the Commonwealth of Puerto Rico and eight states: Arizona, California, Idaho, Louisiana, Nevada, New Mexico, Texas, and Washington. The community-property concept is basically derived from the Napoleonic civil code.[7] The basic tenets of community-property law appear in various statutory forms, but are similar to each other. An example is the Arizona Revised Statutes: "All property acquired by either husband or wife during the marriage, except that which is acquired by gift, devise or descent . . . is the community property of the husband and wife [Secs. 25–211 (A)]."

Since gifts are normally excluded from the definition of community property, there has been extensive litigation in community-property states on the question of whether pension benefits are gifts. The courts have consistently held that retirement contributions and/or benefits are a form of deferred compensation (Dutton, 1972, p. 334). Thus, there is no serious question that pensions or other retirement benefits can be community property.

A pension already being received has been clearly defined as property in community-property states.[8] The treatment of pension expectancies as property (i.e., anticipated but not-yet-vested pension rights), despite their contingency nature, has also emerged in recent years, based on the theory that the contingency can be fulfilled and that a property right that may be gained in the future may be divided upon dissolution of the community. Louisiana reached this conclusion in 1956, where a husband's certificate under a group retirement annuity was held to be community property, divisible upon dissolution, "irrespective of its value or its lack of value . . . at the time of the dissolution."[9] California was the last of the community-

---

[7]See La. Civ. Code Art. 2402.

[8]See, e.g., *Berg* v. *Berg*, 115 S. W. 2d 1171 (Texas Civ. App., 1938).

[9]*Messersmith* v. *Messersmith*, 299 La. 495, 86 S. 2d 169 174–175 (1956).

property states in which courts recognized as community property non-vested pension rights acquired during the period of marriage.[10]

The nature of community ownership of property is that it is held as an undivided interest (i.e., each spouse has an equal interest in the whole). On dissolution of marriage, courts are not obliged to divide each identifiable piece of property in two equal parts. An important result flows from this concept: To achieve the equal division of the whole of community property, a court may award the entire amount of pension property to one spouse while providing an offsetting award to the other spouse.[11]

However, the courts are not reluctant to divide pension wealth. Where a portion of pension credits has been earned prior to the establishment of the community (i.e., prior to marriage), those benefits deemed community property will usually be apportioned according to ratios of dollars or time periods, reflecting the benefit portions earned or accumulated during the period of marriage. Under *defined-contribution plans* (plans in which the monthly contribution rate is fixed as a percentage of salary and benefits to be received by employees after retirement depend upon the accumulated contributions and their earnings), ratios of dollars reflecting the contributions and investment earnings prorated to the period of marriage are simple to calculate and relatively easy to administer. Under *defined-benefit plans* (plans in which the benefit is based on a formula incorporating a stated percentage of final salary and years of service), similar time ratios applied to the benefit formula can effect desired distributions of future annuity payments or death benefits.

The courts have had little difficulty in deciding that spendthrift or alienation clauses that protect pension rights from certain types of assignment do not apply to dispositions involving the joint owners of community property. Two rationales generally prevail. One is that the court divides and awards but does not assign.[12] The other is that the nonassignment provisions apply to creditors in civil actions but not to spouses in matrimonial actions.[13] Louisiana courts have specifically acknowledged that a vested interest in a pension plan that could not be discounted or assigned, nor converted into cash, was nonetheless community property.[14] The Texas courts have held that "the husband is divested

---

[10]*Marriage of Brown*, 15 Cal. 3d 838, 544 P. 2d 566 (1976).

[11]*Marriage of Brown*, cited above, and *Phillipson* v. *Board of Administration, Public Employees' Retirement System*, 3 Cal. 3d 32, 473 P. 2d 765 (1970).

[12]Cal. Civ. Code Sec. 4800.

[13]Adopted by many common-law jurisdictions in matrimonial actions for nonsupport. See, e.g., in New York, *Hodson* v. *New York City Employees' Retirement System*, 243 App. Div. 480 91st Dep't, 1935.

[14]*Lynch* v. *Lynch*, 293 S. 2d 598 (La. App., 1974).

of nothing by recognition of the wife's interest therein, and the 'spend-thrift clause' . . . does not affect her rights, which exist by operation of law, and which do not depend on any action by the employee–husband in contravention of that clause."[15]

Pension fund administrators have not reacted favorably to the additional obligations thrust upon them by payments to former spouses of participant–employees. In three recent California cases, the U.S. Supreme Court rejected the appeals of spokesmen for private pension funds, who had argued that under the antiassignment and alienation provisions of ERISA, pension benefits should go only to an employee and to employee-designated beneficiaries, if any, and not to an employee's former spouse, under state community-property laws. The administrator of the Carpenters Pension Trust Fund for Northern California, recently quoted in *Pensions and Investments*, observed that the decision meant that pension funds not only faced the administrative difficulties of dividing up pension benefits, possibly among several people, but must also pay extra administrative and mailing costs for doing so. According to the article, other administrators were worried that workers who remarried several times could eventually get next to nothing in pension benefits because of multiple payouts of a single benefit (Feb. 4, 1980, p. 19).

A recent California case may serve to illustrate several of the questions that relate to employee and spouse pension entitlements in community-property jurisdictions. In *Phillipson* v. *Board of Administration, Public Employees' Retirement System*, the plaintiff was the divorced wife of a member of the California Public Employees' Retirement System (CPERS).[16] Upon divorce, the plaintiff had been awarded all of the benefits due the employee–participant under the CPERS. When the husband applied for benefits under the terms of the plan, the plaintiff sued the CPERS to enjoin the fund from paying benefits to the husband. Noting its authority to award any asset in community property partially or fully to one spouse in the distribution of an undivided ownership of the whole community property, the California Supreme Court ruled that pension rights accruing from employees' services constituted community property, that such property included pension rights under public plans as well as private pension plans, and that the plaintiff's claim was not as a creditor but as an owner.

A number of further points emerged from this decision. It was held that the court had the power to select the retirement-income option (in order to establish a survivor benefit contingent on the life of the nonemployee

---

[15]*Angott* v. *Angott*, 462 S. W. 2d 74 (Texas Civ. App., 1970).

[16]3 Cal. 3d 32, 473 P. 2d 765 (1970).

spouse), arguing that to leave the right to the spouse whose interest had been terminated could adversely affect the spouse to whom the benefit had been awarded. The court expressed concern that the employee was still empowered to delay the retirement decision, and thus the commencement date of the benefits. The court also held that an award of the entire pension to the nonemployee spouse, where warranted, did not undermine the objective of the public pension system, as claimed by the CPERS, including the objective to induce persons to enter public service and to provide for retired employees and their dependents. Another important point covered by *Phillipson* was the rejection by the court that the pension award to the employee's spouse would be destructive to the actuarial value of the benefit. The court noted that the spouse was to receive exactly and only what the employee would have received.

A later California case emphasized the point that pension benefit awards to a nonemployee spouse do not otherwise effect an alteration of the provisions of pension plans.[17] In *Bensing* v. *Bensing*, the husband had a vested pension that would begin upon retirement, contingent upon his survival to the commencement of retirement. The trial court awarded a portion of the pension to the wife. The Court of Appeals held that the wife would receive her share if and when the husband began receiving the pension. If she predeceased the husband, her portion would revert to him. If he predeceased her, her rights would expire at his death. In this case, the pension fund provided that no payment could be made from the fund prior to an employee's retirement, and it was noted by the court that it did not have the power to order an employee to retire.

STATES UNDER THE UNIFORM
DISSOLUTION OF MARRIAGE ACT

Seven states have adopted the Uniform Dissolution of Marriage Act or similar legislation: Colorado, Illinois, Kentucky, Maine, Missouri, New Jersey, and Oklahoma. This legislation normally has the effect of putting community-property rules into operation when a dissolution of marriage action is filed, even though traditional common-law property concepts otherwise stand. Typical of the statutory language is that of Colorado:

> In a proceeding for dissolution of marriage or for legal separation . . . the court shall set apart to each spouse his property and shall divide the marital property in such proportions as the court deems just.

[17]*Bensing* v. *Bensing*, 25 Cal. App. 3d 889 (1972).

> For purposes of this article only, "marital property" means all property acquired by either spouse subsequent to the marriage [with certain exceptions] . . . [18]

In these states, however, the precise definition of property and whether it is inclusive of pension expectancies or deferred benefits may differ somewhat in different jurisdictions. Consequently, judicial results may not be the same as in community-property states. For example, in New Jersey the courts in the case of *Mueller* v. *Mueller*[19] explored the question, "Is a fully vested pension plan, the proceeds of which are not available to the employee until some future date, subject to equitable distribution [as a marital asset]?" In this case, the employee was age 48, had been employed for approximately 22 years, and was a fully vested participant in a noncontributory pension plan which he could not draw upon until age 65, unless he elected early retirement at 55 or thereafter. Interpreting the applicable statute,[20] the court concluded that for an asset to be subject to equitable distribution in the event of divorce it must be "property . . . which was legally and beneficially acquired by them or either of them during the marriage." In defining "legally and beneficially acquired," the court concluded that it meant that there must be a "right of present enjoyment . . . ." In prior New Jersey cases, the court noted, where pension plan assets were subject to equitable distribution, the husband had the right to the pension money at the time. No future attained age or other condition needed to be met (i.e., the husband had the present control over the funds, since he could either withdraw them or they were being paid as a pension). In the *Mueller* case, the court decided that, though benefits were fully vested, Mueller during his marriage had no power to control, use, or enjoy the asset, and that it was not therefore beneficially available to him. The court concluded: "If the asset is not beneficially acquired in the sense that there is a right of present enjoyment it is not an asset subject to equitable distribution in matrimonial litigation."[21]

The New Jersey case illustrates the exceptions and qualifications that may be applied to the definition of marital property and shows the exceptions that may be made to the definition of what will be property upon dissolution of marriage.[22] Here the result is the opposite of California cases, in which it is clear that nonvested-pension-benefit expecta-

[18]Colorado Revised Statutes, 14-10-113.

[19]166 N.J. Sup., 557, 400 A. 2d 136 (Sup. Ct. Chan. Div. 1979).

[20]N.J. Statutes Annotated 2A:34-23.

[21]*Mueller* v. *Mueller*, 400 A. 2d 138.

[22]For a more complete discussion of this and other cases, see Harris (1979).

tions, as well as vested benefits not yet being received as income, constitute divisible community property.

PURE COMMON-LAW JURISDICTIONS

The pure common-law system prevails in thirteen jurisdictions: Alabama, Florida, Georgia, Maryland, Mississippi, New York, Pennsylvania, Rhode Island, South Carolina, Tennessee, Virginia, West Virginia, and the Virgin Islands (Freed and Foster, 1977–1978, pp. 306–308). In the pure common-law approach, separate property remains such on marriage dissolution and only jointly held property will be divided and distributed (Foster and Freed, 1976–1977, p. 57).

In New York, for example, pension benefits or expectations would normally be classified as separate property and therefore not subject to distribution on divorce. However, this does not mean that pension benefits are not reachable by a former wife in attachment or garnishment proceedings as a resource to be considered in settling alimony or child-support payments (Foster and Freed, 1977–1978, p. 206).

Generally, in common-law jurisdictions, as in others, pension benefits are subject to levy and attachment to enforce alimony and comparable support obligations notwithstanding language in pension plan documents or in state statutes restricting assignment or alienation, or the antiassignment provisions in ERISA.[23] In New York, the governing Domestic Relations Statute for transfers of funds under garnishment proceedings arising out of divorce specifically refers to the obligations of pension funds:

> When a person is ordered by a court of record to pay for the support of his children under the age of twenty-one, and/or spouse, and/or former spouse, the court, at the time an order of support is made or any other time thereafter, upon a showing of good cause, shall order his employer, former employer, the auditor, comptroller, or disbursing officer of any pension fund ... to deduct from all monies due or payable to such person, the entitlement to which is based upon remuneration for employment, past or present, such amounts as the court may find it to be necessary to comply with its order.[24]

OTHER JURISDICTIONS

In 23 states it is not clear what basic tenets apply to the division of property on the dissolution of marriage. In many of these jurisdictions, the

[23]*National Bank of North America* v. *Local 553 Pension Fund of the International Brotherhood of Teamsters and Chauffeurs*, 463 F. Supp. 636 (Ed. N.Y. 1978).

[24]New York Personal Property Law 49-6.

courts are empowered to make an "equitable," "just," or "reasonable" distribution of spouse property, but apparently these courts have been uniformly reluctant to grapple with the complexities of dividing pension rights. The distinction between separate and joint property has been diminished in many of these states and it appears that there is a trend toward the removal of legislative barriers to the recognition of spousal claims to an interest in pension benefits. Efforts to achieve legislative recognition of marriage as an "economic partnership" may be expected to continue, with accompanying statutory language designed to provide for the equitable division of property upon divorce, regardless of which spouse holds title.

VARIETY IN DISPOSITION OF PENSION RIGHTS AT DIVORCE

Pension plan growth and rapidly changing patterns of marriage and family life have extended state judicial actions deeply into the complex area of the disposition of pension entitlements on dissolution of marriage. While several principal jurisdictional approaches can be identified, even within such jurisdictions there are numerous state-by-state variations. Certainly there is no nationwide uniformity in the treatment of pension assets on divorce, which is handled mainly through interpretation of state family-relations and divorce laws. As a result, much of the existing law is case law, and is still evolving. Considerable research remains to be done in order to provide full understanding of the pension rights of spouses of pension plan participants as determined by state courts.

An important public policy question has to do with the role that the pension plans themselves might play in the future with regard to spouse rights on dissolution of marriage. At present, provision for spouse benefits is generally limited to provisions for them as beneficiaries of pre- and postretirement benefits for survivors.

The Future of Spouse Benefits under Occupational Pension Plans

In considering the future of spouse benefits under occupational pension plans, it should be emphasized that the plans have generally developed as individual equity plans under which benefits are regarded as a form of deferred compensation. Thus, public and private pension plans have incorporated two important policy elements: (a) equal pay for equal work regardless of marital status (i.e., benefits the same for equally situated workers); and (b) survivor income options offered as actuarial equivalents of the benefits payable to the employee. Typically, there are no specific provisions in occupational pension plans regarding spouse rights on dissolution of marriage.

If occupational pension plans are to play a greater role than at present in providing for pre- and postretirement benefits for spouses (and perhaps for other dependents as well), a number of policy questions arise:

1. What new benefit objectives should be established?
2. Are there variations in industry practices, employee interests, union objectives, or employer financial resources that should be taken into account?
3. How would the current financial status of the pension plans be affected?
4. How would proposed changes in benefit provisions be related to existing provisions and coverages under group life insurance programs, disability insurance, medical benefits, and the benefits of the social security program?

With respect to setting new objectives, there are numerous options. For example, should there be split ownership for each accrued unit of pension benefit (defined-benefit plans) or in the annuity accumulation (defined-contribution plans)? Should split ownership in pension plans extend to stock option, thrift, bonus, or profit-sharing plans? If there is to be divided ownership of pension plan accruals, what should be the criteria for benefit adequacy for an employee who arrives at retirement, married or unmarried, after two or three divorces? For working couples, should there be arrangements for automatic pension credit sharing (reciprocity) for the exchange of shares of pension benefit between spouses? Should levels of pension benefits be raised for married employees who have lost benefits because they shared pension credits with one or more former spouses (and without reciprocity)? These and other possible questions suggest that there are important basic issues of compensation policy and individual equity involved in the consideration of benefits for spouses under occupational pension plans.

Because benefits for spouses under pension plans constitute just one type of possible improvement, they must be considered in the light of other plan priorities. These may differ among industries, according to the ratio of active to retired employees, according to current union objectives, or for other reasons. Proposed benefits for spouses must necessarily be measured against other desirable changes, including shorter periods of vesting delay, increased benefits, cost-of-living increases for retired employees, and so on.

Nor can present and future financial requirements for the funding of proposed spouse benefits be ignored. The financial condition of a plan will play a vital role in determining the practicality of assuming added costs. A related and equally important factor will be the profitability and future earnings prospects of the industry and the firm.

Proposed changes in pension plans should also take into account possible effects on other benefit plans. Under group life insurance plans there may be a question of adding life insurance coverage for spouses of workers. Dependent coverage under health insurance plans is normally available, but under neither group life nor health insurance coverage is provision made for coverage of divorced spouses. Such provisions might be desirable, especially if the pension plan is amended to provide for former spouses. Pension plans may be integrated with the retirement and survivor benefits under the social security program. (The main purpose of social security integration is to provide benefit replacement ratios that are relatively uniform for all wage and salary levels, given the weighting of social security benefits in favor of lower-paid workers.) Any substantial changes in the social security program, such as earnings sharing, would occasion a review of related provisions of integrated occupational pension plans.

A possible framework for the consideration of further study of recommendations for improved protection of spouses of participants in occupational pension plans is suggested in Table 8.2. Since the status of the employee (salary, service, etc.) under an employer-sponsored pension plan normally determines the treatment of the employee and, directly or indirectly, the treatment of employee dependents, the framework divides the employee's career into various pension-related segments. Prior to retirement, the employee's relation to the pension plan may be defined as progressing through six stages. For postretirement status, the framework expresses the situation of a retired employee and spouse (if any) in terms of the life contingencies involved in benefit payment status.

Column (2) of Table 8.2 shows the current minimum ERISA requirements for death (survivor) benefits for noncontributory plans. A separate column (3) describes the minimum ERISA requirement for contributory plans, under which an employee's right to benefits attributable to his own contributions may not be forfeited on either termination or death, whether or not benefits have been vested.

Higher protection levels than the ERISA minimums may be designed. Space is provided under column (4) for entry of designed improvements on ERISA minimums. An example of the type of benefit that might be substituted for the minimum is that provided under the immediately

Table 8.2
**Framework for Consideration of Spouse Benefits under Occupational
Pension Plans**

(1) Employee Status	Minimum ERISA Requirements for Death (Survivor) Benefit		(4) Improved Survivor Benefits (As Designed)
	(2) Noncontributory Plans	(3) Contributory Plans	
Preretirement			
Employee not eligible for pension plan participation	NA	NA	?
Employee not participating in pension plan	NA	NA	
Employee participating in pension plan but not vested	None	Return of employee contributions	

Employee fully vested but
  not eligible for early or
  normal retirement
	None[a]	Return of
		employee
		contributions[a]	

Employee eligible for early retirement	J&S	J&S	
Employee eligible for normal retirement	J&S	J&S	
Postretirement			
Retired employee living; spouse (if any) living	J&S	J&S	
Retired employee living; spouse (if any) deceased	J&S	J&S	
Retired employee deceased; spouse (if any) living	J&S	J&S	

Notes: NA = not applicable; J&S = automatic joint and survivor annuity unless specifically rejected by employee.
[a]Differs from treatment of terminating employees.

vested TIAA–CREF (Teachers Insurance and Annuity Association–College Retirement Equities Fund) system, under which the survivor benefit at any time prior to retirement is the full annuity accumulation derived from all employer and employee contributions and credited investment earnings; the named beneficiary (normally a spouse) may receive either a lump-sum benefit consisting of the entire accumulation or, alternatively, the actuarial equivalent of a life income. Possible entries in this framework include the splitting of pension credits, provisions for spouses on dissolution of marriage, and increased benefit levels for employees whose shared benefits have become payable to former spouses.

Summary

Occupational pension plans (public and private) share underlying concepts that reflect a century of historical development: pensions as deferred wages, related in amount to employee service and wages and based on reserve funding. These "individual equity" principles differ from the "social adequacy" approach of social security pay-as-you-go transfers of tax revenue. At present, occupational pension benefits for spouses of employees reflect plan concepts by taking the form of pre- and post-retirement survivor benefits based on actuarially equivalent values of the pensions payable to employees. In recent years, pension growth and increased divorce rates have escalated questions of spousal entitlement to employee pension rights on dissolution of marriage; a large body of growing and disuniform case law is the result. Currently, few if any pension plans incorporate provisions relating to spousal rights on dissolution of marriage. A framework is suggested for the consideration of future possibilities for spouse benefits under occupational pension plans, including reference to related policy issues.

ACKNOWLEDGMENT

Mark Feldman, associate general counsel, TIAA–CREF, assisted in the preparation of this paper.

Discussion

JAMES C. HICKMAN

Dr. King has gone far beyond the rather limited scope indicated by the title of his paper. The evolution of the philosophy of private pensions, the history of pension regulation, and an outline for considering the design of pension plan benefits are covered. All of this is in addition to a detailed study of spouse benefits.

In this discussion I will relate some of the demographic and economic trends that are evident in the United States to the spouse-benefit issues raised by Dr. King. The trends that we will examine are (a) price inflation; (b) increased labor force participation by married women; (c) increased rate of divorce; and (d) increasing life expectancy.

Of these trends the most pervasive in its impact on spouse benefits under occupational pension plans is price inflation. The word pervasive is used because inflation threatens the adequacy of all spouse benefits paid under all occupational pension plans. The other trends may require adaptations, but they do not threaten the attainment of the basic goal of providing, in connection with social security and individual saving, adequate retirement and survivor's income.

For example, couples whose retirement income is protected from an unexpectedly long or short lifetime by a joint-and-survivor life annuity find themselves unprotected against inflation. Individuals or couples anticipating retirement income based on vested pension benefits are subject to an even greater threat. Their real retirement income is exposed to erosion before they reach retirement age as well as during retirement. Proceeds paid to a survivor under a group life contract decrease in real value in a similar fashion.

Table 8.3 illustrates the decline in the real value of retirement benefits at various annual price inflation rates. For example, suppose at age 40 a retirement income of $1000 per year, to commence at age 65, becomes vested. If price inflation is at an annual rate of 10%, the annual retirement income commencing at age 65 will have a value of $92.30 in terms of age 40 dollars.

Increased labor force participation by married women creates problems in the design of employee benefits plans. The problems arise because public and private occupational pensions seem to have been established on the implicit assumptions that employees were male breadwinners whose spouses were fully devoted to caring for the home, that the nonemployee spouse was a true dependent, and that couples stayed married for life. When these assumptions are not realized, and to an ever increasing extent they are not, fundamental problems involving the design of all components of employee benefits are created. Family health insurance plans, for example, need to be redesigned to prevent duplicate coverage and, at the same time, avoid gaps for real dependents, such as children. And salary-replacement goals of some private pensions may have to be adjusted to reflect the increasing likelihood that an average employee will need enough retirement income to support only one rather than two persons.

Another adaptation to labor force participation by married women may be the reduction in the required proportion of workers participating in an employer-sponsored group health insurance plan before coverage be-

Table 8.3
Value at Retirement at Age 65 of One Dollar of Vested Benefits at Indicated Age

	Annual Price Inflation Rate				
Age of Vesting	4%	6%	8%	10%	12%
40	.3751	.2330	.1460	.0923	.0588
45	.4564	.3118	.2145	.1486	.1037
50	.5553	.4173	.3152	.2394	.1829
55	.6757	.5584	.4632	.3855	.3220
60	.8219	.7473	.6806	.6209	.5674

Source: Compiled by author.

comes effective by some insurance organizations. This may be necessary because many married women already have health insurance coverage.

The increased rate of divorce has the potential of reordering the risks faced by families and individuals. For example, the attainment of long-term individual and family goals that require income may be more imperiled by divorce than by premature death or unexpected long life. The income stream needed to support children is subject to a greater threat from dissolution of marriage than from the disability or death of the breadwinner.

Dr. King has provided a superb summary of the legal status of pension expectations in the division of property on divorce. It would be useful to augment his summary with some questions and comments on practical problems in evaluating and dividing pension expectations.

For example, what benefits are being evaluated? The amount of vested retirement benefit (the retirement income benefit that cannot be forfeited because of leaving employment before retirement) may be determined at any time. However, there is also the concept of the "accumulated benefit," which in general is equal to or greater than the vested benefit. As defined by the Financial Accounting Standard Board (FASB) in Statement No. 35, accumulated plan benefits are those future benefit payments that are attributable under the pension plan's provisions to employees' service rendered to the benefit information date (FASB, 1980). Their measurement is primarily based on employees' history of pay and service and other appropriate factors as of that date. Future salary changes are not considered. Future years of service are considered only in determining employees' expected eligibility for particular types of benefits, for example, early retirement, death, and disability benefits. To measure their actuarial present value, assumptions are used to adjust those accumulated plan benefits to reflect the time value of money and the probability of payments by means of decrements for death, disability, withdrawal, or retirement between the benefit information date and the expected date of payment.

This lengthy definition of FASB is designed for use in financial reporting for pension plans instead of for use in court-supervised divisions of pension expectations. It is introduced to illustrate some of the elements that must be considered in estimating the value of benefit accumulations of pensions to a certain date. There are plausible lines of reasoning which could lead a court to change many of the elements of the FASB definition. Of course, in the case of defined-contribution plans, the allocation of expected future benefits to particular years of service is not so perplexing.

The key point is that if pension expectations are to be divided by courts in the absence of statutory or plan provisions, we can anticipate increased litigation expense and wide variation in the resulting divisions. In the interest of efficiency, it would seem that a consistent set of principles should be developed to enable the division to be made more automatically. Pressure for a system of earnings sharing in the determination of social security benefits will be accompanied by a drive for a formal system of splitting the allocation of contributions in defined-contribution plans and of accrued benefits in defined-benefit plans.

Much of the discussion has centered on the developing concept that occupational pension entitlements are a property right that may be divided at divorce. It is instructive to recall that the U.S. Supreme Court has been very clear that this concept shall not be applied to social security benefits. The Supreme Court in *Flemming* v. *Nestor* states: "To engraft upon the Social Security System a concept of 'accrued property right' would deprive it of the flexibility and boldness in adjustment to ever-changing conditions which it demands. . . . It was doubtless out of an awareness of the need for such flexibility that Congress included in the original Act and has since retained a clause expressly reserving to it the right to alter amend or repeal any provision of the Act. That provision makes explicit what is implicit in the institutional needs of the program."[1]

The final reality we will discuss is increasing life expectancies. Throughout the history of the United States, mortality rates have shown a somewhat unsteady but persistent tendency to decline. Table 8.4 illustrates the recent history of mortality change as measured by life expectancies. From about 1955 until 1970 female mortality rates continued their long-term decline, but male mortality rates exhibited no significant trend, until, in the most recent decade, cardiovascular disease and

Table 8.4
Life Expectancy in the United States, 1940–1978

Year	At Birth			At Age 65		
	Female	Male	Difference	Female	Male	Difference
1940	65.9	61.6	4.3	13.6	12.1	1.5
1950	71.0	65.5	5.5	15.0	12.7	2.3
1960	73.2	66.8	6.4	15.8	13.0	2.8
1970	74.6	67.0	7.6	16.8	13.0	3.8
1978	77.3	69.6	7.7	18.3	14.1	4.2

Source: National Center for Health Statistics.

[1](U.S. Supreme Court, June 20, 1960) 363US603.

accidents have taken a significantly lower toll. During most of this century the spread between male and female mortality rates has widened.

The primary implication of these trends for spouse benefits is that death during working lifetime is a small and decreasing threat to the fulfillment of family plans.

Pension plans are not the only medium for providing death benefits to surviving spouses. Workers' Compensation and group life insurance are important systems for providing survivor benefits. In these systems it is common for death benefits to be a function of annual pay, thus providing an automatic response to inflation-induced wage changes at a level percentage of payroll. Group term life insurance is almost the only feasible method of providing immediate income to young widows under an employee benefit plan.

Longevity improvement has the unfortunate effect of lengthening the average time a retired person is exposed to the risk of inflation. Thus the declining mortality rate can exacerbate the erosion of retirement income by inflation.

In summary:

1. Inflation is the greatest current threat to adequate spouse benefits under employee benefit plans.
2. Increased labor force participation by women will eventually force a redesign of all employee benefits to eliminate duplication and bridge gaps.
3. Increased rate of family dissolution will hasten the time when a formal system will be used to split accrued pension benefits between former marriage partners.
4. Increased life expectancies, though they make group life insurance cheaper, exacerbate inflation-induced problems by increasing the length of exposure.

9

The Housewife and Social Security Reform: A Feminist Perspective

BARBARA R. BERGMANN

If we were to ponder the list of major complaints which are currently being voiced concerning the present set-up of the social security system— the "inequity" in benefits between one- and two-earner couples, the treatment of the divorced spouse, the "wasted" social security taxes of the working wife—we would find that virtually all of them, in one way or another, involve the housewife. It is the system's method of provision for the housewife—in some instances its lack of provision—that is at the heart of almost all of the complaints.

Paradoxically, it is the *decreasing* number of full-time housewives that has pushed the problem of their treatment under social security onto center stage. As long as most adult men were husbands and most adult women were housewives, the system's provision for a wife through a benefit which was supplementary to her husband's benefit seemed straight-forward to most people. The spouse benefit, which gave a married male retiree 50% more than an unmarried male retiree with the same earnings record, was advantageous to the vast majority of men and the vast majority of women. True, the system's treatment of the working wife was no less anomalous and the system's treatment of the divorced wife was only slightly more shabby than it is today. But working wives and divorced wives were less numerous, and there was little public concern about their problems.

Along with the rise in the labor force participation of married women, the fall in the marriage rate, and the increase in the divorce rate, has come a trend of feminist thinking concerned with the economic, social, and psychological relations between men and women and with the institutions through which those relations are policed and expressed. Feminists now seek redress for what they perceive as previous neglect of women's satisfaction and well-being. They ask that women's interests be more faithfully represented in discussions of issues and that institutional structures be revamped to serve those interests. Whether this wave of feminist thought has been an important part of the cause of these social trends or is in reality more of an effect is something we need not debate here. What needs to be understood, however, is that feminist ideas have a considerable contribution to make to the discussion of issues like social security reform, and in fact are indispensable to a cogent discussion of any set of issues in which gender roles figure prominently. Of course, feminist thought has done more than provide an intellectual framework for the discussion of reform. It has been a source of political action to get the issue of reform onto the national agenda and will be needed to mobilize enough political power to enact reforms.

The role of and treatment of the housewife, which is really the major bone of contention in social security reform, has, of course, a major place in femininst thought. Betty Friedan's book, *The Feminine Mystique* (1963), which was influential in initiating the current wave of feminism in the United States, centered on the disadvantages to women of assuming the housewife's role. All feminists believe that women should not be forced into assuming it, and that alternative choices should be available. Many feminists, such as the present writer, go further and believe that the disadvantages of the role of housewife are so great that it would be better if younger women were to avoid entering the role even temporarily and if the "option" to assume the role were to disappear.

There is a second strand of feminist thought concerning housewives, which derives from the solidarity which feminists feel with all women, housewives included.[1] This solidarity expresses itself in a concern to alleviate injuries (physical and psychological as well as financial) inflicted on housewives by their husbands and by the institutions of society. This second strand is not logically contradictory to the first; it is possible to love the sinner (the housewife herself) while hating the sin (playing the

---

[1] See Lopate (1974), for example, who argues for cash payments to housewives. See also Bergmann (1981).

role). Nevertheless, the two strands do tend to cut different ways in terms of policy. Moreover, individual feminist thinkers differ in the emphasis they place on each.

These two strands of feminist thought inspire two kinds of complaints against the social security system—that some housewives are treated too well and that some housewives are treated not well enough. The housewives who are treated too well are those married to retired men, who are enabled by the system to live at a higher standard than retired working wives whose family had comparable total covered earnings. The housewives who are treated not well enough are those whose dignity is scanted by treatment as a dependent, or those whose marriages end, and whose husbands retain all rights to social security (and private pensions) earned during the marriage.

The solidarity-with-housewives strand of feminist thought results in attitudes which emphasize the housewife's productiveness and give dignity to the position of housewife. It results in policy suggestions which would have the effect of making the woman who becomes and remains a housewife safer, more comfortable, less subject to financial shipwreck, more able to hold up her head as a productive member of society. The most characteristic product of this line of thought is the suggestion that housewives be awarded social security credits for the homemaking work they do. Some credit schemes would require the household to pay taxes in return for the credit; others would not. One merit of homemaker credits in the eyes of the solidarity-with-housewives advocates is that it makes housework and "paid work" more alike, thereby raising the status of housework psychologically and financially. A second merit, of course, is that in the case of divorce the homemaker would keep her credits, and thus would be more financially independent than is the case now.

Earnings sharing, whereby social security credits for paid work are shared between spouses, would also give housewives earnings credits under their own names. In the event of divorce there would be no cases in which the housewife would lose all social security protection, as can happen under present arrangements. While earnings sharing is probably much easier to implement than homemaker credits, it does not go as far in protecting and dignifying housewives. Most earnings-sharing schemes call for sharing 100% of the earnings credit, and no more. For one-earner couples who retire still married, sharing 100% rather than 150% of earnings credit would result in lower pensions than the present spouse benefit or the proposed homemaker credit would provide.

One may also view the two-tiered system (or the double-decker system), in which entitlement is given to all persons of a certain age, regardless of work history, as a protective measure for the housewife and as a potential substitute for the 50% spouse benefit. Homemaker credits are based on the idea that housework should be counted as paid work in figuring pensions. Earnings sharing is based on the idea that housework earns one the right to share the pension entitlement due to the paid work of one's spouse. On the other hand, the two-tiered and double-decker schemes are based on the idea that a pension should be given to all people who reach a certain age, regardless of work history. These two schemes are not based on a concept of the value of housework; rather they are based on the assumption that work history should be less important in determining a person's pension than it now is. This attitude increases the housewife's dignity as a person, if not as a worker. The two-tiered system can also be thought of as bringing the position of the husband closer to the present position of the housewife, instead of moving the position of the housewife towards that of the husband by giving her work a market value, which is the case with homemaker credits.

The role-avoidance strand of feminist thought on the housewife suggests that the concerns of the working wife should get priority over those of the housewife because the wife with a job outside the home works harder than the housewife. The housewife and her family should not get higher benefits than two-earner families who have contributed the same amount to the social security system. This line of thought leads to an advocacy of the abandonment of the 50% spouse benefit. The role-avoidance theme is probably inconsistent with the proposal for untaxed homemaker credits, but not necessarily with any of the other forms of reform that have been mentioned. The role-avoidance strand of thought suggests that it may be detrimental to the long-run interests of women to make the housewife's position a great deal safer and more comfortable then it is now. However, none of the proposals for earnings sharing or a two-tier system would accomplish this in any significant degree and thus do not provoke feminist opposition.

Most informed feminists would probably choose one or another of these two programs of social security reform:

1. The sharing between spouses of earnings credits plus the elimination of the 50% spouse benefit
2. The same as 1 *plus* the provision of a substantial tier or deck of benefits unrelated to work history with concomitant scaling back of benefit dollars awarded per dollar of earnings credit

The first program is more "antihousewife" than the second. While it would insure that housewives get a share of benefits earned by their spouses, it would mean that there would be less to share. The second plan makes the pension less dependent on work history, and so favors those with little or no work history—the housewife, par excellence.

Feminist thought on the housewife is not only a useful guide in organizing our thoughts about social security reform, it is indispensable if certain mistakes are to be avoided. The history of thought on social policy demonstrates that women and their concerns have tended to slip out of sight, even in cases where gender roles are central to the policy being debated. Where the women involved are housewives, the tendency to ignore them is apparently almost irresistible. An egregious example occurred in the debate on welfare reform. When social scientists approached this issue, they apparently forgot that most of the adult clients of the present system are women who stay home with their children— housewives or housewives manqué. This forgetfulness resulted in the concentration of research and thought on the issue of work incentives, with little attention to child-care issues. It also resulted in proposals to expand the number of clients to include anyone of low income, with little attention paid to ways of getting adequate resources to the existing clients of the program. Some of the leading thinkers on welfare reform have recently become interested in social security reform, and once again the problematic issues connected with the housewife are being ignored. This tendency is quite evident in the issues chosen by Lampman and Mac-Donald to be featured in their paper (Chapter 2 in this volume).

Instead of keeping up with feminist thought, social scientists have been busy learning the antifeminist "new home economics," which is for the most part a fatally oversimplified theory of the traditional form of family life. It is the passing away of this traditional form which is occasioning the need for the very reforms we are studying. A familiarity with feminist thought and attitudes is necessary at a minimum as a corrective to ingrained and unexamined sexist attitudes concerning issues which have gender roles at their core, as social security reform does. This does not mean that only women or only feminists are fit to deal with these issues. It does mean, however, that social scientists of both genders and all persuasions need to understand what the feminists are saying.

10

Incremental Change in Social Security Needed to Result in Equal and Fair Treatment of Men and Women

ROBERT J. MYERS

In continuing contemporary discussion of the treatment of men and women in various aspects of our social and economic life, one of the major topics is social security. This paper will examine that subject in depth: its basic nature, past developments, and various proposals.

Nature of OASDI and Medicare

To judge whether or not the social security program provides equal treatment by sex, one must first understand the basic nature of the current program: Old-Age, Survivors, and Disability Insurance and *Medicare*. OASDI and the hospital-insurance portion of Medicare (HI) are social insurance programs, whereas the supplementary medical insurance portion of Medicare is subsidized voluntary insurance (and as such will not be considered further in this paper).

A social insurance program generally is a mix of individual equity and social adequacy, with more emphasis on the latter. Specifically, "individual equity" means that each participant receives protection actuarially equivalent to the contributions or premiums paid on his or her behalf. This does not necessarily involve, in all cases, an exact return of contributions, plus interest. On the other hand, "social adequacy" means that benefits are paid to meet presumptive needs, regardless of length and amount of contribution payments.

Frequently, individuals say that OASDI and HI are improperly structured, because they contain a mix of what they refer to as "insurance" and "welfare." By these phrases, they mean individual equity and social adequacy, although frequently they misuse "insurance" to mean a money-back plan. (Perhaps this view is prevalent among those in the academic community because of their familiarity with TIAA–CREF, which is a defined-contribution plan, a form not widely used throughout the private pension field.) They advocate splitting out the individual-equity and social-adequacy aspects, apparently for purposes of neatness, consistency, and public understanding. Yet most long-time students of social insurance believe that the best results can come from the skillful blending of these two elements into one system.

From the start of social security in 1935, different views have been expressed publicly on how to balance individual equity against social adequacy. Over the years, a gradual trend has occurred toward greater social adequacy and less individual equity. At times, however, this trend has been reversed, such as by the introduction of the delayed-retirement credit in 1972. Nonetheless, there are often general public pressures for instilling more individual equity, such as proposals to eliminate the retirement test and to eliminate the spouse benefit.

I believe that social security has the major role of providing a broad system of social benefits protecting against the long-term risks associated with old-age retirement, disability, and death of insured workers. Such benefits should provide a floor of economic security, with considerable emphasis on social adequacy. As such, the program will effect significant income redistribution (as does any insurance system, to a greater or lesser extent), but it should not be considered that this is its primary purpose—as some assert.

Accordingly, I believe that too much emphasis should not be laid on individual-equity considerations—i.e., on whether people exactly get "their money's worth." I am satisfied that there must be some consideration of individual equity. I believe that, as long as there is not too great a discrepancy between the amount an employee participant pays and the value of the protection furnished, the program is properly balanced.

History of Equal Treatment of Men and Women under Social Security

There have, in the past, been a number of instances where different (unequal) treatment by sex was introduced by OASDI. Interestingly, the original 1935 act had completely equal treatment by sex, essentially because benefits were provided only for retired workers.

Beginning with the 1939 act, which introduced auxiliary and survivor benefits, the sexes were treated differently. Husbands and widowers were protected on the basis of the wife's earnings record *only* if dependency could be proved. Also, benefits to children were payable on behalf of women workers under much more restrictive conditions than were applied to male workers. Further, for a time, women had a lower minimum retirement age for reduced benefits and, for a much longer period, had more favorable conditions as to insured status and computation of retirement benefit amounts (because these were calculated for a shorter period of time—namely, the number of years after 1950, or age 21 if later, and up to age 62 rather than 65 as for men, although for both sexes earnings credits after age 61 could be utilized).

Over the years, owing to both legislative changes and court decisions, virtual equality of treatment of the sexes has now been achieved. The only exceptions are for relatively minor matters—such as that widows can waive payment of federal benefits based on military service before 1957 (so as to count such service under OASDI), but widowers cannot do so. Incidentally, the House version of the 1977 act provided complete equality of the sexes in all respects. However, this provision was dropped in conference, and instead a study by the Department of Health, Education, and Welfare was requested, which resulted in the report *Social Security and the Changing Roles of Men and Women* (1979a).[1]

Criticism of Present Treatment of Men and Women

A number of critics assert that the social security system unfairly discriminates against women. The very foundation for their belief is that the program was constructed almost half a century ago, at a time when the roles of men and women in our society were completely different from those that obtain at present. They seem to assume that no married women worked in the paid labor market in the mid-1930s whereas now (or certainly in the near future) the reverse is the case. This is not true, of course, although admittedly there has been a rapidly growing trend of employment of married women and of women reentering the paid labor force after their children have grown up or after widowhood. But this trend was anticipated by the original planners of the social security system, and the benefit structure was developed taking it into account.

Some people assert that, even though the benefit provisions might

[1]For more detail on how equality of treatment of the sexes has developed over the years, see Myers (1975).

apply equally in all respects between men and women, equal treatment is still not present because women have both lower wages and more breaks in service, as a result of unfair discrimination in the marketplace. The solution to this problem should not be sought from OASDI. Rather, the remedies should come through altering the underlying causes. (Moreover, this argument has no validity when HI is considered, because all insured persons receive exactly the same benefit protection.)

Other people are concerned about what they believe to be the unfair treatment of two-worker families compared to one-worker families under OASDI. Any such unfairness is equally present when the one-worker family consists of a male worker and spouse or when it consists of a female worker and spouse, so there is no question of unequal treatment by sex. In this discussion, "worker" is used to refer only to workers in paid employment in the labor market outside the home.

As to relative treatment of one-worker and two-worker families, consider what the problem is stated to be by those who believe there is one. Usually, very simplistic assumptions are made, such as that the husband and wife are the same age and both retire at age 65 and that the one-worker family and the two-worker family have the same total combined earnings, but in the two-earner family the earnings are split equally. The total of the two primary benefits for the latter family is generally smaller than the primary benefit plus the spouse benefit for the former family. For example, for the cohort of persons attaining age 62 or becoming disabled or dying before age 62 in 1980, Average Indexed Monthly Earnings (AIME) of $1000 produce a primary benefit of $432.60 in the early part of 1980, so that the combined primary and spouse benefit for both, retiring at age 65, is $648.90. In contrast, an AIME of $500 produces a primary benefit of $272.60, so that the total benefit for the two workers in a two-worker family is $545.20, or 16% less than the benefits for the one-worker family. Because both families paid the same amount of social security taxes, it is then argued that the two-worker family is treated unfairly.

The weaknesses of the argument are that it is based solely on the individual-equity principle and that the advantages accruing to the two-worker family are not considered. The argument for individual equity is faulty because in many other instances it can be shown that one person is not receiving as good an "actuarial" deal from OASDI as another. This is inevitable in a system that, desirably, is founded primarily on social-adequacy principles. If individual equity were the overriding aim of social security, there would be no need for a governmental program, because the private sector could just as readily handle it. Therefore, just because complete individual equity is not present in a particular situation is no reason why an injustice is present and why a change should be made.

Moreover, I would argue that, although the one-worker family and two-worker family have the same total income, from an economic standpoint they are not really in equivalent positions. The one-worker family actually has a higher real income, because of the greater time at home of the "nonworker" spouse and the resulting increased productivity for home-consumption items (and thus the lessened need for expenditures). As a result, in keeping with the principle that benefits should be somewhat greater as earned income increases, there is no reason to be disturbed about the one-worker family versus the two-worker family.

Still further, it could be argued that the two-worker family with each having equal earnings is unduly advantaged as compared with a one-person, one-worker family with the same total earnings. Although both families contribute the same, the total benefits for the former are $545.20, or 26% more than the benefit of $432.60 for the latter. Once again, this absence of individual equity is nothing to be disturbed about!

But is the two-worker family in any sense receiving less than its fair share? The two-worker family in fact receives more insurance protection for its "investment" than does the one-worker two-person family with an equal income. If one worker in such a family retires before the other, then benefits will be paid to that worker. On the other hand, in the one-worker family, no benefits are payable to the nonworker unless the worker retires. Also, child survivor benefits are payable in the event of the death of *either* spouse in a two-worker family, but only on the death of one spouse (the worker) in the one-worker family. Further, prior to retirement, both spouses in the two-worker family have disability insurance, whereas in the one-worker family only the working spouse does.

Finally, I think that an important social principle requires that a nonworking spouse who is taking care of the home and raising the children have an OASDI benefit. Then, if such a spouse also has a benefit based on earnings outside the home, it is only fair that the larger of the two available benefits should be paid—without consideration of the taxes that were or were not paid.

Proposed Solutions and Their Weaknesses

Several proposals have been made (U.S. Department of Health, Education, and Welfare, 1979a) to remedy what are believed to be either the unequal or inequitable treatment of women under OASDI. Little discussion has been given to the similar situation under HI, but this too should be considered.

Those who believe that gross inequities are involved recommend what might be called sweeping structural changes. There are three general types of such proposals—earnings-sharing credits, wage credits for home-makers, and the "double-decker" approach. All of these proposals would, to one extent or another, provide social-benefit protection for the "non-working" wife (or full-time homemaker), but so too does the present spouse benefit. Which approach is best depends upon many factors, some objective and some subjective. Among these factors are cost, administrative feasibility, public understanding, and (very important) the problems involved in any transition required from the existing provisions.

Before discussing each of these proposals in turn, I want to clear up one matter. It is frequently argued that it is degrading for persons who have made a life career as a homemaker to receive OASDI and HI benefits on the basis of dependency. As I see it, a straw-person has been set up by terming these auxiliary benefits as "dependent benefits." The law does not contain (and never has contained) the designation of these auxiliary benefits as "dependent benefits." Nor, for that matter, has there ever been any dependency requirement for wives and widows. The various types of spouse benefits are now payable as a right on the basis of legal status (although 10 years of marriage is required for divorced spouses); they are not based on proof of dependency.

Now consider the proposals which have been made to solve what is said to be the inequitable treatment of two-worker families compared to one-worker families. These proposals have usually been quite simplistic. They have not considered all the complex situations that can arise, including not only those mentioned previously, but also termination of the marriage through divorce or death. Separation, too, can cause serious problems under these proposals.

Usually involved are either equally splitting the combined earnings records of the couple (earnings sharing) or providing wage credits for homemakers. The earnings-sharing approach, even though superficially attractive, would create other anomalies and inequities. If all benefit rights, both accrued and expected, were preserved for present partici-pants, the costs involved would be very high. If such rights are not preserved, there would be grave, divisive political and social problems. Furthermore, regardless of how an earnings-sharing plan was instituted and phased in, there would be tremendous administrative problems and difficulties in explaining the program to the public (in a system which is already having troubles with public relations).

The earnings-sharing proposals would result in giving higher benefits to two-worker families by *reducing* the benefits for one-worker families. In some ways, this could be viewed as taking benefits away from men to give them to women. However, in actuality, what is involved is taking benefits away from certain women (traditional homemakers) and giving them to other women (married women working in the paid labor market).

Some might say that such a result would be good, while others would say that this would be bad. In my opinion, if one group is to be favored over another (but not to an unfairly great extent), it should be the traditional homemaker, because otherwise we *may* be endangering the familial structure of the nation and its future development. And, once again, I question whether we should care so much about apparent individual equity in a social-insurance program that we create divisive situations of benefit losses. I strongly believe that any resulting gain in individual equity is not worth the loss, especially a loss bound to shake the public's confidence in the viability and integrity of the system. If the OASDI system had just now been initiated, it might have been possible to develop a satisfactory earnings-sharing plan. However, with OASDI having been in operation for over 40 years, it just is "not possible to get from here to there!"

Some have said that earnings sharing would eliminate the alleged demeaning nature of the present program. I fail to see any difference in this respect between getting *earnings credits* from a spouse's earnings record and getting *benefit rights* from a spouse's earnings record. Some might point out that, in the case of divorces, the earnings credits would always be available under earnings sharing, but that benefit rights would not be if the marriages lasted less than 10 years. The answer to this, essentially, is that such a requirement should be reduced to 5 years (the House version of the 1977 amendments). The absence of deferred-benefit rights for very short marriages broken by divorce does not seem vital, because the individuals involved will almost certainly obtain OASDI benefit rights in other ways.

Concern has also been expressed over the unfair treatment of homemakers under OASDI. It has been argued that homemakers should receive earnings credits for their home work which reflects the value of the services they render, because the present basis of OASDI benefits as "dependents" is degrading. Although this proposal has considerable appeal, it involves insurmountable problems of administration and/or costs. If it is offered on a voluntary basis, few will elect it—and those who do so will be the high-cost cases (i.e., women who are near retirement age or who have eligible children and are in very poor health). If it is on a compulsory contributory basis, great difficulties will arise in devising an equitable method of determining the earnings to be attributed—and then also in collecting the applicable taxes, which could be heavy financial burdens for many families. If a homemaker-credit plan is on a compulsory noncontributory basis, with the credits financed from the general treasury, a large cost is involved.

Another proposal intended to solve the alleged discrimination of OASDI against women is the so-called double-decker approach. This is by no means new, having been discussed first some 40 years ago. A flat benefit would be paid to all persons who are eligible by reason of age or other demographic condition, to be financed from general revenues. The second deck would provide wage-related benefits, financed by payroll taxes.

Although there is a certain appeal to this approach, I do not favor it. Under some circumstances, the benefit level of the first deck could become too high, and thus too costly, because of the absence of fiscal constraints (such as are inherent in earmarked, highly visible payroll-tax financing). Under other circumstances, there might be pressures to make the first deck subject to a needs test, which would be undesirable because it would discourage private savings and private pension plans.

Solutions Through Incremental Change

Despite the foregoing discussion, I believe that certain changes should be made to alleviate the problems of homemakers under OASDI. These involve such matters as the distribution of OASDI benefits between spouses, more consistent and equitable treatment with regard to termination of benefits because of marriage or remarriage, and computing average earnings by taking into account child-care years.

At present, a retired worker and a spouse who has not worked in the paid labor market can receive, at their choice, either a combined benefit check or two separate ones. In the latter case, the amounts of the checks will not be equal, being larger for the retired worker than for the spouse. I propose that, when spouses are living together, the total family benefit amount should be divided equally between them. This would apply in all cases of retirement benefits when an auxiliary spouse benefit is payable, including those cases in which both spouses are eligible for benefits on their own earnings and those in which children's benefits are payable. There would, of course, be no cost effect on OASDI.

At present the marriage (or remarriage) of a beneficiary can in some instances terminate benefits. Marriage after age 60 is not a terminating event, and neither is marriage between two survivor beneficiaries. However, when a survivor beneficiary under age 60 marries a retired worker, the survivor benefit terminates, and any subsequent benefit eligibility is based on the benefit of the new spouse as long as that spouse is living. Also, when a young survivor beneficiary (with eligible child or children) marries any person (other than certain categories of beneficiaries), her or his benefit rights end. Considering that, currently, there are widely different ethical and moral views about living together without benefit of marriage, it is unfair to penalize those who hold to tradition. Accordingly, both marriage and remarriage should be eliminated as causes of termination of benefit rights. Such a change would have a favorable effect for others beside homemakers (e.g., child student beneficiaries). There would be the continuing cost control for OASDI in that individuals can, in essence, draw only the largest of any benefits to which they are entitled, so that overlapping of benefits will not occur.

Also, as mentioned previously, the duration-of-marriage requirement for a divorced spouse to be eligible for benefits on the earnings record of the insured worker should be reduced from 10 years to 5 years.

Persons who do not engage in paid gainful work while caring for their young children can be at a disadvantage under the present benefit-computation methods. This is so because the average earnings used in the calculations are determined over a long period. This period should be shortened somewhat by allowing "child-care drop-out years"—years to be skipped in making the calculation—for periods during which the individual takes full care of a preschool child at home or a child under age 16 in school. The number of child-care drop-out years should be limited to, say, 20 years. Thus, over the long run, the average earnings for retirement cases would be computed over not less than 15 years (and not more than 35 years, as at present).

A problem in connection with child-care drop-out years is how to define such years so that the provision can be properly administered and well understood by the public. It may perhaps be the case that, although the principle is good, it is not operable. In lieu thereof—but only partially solving the problem—the period for computing the AIME could be shortened somewhat (say, for retirement benefits, from 35 years ultimately to 25 or 30 years).

Provisions for child-care drop-out years are contained, to a limited extent, in P.L. 96-265, enacted on June 9, 1980 (which deals with changes in the DI program). This law *reduces* the normal drop-out years for computing the Primary Insurance Amount for disabled-worker cases from the previous uniform 5 years to less than this for persons disabled in the year in which age 46 is attained or in an earlier year (e.g., 4 years for ages 42–46, 3 years for ages 37–41, 2 years for ages 32–36, 1 year for ages 27–31, and none for ages 26 and under). Child-care years with respect to children under age 3 can be used to "build up" the drop-out years to a maximum of 3 years (i.e., this is applicable only to those disabled at ages 36 and under). A child-care year is defined as one in which a child under age 3 was living in the same household as the individual substantially throughout the entire year, during which time the individual did not engage in *any* outside employment.

Persons who are widowed before age 60 will probably be at a disadvantage, because the indexing of the deceased spouse's pension in the deferred period (from age at widowhood to age 60) is now by prices, rather than by wages. This could be remedied by indexing the deceased worker's earnings record by wages up to the earlier of (a) when the worker would have attained age 60; or (b) when the survivor beneficiary attains age 58. This will produce a larger widow's or widower's benefit and is quite logical. (Under the present unusual economic conditions, a larger benefit would not result—but it is to be hoped that such conditions will not prevail over the long run.)

If it is felt imperative to solve the putative "equity" problem between one-worker and two-worker families, the best approach is to provide an *additional* "working-spouse" benefit for the spouse who has the smaller primary benefit. This benefit would be 25% of the smaller of (a) the spouse's own primary benefit, or (b) the benefit coming from the other spouse's earnings record. This provision was contained in the Republican alternative bill put forth when the House of Representatives was considering the 1977 amendments. The principal drawback is that it involves substantial additional cost—an estimated long-range cost of approximately 0.8% of taxable payroll.

Conclusion

I have a moderate philosophy of social security. I hold that the existing program—and especially its scope and level of benefits—is more or less proper and adequate. In contrast, holders of an expansionist philosophy feel that the benefit level particularly should be increased significantly, so as to provide for the full economic needs of covered workers. The other extreme, the contractionist or laissez faire proponents, oppose governmental social insurance and support only a limited public assistance program. They feel that individuals should provide for their own economic security through the private sector (or at least have the opportunity of opting out of social security and using this alternative).

I believe that a moderate social security program is not just desirable, it is essential. Such a program must meet presumed social needs and therefore must be primarily based on principles of social adequacy rather than individual equity. This is the kind of social security program we now have.

There is no need for radical changes in the structure of the program to solve existing problems. In fact, many things which are seen as problems by some individuals are not really problems at all.

I realize that, in intellectual circles, the defense of the status quo is often assailed on the grounds that change is always desirable and that criticism is always constructive. However, change is not always necessarily beneficial, and even when it may be beneficial in some ways, the net effect produced may be harmful. Further, although those advocating radical change in the structure of social security may see the system's problems as serious, I believe the "solutions" examined in this volume would, on balance, be damaging to our whole social security system. Who can say that the repudiation of the Ten Commandments, which have borne the test of time, would be desirable for the sake of change?

11

The Changing Nature of
Social Security

STANFORD G. ROSS

The social security program has changed dramatically over the past 45 years and is today at a critical point in its history. The underlying economic and social conditions which nurtured the development of social security have changed in ways adverse to the program. The program grew rapidly in a period of optimism that forecast relatively unlimited economic growth, favorable demographic trends, and great faith in the federal government's ability to solve social problems effectively. This optimistic view of the future has today given way to acceptance of the realities of limited economic growth and unfavorable demographic developments, and a deep suspicion that government cannot deal effectively with social problems. The basic issue for social security today, stated simply, is whether this fundamental institution of our society can adjust successfully to a changing and increasingly difficult environment (Ross, 1979a; 1979b).

Enacted in 1935 as a moderate program to provide future retirement benefits, social security enjoyed remarkable growth during its first 37 years. The strategy of the framers of the program was one of incremental expansion. Before the first benefits were even paid in 1939, the scope of the program was enlarged to include benefits for dependents and survivors. Following World War II, there were some eight *ad hoc* benefit increases from 1950 to 1971, and additional categories of workers became covered by the program, bringing more than 90% of all employment under social security. Finally, in 1972, benefits were increased by 20% and an automatic benefit adjustment for increases in the cost of living was introduced. Incremental expansions had by 1972 produced a mature program of enormous size and importance.

No sooner had this last dramatic expansion in 1972 taken place than serious problems underlying the financing of social security began to be apparent. A serious recession coupled with inflation demonstrated that the optimistic assumptions that had been used to justify and promote past expansions were gravely in error. By 1977, it was clear that projected payroll tax revenues would not be sufficient to pay projected benefits. Funds to pay benefits would not be available unless action was taken. This threat to social security reverberated through a shocked public that had a long history of pride and confidence in the program.

The Congress moved quickly in 1977 to enact the largest peacetime tax increase in history, but the payroll tax increases were scheduled to take effect over a period of years, commencing in January 1981. At the same time, Congress revised the benefit structure to slow the growth of benefits prospectively. These difficult acts of fiscal responsibility, particularly during a time of growing public unrest with tax levels in general, were heralded as adequate to ensure a soundly financed program well into the next century. The prospect of a longer-term deficiency was left to be dealt with by later congresses.

However, unpredicted further inflation and another recession, fueled by sharp increases in oil prices and other events, now indicate that the scheduled payroll tax increases enacted in 1977 will not enable us to avoid serious deficits in social security financing in the early 1980s. Thus we are again faced with the need for fiscally responsible actions by our political leadership to maintain the short-run integrity of the social security system and with developments that further undermine the public's confidence in the program.

In addition to immediate financial problems, the long-range deficit in social security, which was not dealt with in 1977, continues to hang as a cloud over the entire system. Lowered fertility rates and longer life spans combined with trends toward shorter work lives are leading us toward a working generation in the early part of the next century that may have to devote as much as 25% or more of its entire payroll to finance the social security benefits provided for under present law. This prospect should provoke a series of questions about the presently legislated benefit and tax structure, and the appropriate direction for public policy guiding work and retirement behavior.

It would be a mistake, however, to identify the problems of the social security program as being rooted only in the system's financing. Indeed, the financing issues are primarily symptoms of the problems inherent in the system as a whole. The benefit structure itself requires reconsideration, regardless of how it is financed. Only when the benefit and tax structures are reconciled and the appropriate tax levied to finance the appropriate set of benefits will the system as a whole be set right for the future.

To begin this difficult task of reassessment, we must shed the mythology that was developed in simpler days, when the public was encouraged to view social security as each individual worker's "investment" in a particular benefit package to which he or she had "an earned right" by virtue of making social security "contributions." This notion of an earned right permeates the public's thinking about social security. It has been described as a social contract between the government and workers, invoked to justify outrage toward any suggestion of a reshaping of benefit protection already enacted into law. Once enacted, those who promulgate this view argue, benefits become part of the contract that a worker enters into with the government when he or she makes "contributions"; altering those benefits serves as a breach of that contract.

On the contrary, social security is a social welfare program of tax transfers from current workers to those who do not work because of retirement, disablement, or the death of a breadwinner. Workers' taxes are set at a level to finance the benefit levels for those currently on the rolls. If those paying social security taxes today have earned a right to every piece of the currently legislated benefit package, then we have effectively mandated, without their consent, ever higher tax payments for tomorrow's workers. A program that increasingly burdens succeeding generations must face the reality that the legitimacy of that narrow interpretation of earned right will inevitably be challenged. Young taxpayers today have already begun to resist increasing social security taxes for a program they doubt will endure to pay them benefits.

The doctrine of earned right contains an important reality because a worker's earnings are compulsorily set aside to pay for benefits, and there is a corresponding obligation of the government to maintain a comprehensive and viable program to protect today's workers in the future. But the taxes today's workers pay are not earmarked for specific individuals' future benefits, nor do they necessarily cover the full cost of benefits that any particular individual can expect to receive. Thus, even though there is an undeniable moral obligation on the part of the government to pay promised benefits, the size of the benefit—and, therefore the transfer between generations—does not flow inexorably from the amount paid in. Rather, the size of the transfer is properly a matter of political choice.

Thus, the right that is earned is the right to basic protection, not the right to every feature of the present law. To argue that it is more is to mislead younger generations and obstruct thoughtful change.

Taxes have been called "contributions" to further imbed in the public mind the notion that workers are contributing to their own future security rather than being taxed to finance the security of present beneficiaries. Benefit formulas that painstakingly relate benefit amounts to wages earned in employment covered by social security have led to even deeper acceptance of the notion that an individual's work effort will be rewarded with benefits in an amount directly related to that effort. These so-called contributions have become, because of the expansion of the program, the second largest tax burden on the American public—second only to the individual income tax. Unless the public understand how the program works, they will be unable to judge the appropriate directions for change. The contributory, earnings-related description of social security disguises one of the program's most fundamental features: a benefit formula weighted to favor low-income workers. Describing social security taxes as contributions leads the worker to logically ask if he or she is getting a fair return on those contributions. The answer will be "no" for the average or above-average earner in contrast to the low earner, whose rate of return will have been enriched by the weighting in the formula.

If social security is understood as a tax–transfer program, the rate-of-return question becomes irrelevant. The question is not what every individual participant gets back in individual benefit payments, but whether the social value of the program is worth its costs. We can build support for the program in today's more sophisticated world only by being straightforward about its workings.

Probably the most significant test of our willingness to restructure the system to make it more acceptable to future generations will be the way we alter the program to improve the treatment of women. This issue forces us to rethink the fundamental bases of social security. It requires us to look at the workings of the entire system and focus on its internal equities. Women are at once high-wage earners and low-wage earners with intermittent attachment to the labor force; they are single and married, divorced and widowed, disabled and very aged. Improving their treatment provides a focus for studying all the ramifications of making basic structural changes to this vast and complex social mechanism.

Challenges to the traditional mythology are now occurring. Questions are being raised about the appropriateness of reducing future benefits for certain categories of people; whether a homemaker's work constitutes a "contribution" to society that should be rewarded with social security protection for herself and dependents; whether people should gain independent entitlement to social security benefits even if they have had no "wages" of their own to which the benefit amount could be directly related; whether public policy should encourage women to work in the paid labor force or to stay home with young children; whether adults should be treated as individuals rather than units of a family. The weighting in the benefit formula will come under serious scrutiny as differing benefit amounts for couples with the same total earnings are examined. And the trade-off of adequacy for improved equity in a period of limited resources will be difficult if it reduces benefits for certain categories of recipients, such as aged widows, who are among the poorest of the poor.

All of these issues will require a great deal of careful thought about ultimate values, an effort toward which this volume makes a significant contribution. Certain directions seem clear to me at this point, however. The basic concept of adult dependency, which has guided the system until now, is out of touch with current social realities. Women should be regarded as workers and full participants in society whether they are in the paid work force or performing homemaker and child-rearing functions. The social security system must be restructured so that its underlying concepts treat each adult as an individual with an independent right to benefits.

Further, I believe the earnings-sharing approach has considerable merit, with its premise that marriage is an economic partnership in which each spouse gains independent entitlement to benefits based on one-half the total earnings of the couple during the marriage. This approach is particularly interesting when viewed as a part of a two-tier or double-decker system. A double-decker structure could clarify the dual purpose of the present benefit formula by separating the elements of social security that benefit low-wage workers from the wage-related elements of the program, which provide insurance-type benefits. The appropriate revenue source would finance each element; general revenues for the first-tier flat-grant benefit and a payroll tax to finance the second-tier benefit, which would be proportional to wages.

Surely a transition to a new system must be gradual, with great care taken to protect individual rights. But unless we chart long-term directions—even as we recognize that basic change must be implemented gradually—any incremental changes, however well-intentioned, could be harmful to the system and to society.

Moreover, development of a comprehensive reform plan must take into account not only the social security program but the fact that we have developed in this country an income-security sector, the management of which is the single largest domestic activity of government. Roughly one out of four Americans is dependent on a government check for his major, if not sole, source of income. Roughly $500 billion, 20% of the gross national product, is transferred annually from the working to the nonworking population directly through government programs or other mechanisms that are structured and regulated by the government. We need to do a much better job of studying and understanding this income-security sector, of which social security is the heart, if we are truly to ensure economic justice in our society. We should not shy away from recognizing the need for change, no matter how painful it may be to achieve such change. But we must also take into account that we are dealing with a phenomenon that has deep political roots. Change can only take place if it is supported by broad constituencies. Unfortunately the constituencies in the income-security area have historically been special-interest consti- tuencies, which do not always take positions that reflect the larger public interest. To the extent that work is done on a subject like the changing roles of women, progress can be made because we are addressing the problems of a constituency that is broader than the customary groupings.

No one looking even briefly at the history of the social security program and the dilemmas which face us today can doubt that this program, which has changed continually in the past, will continue to change in the years ahead. The question is only about the nature of the change. Will it be principled and orderly, and will it improve the efficiency and equity of the system?

Progress cannot be taken for granted. History provides many instances of nations unable to adapt to the changing needs of their citizens. We must work through the challenges that face social security in this country so that it can continue to fulfill urgent national needs.

Glossary

Many of the definitions below are based on—though not as detailed as—those to be found in *Social Security Bulletin; Annual Statistical Supplement, 1977–1979*, pp. 5–14.

Actuarial reduction. Reduction in monthly benefit amount payable (*a*) on entitlement at ages 62–64 if the beneficiary is a retired worker, a wife of a retired or disabled worker, a husband or a divorced spouse; (*b*) on entitlement at ages 60–64 if the beneficiary is a widow, widower, or surviving divorced wife; or (*c*) on entitlement, in case of disability, at ages 50–59, if the beneficiary is a widow, widower, or surviving divorced wife. The benefit continues to be paid at a reduced rate even after age 65, except that the reduced rate is refigured at age 65 for all beneficiaries and also at age 62 for a widow, widower, and a surviving divorced wife to omit months for which the reduced benefit was not paid and to take into account any additional earnings.

Aging effect. A term used by Warlick, Berry, and Garfinkel to describe an increase over time in the size of benefits from a double-decker system relative to the current system, caused by indexing the demogrant by average wage growth rather than inflation, and assuming that wages will grow faster than prices.

Average indexed monthly earnings (AIME). The amount of earnings used as the basis for determining the primary insurance amount (PIA) for most workers who attain age 62, become disabled, or die after 1978. Indexing creates an earnings record that reflects the value of the individual's earnings relative to national average earnings in the indexing year. Earnings after the indexing year are counted at their nominal value.

Average monthly wage (AMW). The amount of wages used as the basis for determining the primary insurance amount (PIA) for workers who attain age 62, become disabled, or die before 1979, and also under a special guarantee computation for workers who attain age 62 or die in 1979–1983. The average is computed by dividing the sum of earnings in the computation years by the total number of months in the computation years. After 1978 the average indexed monthly earnings (AIME) are used to compute PIA.

Bend points. The AIME levels at which the coefficient used in the PIA calculation changes. These levels are adjusted each year to reflect inflation. In 1981 the first AIME bend point was $422 and the second was $1274.

Benefits to dependents. Benefits paid to a family member of a retired, deceased, or disabled person. Entitlement to these benefits is based on the relationship to the retired, deceased, or disabled person and does not depend on the dependent having worked in covered employment. These benefits include spouse, survivor, and divorced-spouse benefits.

Child-care drop-out years. A proposed change in the method of calculating OASI benefits by which the number of years over which the AIME is calculated is reduced to account for those years during which a person remained at home to care for (usually, young) children.

Defined-benefit plan. A pension plan in which benefits are defined by a benefit formula and not tied directly to prior contributions. Benefits are usually based on earnings and on years of service, and are funded according to actuarial principles over the employee's period of participation.

Defined-contribution plan. A pension plan in which benefits are directly based on prior contributions made by the individual to the benefit plan. The size of the benefits received at retirement depends upon past contributions, earnings on these contributions, and expectation of life at the age when benefits begin.

Delayed-retirement credit. A credit due a worker for delaying retirement after attaining age 65 for each month the worker (a) was fully insured, (b) had attained age 65 but was not yet age 72, and (c) did not receive benefits because the worker had not filed an application or was working. The increase is applicable to the worker's monthly benefit amount but not to his PIA. Hence, auxiliary benefits are generally not affected. The exception is that a surviving spouse (including divorced) receiving widow(er) benefits is entitled, for months after May 1978, to the same increase that had been applied to the benefit of the deceased worker or for which the worker was eligible at the time of death.

Demogrant. A flat payment made to all persons with some well-defined demographic characteristic. As used in this volume it refers to a flat benefit payable to all persons of a given age.

Dependent benefits. *See* Benefits to dependents.

Disabled-widow benefit. Benefit payable to a disabled widow(er) of a deceased worker. These benefits are payable at ages 50–59 under certain conditions or at age 60.

Disability insurance benefit. A monthly benefit payable to a disabled worker under age 65 who is insured for disability. These benefits automatically convert to retired-worker benefits at age 65. Eligibility also requires that a disabled person be fully insured and have worked at least 20 quarters of coverage during the 40-quarter period ending with the quarter in which the worker became disabled.

Divorced-spouse benefit. A benefit payable to a divorced spouse of a retired or disabled worker. Monthly benefits are calculated as are spouse benefits. Benefits are payable only if the marriage lasted at least 10 years.

Double-decker system. A proposed system in which social security benefits would be the sum of benefits from two so-called decks. The first deck would consist of a demogrant paid to all aged persons regardless of income status. The second deck would consist of a benefit strictly proportional to covered earnings.

Dual entitlement. Entitlement to and actual receipt of two types of benefits for the same month. A woman may, for example, be entitled to payments both as a retired worker and as a wife. Entitlement to a retired-worker or disabled-worker benefit and a secondary benefit results in dual entitlement only if the secondary benefit is larger. When there is dual entitlement, the larger of the two benefits is paid only in the amount by which it exceeds the smaller benefit.

Earnings sharing. A proposed system of sharing social security earnings records between married partners. Under such a system total covered earnings of a couple would be shared equally during marriage. Earnings could be split either annually or at divorce, disability, or retirement. Social security benefits would be calculated by a formula based on the individual's earnings record obtained through this split.

Earnings test. A restriction on the amount of earnings a beneficiary may receive from covered or noncovered employment without facing a reduction in these benefits. Earnings above a permitted amount result in a reduction in monthly benefits of $1.00 for every $2.00 of earnings.

Employee Retirement Income Security Act (ERISA). This 1974 legislation regulates coverage, funding, and vesting provisions of private pension plans. It also requires that retiring employees be able to choose an actuarially equivalent form of retirement income that will continue income benefits to a survivor. A private pension plan must automatically provide married persons with an actuarially equivalent joint–survivor annuity option if the employee does not specifically elect a single life annuity.

Entitlement. The state or condition of meeting the applicable requirements for receipt of benefits, including the filing of a claim. A person can become entitled to one benefit, to two benefits simultaneously (dual entitlement) or, in a few cases, to three benefits simultaneously.

Expected present value. The value of all future streams of income or costs, discounted to the present.

Functional limitation scale (FLS). A measure Johnson and Burfield developed by applying American Medical Association guidelines for the evaluation of permanent-partial impairment to data from the 1972 Social Security Survey of Health and Work Characteristics to measure the functional limitations of the respondents. The FLS values are constructed by adding limitation percentages for separate body functions. Someone is classified as 25% limited, for example, if he is able to perform one or two of the following functions but with difficulty: walking, using stairs, or lifting less than 10 pounds.

Homemaker credit. A proposed system in which a homemaker would be credited with some amount of annual earnings even though no covered earnings were actually made. Under some proposals a homemaker would pay OASI taxes as if earnings were actually made, under others such a credit would be financed through the contributions of covered earners. At retirement or disability the person's PIA would be calculated as under the current system, based on the sum of the credits and actual covered earnings.

Individual account plan. *See* Defined-contribution plan.

Inherited credit. A proposed method of calculating a survivor benefit, recommended by the 1979 Advisory Council on Social Security, which would provide a surviving spouse with a benefit based on her (or his) own earnings record combined with that of a deceased spouse. The total of combined annual earnings on the survivor's record would be limited to the annual maximum earnings creditable to an individual.

Insured status. The state or condition of having sufficient quarters of coverage to meet the eligibility requirements for retired-worker or disabled-worker benefits or to permit the worker's dependents or survivors to establish eligibility for dependent or survivor benefits in the event of his disability, retirement, or death. *See* Quarters of coverage.

Joint—survivor benefit. An option offered by pension plans by which benefits to a retired worker are actuarially reduced in order that the survivor will be assured a continuing benefit in the event of the death of the worker.

Maximum family benefit. The maximum monthly amount (varying with the PIA) that can be paid on a worker's earnings record. A benefit to a divorced spouse or to a surviving divorced spouse is not included.

Medicare. A program enacted in 1965 to provide hospital insurance (HI) and supplementary medical insurance (SMI) to persons entitled to OASDI benefits. The HI program is financed through a proportion of the total OASDHI payroll tax. SMI enrollment is on a voluntary basis and paid by monthly premiums from the eligible person.

Negative income tax. An income-redistributive plan which would mirror the income tax system by giving money payments directly to persons earning below some given amount. Payments would fall, the greater the income of the person. Above some income level the person would begin to pay positive taxes.

New home economics. The view of marriage as an economic enterprise in which a family produces goods and services by combining home and market work in order to maximize the well-being of all family members.

Primary insurance amount (PIA). The monthly amount that would be payable to a retired worker who begins to get benefits at age 65 or to a disabled worker. This amount, which is related to the worker's average monthly wage or average indexed monthly earnings, is also the amount used as a base for computing all types of benefits payable on the basis of one individual's earnings record.

Quarters of coverage. The crediting of coverage needed for insured status has changed from a quarterly to an annual basis. In 1982, a worker received 1 quarter of coverage (up to a total of 4) for each

$340 of annual earnings reported from employment or self-employment. This dollar amount is subject to annual automatic increases in proportion to increases in average earnings. Before 1978, a quarter of coverage was a calendar quarter in which a worker was paid $50 or more in wages for covered employment.

Spouse benefit. A benefit to a dependent payable to a husband or wife, at least 62 years of age, of a retired or disabled worker. Entitlement is based on marriage to a retired or disabled worker and does not depend on the spouse having worked in covered employment. The monthly benefit payable is equal to 50% of the PIA of the insured worker, although the actual amount paid may be reduced if the dependent initiates benefits prior to age 65 or continues to work.

Supplemental spouse benefit. A benefit defined by Holden as the additional amount for which a spouse of a retired beneficiary is eligible above her own retired-worker benefit.

Supplemental widow benefit. A benefit defined by Holden as the additional amount for which a widow of a deceased insured worker is eligible above her own retired-worker benefit.

Survivor benefit. A benefit payable to a dependent who is a survivor of a deceased insured worker. Monthly benefits payable to an aged widow or widower are equal to the PIA of the deceased insured worker. Actual benefits may be reduced if the widow(er) is not disabled and between 62 and 65 years of age or if earnings are greater than allowed under the earnings test.

Two-tier system. A proposed system in which social security benefits would be the sum of benefits from two so-called tiers. The first tier would consist of a means-tested benefit. The second tier would be a benefit strictly proportional to covered earnings.

Workers' Compensation Insurance program. A disability insurance system, run by individual states, which provides compensation for work-related injuries or occupational disease. It is based on the presumption that employers are liable for compensation at some level, but with no presumption of fault, and is financed by a tax on employers. While each state program is run differently, typically benefits are paid to covered workers who are temporarily disabled, whether partially or totally, and to those whose impairments are permanent, whether partial or total.

Work recency test. The requirement that in addition to lengh-of-covered-work requirements, disabled workers must have earned 5 years of the required work credit in the 10 years ending when they became disabled in order to receive monthly disability benefits. The years need not be continuous or in units of full years.

References

Allan, K. H. 1976. First findings of the 1972 Survey of the Disabled: General characteristics. *Social Security Bulletin*, October, pp. 18–37.

Altmeyer, A. 1966. *The formative years of social security.* Madison: University of Wisconsin Press.

American Council of Life Insurance. 1978–1979. *Pension facts.* Washington, D.C.: ACLI.

Ball, R. M. 1978. *Social security: Today and tomorrow.* New York: Columbia University Press.

———. 1979. Social security and women. Testimony before the U.S. Congress, House of Representatives, Committee on Ways and Means, Subcommittee on Social Security, November 2.

Bankers Trust Company. 1975. *1975 study of corporate pension plans.* New York: Bankers Trust Company.

Barth, P.S., with Hunt, H.A. 1980. *Workers' Compensation and work-related illness and diseases.* Cambridge, Mass.: MIT Press.

Bennett, C. T. F. 1979. The social security benefit structure: Equity considerations of the family as its basis. Papers and proceedings of the ninety-first annual meeting of the American Economic Association. *American Economic Review, 69*, 227–239.

Bergmann, B. R. 1981. The economic risk of being a housewife. Papers and proceedings of the ninety-third annual meeting of the American Economic Association. *American Economic Review, 71*, 81–86.

Berkowitz, E. (ed.) 1979. *Disability policies and government programs.* New York: Praeger.

Berry, D., Garfinkel, I., and Munts, R. Forthcoming. Income testing in income support programs for the aged. In I. Garfinkel (ed.), *Income-tested transfer programs.* New York: Academic Press.

Board of Trustees of the Federal Old-Age and Survivors Insurance and Disability Insurance Trust Funds. 1979. *Annual Report.* Washington, D.C.: U.S. Government Printing Office.

Boskin, M. J. 1973. The economics of labor supply. In G. G. Cain and H. W. Watts (eds.), *Income maintenance and labor supply.* Chicago: Rand McNally.

Boston University, Center for Applied Social Science. 1981. Disability analysis of health data. Mimeo.

Boulding, K. 1958. *Principles of economic policy.* Englewood Cliffs, N.J.: Prentice Hall.

Brown, J. D. 1972. *An American philosophy of social security.* Princeton, N.J.: Princeton University Press.

_____. 1977. *Essays on social security.* Princeton, N.J.: Princeton University Press.

Burfield, W. B. 1978. A scale for measuring functional limitations. Health Studies Working Paper No. 26, Syracuse University, Syracuse, N.Y.

Burkhauser, R. V. 1979. Are women treated fairly in today's social security system? *Gerontologist, 19,* 242–249.

Burkhauser, R. V., and Warlick, J. 1981. Disentangling the annuity from the redistributive aspects of social security. *Review of Income and Wealth,* Series 27, pp. 401–421.

Burns, E. 1965. Needed changes in welfare programs. Institute for Government and Public Affairs Paper MR-44. University of California, Los Angeles.

Cain, G. G. 1966. *Married women in the labor force: An economic analysis.* Chicago: University of Chicago Press.

California Public Employees' Retirement System. 1977. *Benefits for state miscellaneous members.* Sacramento: Cal. PERS.

Cohen, W. J. 1957. *Retirement policies under social security.* Berkeley and Los Angeles: University of California Press.

Commerce Clearing House. 1978. *1978 social security and Medicare explained.* Chicago: Commerce Clearing House.

Conant, L. 1922. *A critical analysis of industrial pension systems.* New York: Macmillan.

Cook, T. J. 1979. *Public retirement systems: Summaries of public retirement plans covering colleges and universities.* New York: TIAA–CREF.

Dearing, C. 1954. *Industrial pensions.* Washington, D.C.: Brookings Institution.

Derthick, M. 1979. *Policymaking for social security.* Washington, D.C.: Brookings Institution.

Dixon, R. G., Jr. 1973. *Social security disability and mass justice.* New York: Praeger.

Dunlop, J. T. 1950. Appraisal of wage stabilization policies. In *Problems and policies of dispute settlements and wage stabilization during World War II.* Bulletin 1009. Washington, D.C.: U.S. Department of Labor (BLS).

Dutton, D. 1972. The wife's community interest in her husband's qualified pension or profit-sharing plan. *Texas Law Review, 50,* 334–350.

Federal Register. 1978. Vol. 43, no. 251, December 29.

Feldstein, M. 1977. Social insurance. In C. D. Campbell (ed.), *Income redistribution.* Washington, D.C.: American Enterprise Institute.

Ferrara, P. J. 1980. *Social security: The inherent contradiction.* San Francisco: Cato Institute.

Financial Accounting Standards Board. 1980. *Statements.* Stamford, Conn.: FASB.

Florida Retirement System. 1975. *The Florida Retirement System.* Tallahassee, Florida: FRS.

Flowers, M. R. 1977. *Women and social security: An institutional dilemma.* Washington, D.C.: American Enterprise Institute.

_____. 1979. Supplemental benefits for spouses under social security: A public choice explanation of the law. *Economic Inquiry, 17,* 125–131.

Foster, H. H., Jr., and Freed, D. J. 1976–1977. Marital property and the chancellor's foot. *Family Law Quarterly, 10,* 55–73.

_____. 1977–1978. Spousal rights in retirement and pension benefits. *Journal of Family Law, 16,* 187–211.

Freed, D. J., and Foster, H. H., Jr. 1977–1978. Divorce in the fifty states: An outline. *Family Law Quarterly, 11,* 297–313.

Friedan, B. 1963. *The feminine mystique.* New York: Norton.

Frohlich, P. 1972. Economic resources of institutionalized adults. In *Social Security Survey of Institutionalized Adults: 1967.* Report No. 3 (April). Washington, D.C.: HEW.

Garfinkel, I. (ed.). Forthcoming. *Income-tested transfer programs.* New York: Academic Press.

Gordon, N. M. 1979. Institutional responses: The social security system. In R. E. Smith (ed.), *The subtle revolution, women at work.* Washington, D.C.: Urban Institute.

Grimaldi, P. L. 1980. *Supplemental Security Income: The new federal program for the aged, blind, and disabled.* Washington, D.C.: American Enterprise Institute.

Haber, L. D. 1968. The effect of age and disability on access to public income-maintenance programs. In *Social Security Survey of the Disabled, 1966.* Report No. 3 (July). Washington, D.C.: HEW.

Harris, E. F. 1979. The non-employee spouse's rights in pension and profit sharing plans after ERISA. *The Compensation Planning Journal,* November, pp. 3–12.

Hodgens, E. L. 1973. Survivor's pensions: An emerging employee benefit. *Monthly Labor Review,* July, pp. 31–34.

Hodgens, E. L. 1975. Key changes in major pension plans. *Monthly Labor Review,* July, pp. 22–27.

Holden, K. C. 1979a. Spouse and survivor benefits. *Research on Aging, 1,* 301–318.

_____. 1979b. The inequitable distribution of OASI benefits among homemakers. *Gerontologist, 19,* 250–256.

Johnson, W. G. 1979. Disability, income support and social insurance. In E. Berkowitz (ed.), *Disability policies and government programs.* New York: Praeger.

Johnson, W. G., Cullinan, P. R., and Curington, W. P. 1980. The adequacy of Workers' Compensation payments. In *Research reports to the Interdepartmental Task Force on Workers' Compensation,* vol. 6. Washington, D.C.: U.S. Government Printing Office.

Johnson, W. G., Mudrick, N., and Wai, H. S. 1980. Applications for Social Security Disability Insurance. Health Studies Program Working Paper, Syracuse University, Syracuse, N.Y.

Kestenbaum, B. M. 1979. Fertility and work history: Findings from the 1973 Exact Match. *Review of Public Data Use, 7,* 73–79.

Kotlikoff, L. J. 1978. Social security, time to reform. In M. J. Boskin (ed.), *Federal tax reform: Myths and realities.* San Francisco: Institute for Contemporary Studies.

Kyrk, H. 1953. *The family in the American economy.* Chicago: University of Chicago Press.

Latimer, M. W. 1932. *Industrial pension systems in the United States and Canada.* 2 vols. New York: Industrial Relations Counselors.

Lopate, C. 1974. Pay for housework. *Social Policy, 5,* 27–31.

Mashaw, J. 1979. Administrative justice, Yale University School of Law. Mimeo.

Moon, M. 1977. *The measurement of economic welfare: Its application to the aged poor.* New York: Academic Press.

Munnell, A. H. 1977. *The future of social security.* Washington, D.C.: Brookings Institution.

Myers, R. J. 1975. Social security and sex discrimination. *Challenge,* July–August, pp. 54–57.

Nagi, S. 1979. The concept of disability. In E. Berkowitz (ed.), *Disability policies and government programs.* New York: Praeger.

National Industrial Conference Board. 1925. *Industrial pension plans in the United States.* New York: NICB.

_____. 1931. *Elements of industrial pension plans.* New York: NICB.

Organisation for Economic Cooperation and Development. 1977. *The treatment of family units in OECD member countries under tax and transfer systems,* a report for the Committee on Fiscal Affairs. Paris: OECD.

Orshansky, M. 1965. Counting the poor: Another look at the poverty profile. *Social Security Bulletin,* January, pp. 3–29.

Pechman, J., Aaron, H., and Taussig, M. 1968. *Social security: Perspectives for reform.* Washington, D.C.: Brookings Institution.

Pensions and Investments. 1980. Pension benefit legal order creates snare, February 4, p. 19.

Peterson, F. 1945. *American labor unions.* New York: Harper and Brothers.

Pratt, H. 1977. *The gray lobby.* Chicago: University of Chicago Press.

President's Commission on Pension Policy. 1981. *Coming of age: Towards a national retirement policy.* Washington,D.C.: U.S. Government Printing Office.

Rosen, S. 1977. Social security and the economy. In M. J. Boskin (ed.), *The crisis in social security: Problems and prospects.* San Francisco: Institute for Contemporary Studies.

Ross, S. G. 1979a. *Social security: A worldwide issue.* Washington, D.C.: HEW, Social Security Administration.

_____. 1979b. *New directions in social security: Considerations for the 1980's.* Washington, D.C.: HEW, Social Security Administration.

Schorr, A. 1977. The strategy and hope. In A. Schorr (ed.), *Jubilee for our times.* New York: Columbia University Press.

Schulz, J. H. 1980. *The economics of aging* (2nd ed.). Belmont, Calif.: Wadsworth.

Snee, J., and Ross, M. 1978. Social security amendments of 1977: Legislative history and summary of provisions. *Social Security Bulletin,* March, pp. 3–20.

Social Security Bulletin. 1979. Men and women: Changing roles and social security, May, pp. 25–32.

Social Security Bulletin. Annual Statistical Supplement, 1975. 1975.

Social Security Bulletin, Annual Statistical Supplement, 1977–1979. 1980.

Stein, B. 1980. *Social security and pensions in transition.* New York: Free Press.

Teachers Insurance and Annuity Association of America (College Retirement Equities Fund). 1979. *Report of annuity premiums and benefits,* December 31. New York: TIAA.

Thompson, G. B. 1977. Aged women OASDI beneficiaries: Income and characteristics, 1971. *Social Security Bulletin,* April, pp. 23–48.

Tissue, T. 1978. Response to recipiency under Public Assistance and SSI. *Social Security Bulletin,* November, pp. 3–15.

Treitel, R. 1979. Disability claimants who contest denials and win reversals through hearings, U.S. Department of Health, Education, and Welfare, Social Security Administration, ORS, Division of Disability Studies, February.

U.S. Congress, House of Representatives. 1974. *Committee staff report on the Disability Insurance program.* Prepared by the staff of the Committee on Ways and Means, July. Washington, D.C.: U.S. Government Printing Office.

_____. Committee on Education and Labor. 1978. Pension task force report on public employment retirement systems. 95th Congress, 2nd Session, *Committee print.* Washington, D.C.: U.S. Government Printing Office.

U.S. Department of Commerce (Bureau of the Census). 1979a. *Current Population Reports,* P-60, No. 118, March. Washington, D.C.: U.S. Government Printing Office.

U.S. Department of Commerce. 1979b. *Statistical abstract of the United States.* Washington, D.C.: U.S. Government Printing Office.

U.S. Department of Health, Education, and Welfare (Social Security Administration). 1973. *Disability evaluation under social security: A handbook for physicians* (reprint of 1969 ed.). Washington, D.C.: HEW.

_____. 1975. *Studies from Interagency Data Linkages*, Nos. 4, 5, and 6. Washington, D.C.: HEW.

_____. 1978. *Social security handbook* (6th ed.), publication no. 77-10135. Washington, D.C.: HEW.

U.S. Department of Health, Education, and Welfare. 1979a. *Social security and the changing roles of men and women.* Washington, D.C.: HEW.

U.S. Department of Health, Education, and Welfare (Social Security Financing and Benefits). 1979b. *Report of the 1979 Advisory Council on Social Security.* Washington, D.C.: HEW. (A final version of this report, with different pagination, was printed by the Government Printing Office in 1980.)

U.S. Department of Health and Human Services (Social Security Administration). 1980. *Social security programs throughout the world, 1979.* Research Report no. 54. Washington, D.C.: U.S. Government Printing Office.

U.S. Department of Labor (Office of the Assistant Secretary for Policy, Evaluation, and Research). 1980. *An interim report to Congress on occupational diseases,* June. Washington, D.C.: U.S. Government Printing Office.

U.S. National Commission on Social Security. 1981. *Social security in America's future.* Washington, D.C.: U.S. Government Printing Office.

Warlick, J. 1979. An empirical analysis of participation in the Supplemental Security Income program among aged, eligible persons. Ph.D. dissertation, Department of Economics, University of Wisconsin–Madison.

Webb, S., and Webb, B. 1894. *Industrial democracy.* London: Longmans, Green.

Witte, E. E. 1962. *Social security perspectives.* Madison: University of Wisconsin Press.

_____. 1963. *The development of the Social Security Act.* Madison: University of Wisconsin Press.

Index

Institute for Research on Poverty
Monograph Series

Richard V. Burkhauser and Karen C. Holden, Editors, *A Challenge to Social Security: The Changing Roles of Women and Men in American Society.* 1982

Jeffrey G. Williamson and Peter H. Lindert, *American Inequality: A Macroeconomic History.* 1980

Robert H. Haveman and Kevin Hollenbeck, Editors, *Microeconomic Simulation Models for Public Policy Analysis, Volume 1: Distributional Impacts, Volume 2: Sectoral, Regional, and General Equilibrium Models.* 1980

Peter K. Eisinger, *The Politics of Displacement: Racial and Ethnic Transition in Three American Cities.* 1980

Erik Olin Wright, *Class Structure and Income Determination.* 1979

Joel F. Handler, *Social Movements and the Legal System: A Theory of Law Reform and Social Change.* 1979

Duane E. Leigh, *An Analysis of the Determinants of Occupational Upgrading.* 1978

Stanley H. Masters and Irwin Garfinkel, *Estimating the Labor Supply Effects of Income Maintenance Alternatives.* 1978

Irwin Garfinkel and Robert H. Haveman, with the assistance of David Betson, *Earnings Capacity, Poverty, and Inequality.* 1977

Harold W. Watts and Albert Rees, Editors, *The New Jersey Income—Maintenance Experiment, Volume III: Expenditures, Health, and Social Behavior; and the Quality of the Evidence.* 1977

Murray Edelman, *Political Language: Words That Succeed and Policies That Fail.* 1977

Marilyn Moon and Eugene Smolensky, Editors, *Improving Measures of Economic Well-Being.* 1977

Harold W. Watts and Albert Rees, Editors, *The New Jersey Income—Maintenance Experiment, Volume II: Labor-Supply Responses.* 1977

Marilyn Moon, *The Measurement of Economic Welfare: Its Application to the Aged Poor.* 1977

Morgan Reynolds and Eugene Smolensky, *Public Expenditures, Taxes, and the Distribution of Income: The United States, 1950, 1961, 1970.* 1977

Fredrick L. Golladay and Robert H. Haveman, with the assistance of Kevin Hollenbeck, *The Economic Impacts of Tax–Transfer Policy: Regional and Distributional Effects.* 1977

David Kershaw and Jerilyn Fair, *The New Jersey Income-Maintenance Experiment, Volume I: Operations, Surveys, and Administration.* 1976

Peter K. Eisinger, *Patterns of Interracial Politics: Conflict and Cooperation in the City.* 1976

Irene Lurie, Editor, *Integrating Income Maintenance Programs.* 1975

Stanley H. Masters, *Black–White Income Differentials: Empirical Studies and Policy Implications.* 1975

Larry L. Orr, *Income, Employment, and Urban Residential Location.* 1975

Joel F. Handler, *The Coercive Social Worker: British Lessons for American Social Services.* 1973

Glen G. Cain and Harold W. Watts, Editors, *Income Maintenance and Labor Supply: Econometric Studies.* 1973

Charles E. Metcalf, *An Econometric Model of Income Distribution.* 1972

Larry L. Orr, Robinson G. Hollister, and Myron J. Lefcowitz, Editors, with the assistance of Karen Hester, *Income Maintenance: Interdisciplinary Approaches to Research.* 1971

Robert J. Lampman, *Ends and Means of Reducing Income Poverty.* 1971

Joel F. Handler and Ellen Jane Hollingsworth, *"The Deserving Poor": A Study of Welfare Administration.* 1971

Murray Edelman, *Politics as Symbolic Action: Mass Arousal and Quiescence.* 1971

Frederick Williams, Editor, *Language and Poverty: Perspectives on a Theme.* 1970

Vernon L. Allen, Editor, *Psychological Factors in Poverty.* 1970